DISCOURS

Multimodal Dis

Georgetown University Round Table on Languages and Linguistics series
Selected Titles

Linguistics, Language, and the Real World: Discourse and Beyond
DEBORAH TANNEN AND JAMES E. ALATIS, EDITORS

Linguistics, Language, and the Professions: Education, Journalism, Law, Medicine, and Technology
JAMES E. ALATIS, HEIDI E. HAMILTON, AND AI-HUI TAN, EDITORS

Language in Our Time: Bilingual Education and Official English, Ebonics and Standard English, Immigration and Unz Initiative
JAMES E. ALATIS AND AI-HUI TAN, EDITORS

DISCOURSE AND TECHNOLOGY
Multimodal Discourse Analysis

Philip LeVine and Ron Scollon, *Editors*

GEORGETOWN UNIVERSITY PRESS
Washington, D.C.

Georgetown University Press, Washington, D.C.

Printed in the United States of America

10 9 8 7 6 5 4 3 2 1 2004

This book is printed on acid-free paper meeting the requirements of the American National Standard for Permanence in Paper for Printed Library Materials.

Library of Congress Cataloging-in-Publication Data

Discourse and technology : multimodal discourse analysis /
Philip LeVine and Ron Scollon, editors.
p. cm. — (Georgetown University round table on languages and linguistics)
Includes bibliographical references.
ISBN 1-58901-101-5 (pbk. : alk. paper)
1. Discourse analysis. 2. Technological innovations. 3. Interactive multimedia.
4. Multimedia systems. I. LeVine, Philip, 1959– . II. Scollon, Ron. III. Series.
P302.865.D57 2004
401′.41—dc22 2003024544

Contents

Preface

This volume contains a selection of papers from the 2002 Georgetown University Round Table on Languages and Linguistics, which has also been known as the Round Table and, perhaps most frequently, simply GURT. The theme for this fifty-third GURT was "Discourse and Technology: Multimodal Discourse Analysis." The papers were selected by peer review from among more than one hundred presentations and seven plenary addresses given during this groundbreaking conference. The editors of this volume are Philip LeVine and Ron Scollon.

The joint chairs for the conference itself were James E. Alatis, dean emeritus of the School of Languages and Linguistics at Georgetown University, and Ron Scollon, professor of linguistics at Georgetown. Professor Alatis has been the driving force behind GURT for many years, and we would like to thank him for his work in establishing the important tradition that these Round Tables have become.

Many of the talks given at GURT 2002 required complex presentation technologies. Arranging for the smooth display of sound and image demanded the coordinated efforts of students, faculty, and staff. Our thanks go out to all of the student and faculty volunteers, and to Georgetown Technology Services for their assistance. Our thanks to Jackie Lou for giving her time and considerable talents to the design of the GURT program. We would also like to express our appreciation to assistant coordinators Sylvia Chou and Pornpimon Supakorn for efforts that began months before the conference took place.

Multimodal Discourse Analysis as the Confluence of Discourse and Technology

RON SCOLLON AND PHILIP LEVINE
Georgetown University

THAT DISCOURSE AND TECHNOLOGY are intimately related is not a new perception. Even the philosopher Nietzsche got in a word on the subject—"Our writing tools are also working on our thoughts"—according to Arthur Krystal (2002). Our interest in this volume is not to try to demonstrate that discourse and technology live in a symbiotic relationship. Our interest is in presenting a selected set of papers from the Georgetown University Round Table 2002 (GURT 2002), which opened up a discussion among discourse analysts and others in linguistics and in related fields about the twofold impact of new communication technologies: The impact on how we collect, transcribe, and analyze discourse data, and, possibly more important, the impact on social interactions and discourses themselves that these technologies are having.

Discourse analysis as we now know it is in many ways the product of technological change. At the time of the epoch-making 1981 GURT (Tannen 1982), Deborah Tannen chose as her theme "Analyzing discourse: Text and talk." Discourse analysis was just then emerging as a subject of linguistic research. The papers in that conference and in that volume were about equally divided between studies of text (discourse in the form of written or printed language) and talk (discourse in the form of spoken language captured *in situ* by means of the tape recorder).

As Frederick Erickson has noted, small, inexpensive cassette tape recorders made it possible to capture language in use in a way that was prohibitively difficult before the 1960s. He was one of the very few at GURT 1981 who was already using sound film in his research. Now we are seeing the proliferation of communication technologies from palm-sized digital video recorders to cell phones and chat rooms on the Internet. Journals are going online, and theses are being submitted in multimedia formats. The term "multimodality" is coming to be used across many fields within which linguists work to encompass these many new technological changes. It was our goal in this fifty-third annual conference at Georgetown University's Department of Linguistics to bring together scholars working in a variety of fields and in subdisciplines of linguistics both to assess the state of the art in different areas of research and to facilitate cross-disciplinary and cross-subfield links in the development of research in discourse and technological change.

Multimodal Discourse Analysis

The subtheme of GURT 2002, multimodal discourse analysis, was intended to highlight the recognition discussed in many of the papers in this volume that all discourse is multimodal. That is, language in use, whether this is in the form of spoken language or text, is always and inevitably constructed across multiple modes of communication, including speech and gesture not just in spoken language but through such "contextual" phenomena as the use of the physical spaces in which we carry out our discursive actions or the design, papers, and typography of the documents within which our texts are presented.

One of the problems of GURT 2002 that was at least partly addressed in these papers is the question of how we should understand words such as *multimodality* or, more simply, *modality*. For example, in Theo Van Leeuwen's chapter, "modality" is derived from the concept of modality in grammatical studies of language where the primary notions carried by the "modal" verbs ("might," "could," "should," and so forth) are extended to mean any of a wide array of stances that may be taken to the existential status of a representation. In his thinking, "modality" in this traditional grammatical sense needs to be kept clear from the concept of a "mode" of communication—any of the many ways in which a semiotic system with an internal grammaticality, such as speech, color, taste, or the design of images, may be developed. "Modality" in the grammatical sense may be realized within any of the many "modes" that may be used to communicate. Thus, "modality" is polysemous in that it might make reference either to the grammatical system of existential stances or simply to the presence or use of modes of communication.

Carey Jewitt's chapter takes up a second terminological problem in discussions of multimodality, the problem of mediation. She argues for making an analytical distinction between a mode of communication and a medium of communication, though, of course, there can be no mode that does not exist in some medium. The former is a semiotic system of contrasts and oppositions, a grammatical system, as Van Leeuwen has noted; the latter is a physical means of inscription or distribution such as a printed or handwritten text, making the sounds of speech (in the physical sense), body movements, or light impulses on a computer screen.

The notion of multimodal discourse analysis in the papers in this volume varies quite considerably from papers that focus primarily on technological media to ones that focus on what might more traditionally have been called nonverbal communication. Although we believe that this polysemy and ambiguity may ultimately need to be resolved, at least for individual scholars within their own research projects, we feel that this collection makes for a suitably rich and varied treatment of the current state of the art in the study of multimodal discourse analysis.

GURT 2002 as a Multimodal Discourse

Discourse and technology was not only the conceptual theme of GURT 2002, but it was also a practical problem for the management of the conference. The use of webpage design software, the Internet, instant messaging, and the capture and transfer of digital images would in itself make an interesting study of how new technologies and associated discursive practices culminate in and sustain an event. Although the readers of this volume hardly need to be reminded of the changes brought about by email, it is worth noting not only the volume of electronic messages sent in preparation for the conference, but also the speed and global access this technology afforded. As some of these emails made clear, information provided (or not provided) on the GURT webpage had a good deal to do with the actions taken by participants prior to the conference. In short, one of the lessons of this conference was that the effect of new technologies is most clear when it becomes difficult to imagine communicating without them.

Multiple Threads of the Discourse at GURT 2002

The papers in this volume most often treat several themes; indeed, it would be difficult for them not to do so. Five themes, however, may be pulled out that were central in the conference and are well represented here.

Why should we study discourse and technology and multimodal discourse analysis?

The central argument made here is made in most of the chapters of this book. These authors argue that discourse is inherently multimodal, not monomodal. A monomodal concept of discourse is distorting, and therefore, now that we can, we should open up the lens to discover a fuller view of how humans communicate. Erickson's chapter is particularly adroit in suggesting that the somewhat narrowed compass of discourse analysis in the past two decades derives from the coupling of the inexpensive audiotape recording and the IBM Selectric typewriter. The recorder narrowed the focus to the audible soundtrack and the IBM Selectric enabled the careful transcription of that track onto standard 8.5 x 11-inch sheets of paper. In his view, this is less than we were able to do using the admittedly more expensive sound film and much less than we are now able to do using handheld video cameras and laptop software suites for analysis. The chapter by Marilyn and Jack Whalen et al. illustrates the usefulness of multimodal analysis in workplace settings, what they call "workscapes."

The second argument for why we should study discourse and technology is that there are, in fact, new forms of discourse. The chapters by Rodney Jones, Angela Goddard, Boyd Davis and Peyton Mason, and Hsi-Yao Su point to the proliferation of new forms of discourse on the Internet and in "chat" settings. Jewitt and Erickson discuss many ways in which educational discourse is being transformed from the traditional teacher-student-textbook model of mediation to much more complex forms of mediation that bring software designers into the equation as well as educators themselves as developers of these new forms of discourse. Lilie Chouliaraki gives an extended account of the way "live" television broadcasts of the events of September 11, 2001, reconstructed Danish viewers within a new discourse of periphery and center. Whalen et al. focus directly on the problems of technology-mediated human discourse in call centers and service encounters.

The role of the web in discourse analysis

Not only is the World Wide Web enabling new forms of discourse, it is enabling new forms of discourse analysis. Jones, Goddard, Davis and Mason, and Su all use their analyses of web-based or web-centered discourse as a means of analyzing phenomena that extend considerably beyond just the interactions mediated by the web. Jones, for example, uses web-based software such as "screen movies" to capture extended and very complex strings of social interactions among multiple identities. Goddard, Davis and Mason, and Su take advantage of the text-based medium to look into identity production and indexicality, the appropriation of professional social roles, and mock-accented Taiwanese Mandarin, phenomena that might be rather ephemeral and certainly difficult to capture in some other medium or contexts.

Multimodal discourse analysis in studies of social actions and interactions

A third theme, again evident in many of the chapters of this book, is the study of social actions as multimodal phenomena. Some, such as Ingrid de Saint-Georges, Sigrid Norris, Alexandra Johnston, and Elisa Everts, take advantage of convenient video recording to capture social interactions in which there is relatively little talk (e.g., Johnston's study of immigration service interviews or de Saint-Georges' study of manual-labor work sites), where there are a multiplicity of constantly shifting participant structures and identities (e.g., Norris's study of two women working and living within their homes and families), and where there is a limit placed on the use of a particular mode (Everts's study of interactions between blind and sighted friends). Laurent Filliettaz uses perhaps the least technology of all the papers but carefully theorizes relations between discourse and actions across modes. Joel Kuipers argues that the use of video technology in conducting ethnography of speaking research shows that we have both underestimated and overestimated the play of multiple modes in our analyses. Video records, he argues, have shown that in some cases participants in rituals are actually attending *less* to the audible track than we might be led to imagine if that were the only mode of recording available. This argument is corroborated in Norris's chapter.

Multimodal discourse analysis in educational social interactions

It is natural, of course, because so many academic researchers are themselves working within educational environments that their research themes would encompass educational social interactions. Thus Jones, Goddard, Davis and Mason, and Yakura all use data that involve students in educational institutions. Jewitt and Erickson, however, address the use of technology in education more directly. Jewitt's paper, though primarily focused on elucidating the distinction between mode and media in terms such as "multimodality" and "multimediality," provides a window on a project in which the whole educational environment of students from texts and technology to the structure of schoolrooms is taken up in an integrated multimodal discourse analysis. Erickson's chapter argues that the use of new recording technologies assists educators and educational researchers to open up the time frame to which they may apply their analyses. Early film studies were restricted to stretches of continuous data that were just minutes long. Audiotape data might extend to sixty minutes at a stretch. Now suites of technology and software enable comparisons of events across whole school years, and these are providing insights into rhythms of a periodicity that were all but invisible just a few years ago.

The use of MMDA in doing our analyses in workplaces

Schools are, of course, workplaces for teachers and administrators but because of very great differences in purposes, participant structures, and the common places in the life cycle of the participants, research on schools may not easily be transferred to studies of the workplace. The chapter by Whalen et al., like that of de Saint-Georges, focuses on sites where multiple participants are focused on accomplishing tasks with real-world material outcomes—the filling of work or service orders, for example, in the case of Whalen et al., or the cleaning of an attic in the case of de Saint-Georges. These studies point out, by comparison, some of the inherent weaknesses in more traditional forms of discourse analysis, which tend to be focused upon short, talk- or text-dominated social interactions. Common problems of intersubjectivity and coherence may be spread over multiple interactions and across several participants working jointly or in sequence. In both cases, social interaction is not only mediated by but also carried out through the use of a multiplicity of tools, objects, and technologies, from work-order forms in Whalen et al. to buckets, cleanser, and cleaning rags in de Saint-Georges. These chapters demonstrate that the use of new technologies of video recording and data extraction are now opening up new areas of research that extend beyond the talk-centered genres upon which much contemporary discourse analysis has been based.

Discourse Analysis Going Forward from GURT 2002

Each of the authors in this volume has taken a somewhat different perspective on discourse and technology and on multimodal discourse analysis. Their papers, like the conference itself, exude an enthusiasm for opening up the lens, for greater inclusion of more modes of communication within the purview of discourse analysis, and for enabling this expansiveness through the full use of current and yet-to-come technologies of communication. We editors also share this enthusiasm, of course, but in closing would like to introduce two thoughts, the first having to do with the sociopolitical circumstances of the period within which we live and the second a simple reminder that we follow in the steps of researchers whose examples are genuinely humbling.

In the first case, as Yakura's chapter has noted, we now work under a heightened awareness of the intrusiveness of our own research behaviors in the lives of others. The better the technology for capturing the full subtlety of human communication, the more easily that technology may abuse the rights to privacy of those whom we would wish to study. The primary question now is not: Do we have or can we develop the technology needed to record the behavior of others? The primary question is: What rights does an academic researcher have in relationship to and in negotiation with her or his subjects of study? And we ask this question knowing that it might be extended considerably further into domains of political analysis, in short: Can our data collection and our analyses do others good or harm, and can we control those outcomes?

Although it might seem that these questions could have a dampening effect on research in multimodal discourse analysis, a second reminder might be useful in conclusion. No author may be cited in these pages more than Erving Goffman. His thinking is central to our understanding of discourse in its full panoply of social and situational meanings, and his writings are replete with sharply observed examples of multimodality in the analysis of discourse. As far as we know, Goffman's research technology did not extend much beyond his own acute observations and the pens and pencils with which he wrote his notes and the scissors he used to clip examples from published sources such as newspapers and magazines.

A second but less well-known researcher also deserves mention. One of the highlights in the preparation of the conference was the acquisition of several films by Weldon Kees, the poet, musician, and filmmaker who collaborated with Jürgen Ruesch and Gregory Bateson on a number of projects. Of special note is *Approaches and Leavetakings,* a twelve-minute collection of clips shot on 16mm film. The film depicts the kind of structured interaction Goffman was soon to write about with such precision: students on a college campus "holding forth," and "moving in fast"; children dropped off for their first day at school; businessmen, pedestrians, and shopkeepers greeting, chatting, and parting company.

Shot in 1955, the film is a remarkably adept use of technology as a means to capture expressive behavior in public encounters. The role of technology was not lost on Kees, who notes in the opening frames that "the camera records the signals by which people announce their conscious or unconscious intentions of approaching, meeting, leaving, or avoiding one another." At least two of the themes discussed earlier in this chapter surface in the film. There is the multimodality of social action, evident in the coordinated use of gesture, speech, body orientation, and gaze. And there is the issue of intrusion, undeniably reflected in the suspicious glances occasionally thrown back at the lens of Kees's camera. The film is also a reminder of a period that preceded the development of the technologies that have since shaped discourse analysis and discourse in use. We hope the papers in this volume make a useful contribution to the discussion of issues these new technologies have raised.

REFERENCES

Krystal, A. 2002. Against type? What the writing machine has wrought. *Harper's* 305(1831): 82–88.

Ruesch, J., and W. Kees. 1955. *Approaches and leavetakings.* 16mm film. San Francisco: Langley Porter Clinic.

Tannen, D. 1982. *Georgetown University Round Table on Languages and Linguistics 1981: Analyzing discourse—Text and talk.* Washington, DC: Georgetown University Press.

Ten Reasons Why Linguists Should Pay Attention to Visual Communication

THEO VAN LEEUWEN
Centre for Language and Communication Research, Cardiff University

THE TEXT OF THE FAMOUS KITCHENER POSTER (fig. 2.1) realizes a speech act. Four linguistic features combine to create a kind of demand: the direct address; the declarative; the verb, which lexicalizes a request ("need"); and the fact that the agent whose needs are expressed here has, in the given context, the right to demand something from the addressee (a moral right, based on patriotism). Taken together, these features create a hybrid speech act, a speech act that oscillates between bluntness and formality, directness (the direct address) and indirectness (the indirect demand). And then we haven't even mentioned the typography, with its highly salient, large "you."

But the poster also realizes an *image act,* again through a combination of features. The pointing finger and the look at the viewer realize a visual demand (Kress and Van Leeuwen 1996:122), and the other features (the imperious nature of the look, and the uniform and Prussian moustache, both symbols of authority) modulate this demand into a very direct, maximally authoritative visual summons.

The question is, what do we have here? One or two speech acts? The same demand formulated twice, once visually, in a rather direct way, and once verbally, in a more indirect, less personalized and more formal way? Or one single multimodal communicative act in which image and text blend like instruments in an orchestra?

If we take the first approach, we will have to sequentialize what we in fact see in one glance, and posit a reading path that leads our eye from the picture to the text. This will make us see the sequence as structured by some kind of "elaboration" (Halliday 1985:202), in which the message of the text becomes a polite restatement of the pictorial message.

In the everyday face-to-face equivalent of this poster, we would not dream of doing so. Imagine an actual uniformed man addressing us in this way. Clearly we would experience this as a single, multilayered, multimodal communicative act, whose illocutionary force comes about through the fusion of all the component semiotic modalities: dress, grooming, facial expression, gaze, gesture. Perhaps we should view posters and similar texts (e.g., display advertisements) in the same way—as single, multimodal communicative acts, especially inasmuch as the cohesion between the verbal and the visual is usually enhanced by some form of stylistic unity between the image, the typography and the layout.

Figure 2.1. Kitchener Recruitment Poster (1914).

So here is the first of my ten reasons why linguists should pay attention to visual communication:

1. Speech acts should be renamed communicative acts and understood as multimodal microevents in which all the signs present combine to determine its communicative intent.

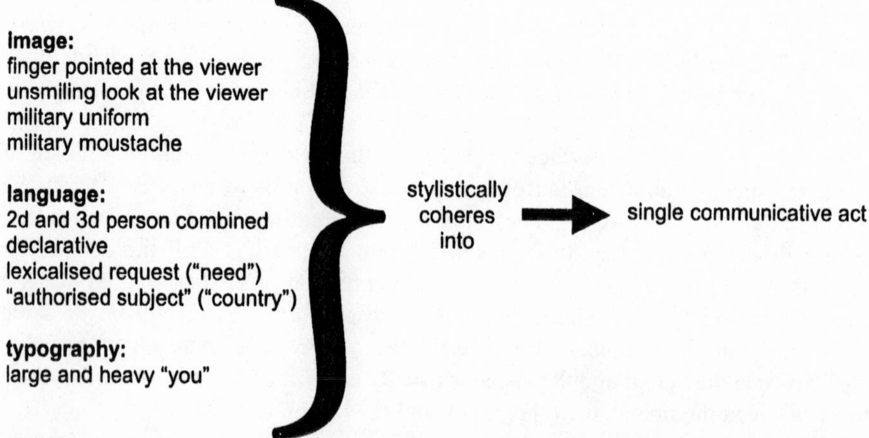

Figure 2.2. Coherence of Image, Language, and Typography into a Single Communicative Act.

An influential early study of the generic structure of service encounters (Hasan 1979) used the following key example:

Who's next?	[Sale initiation]
I think I am	
I'll have ten oranges and a kilo of bananas please	[Sale Request]
Yes anything else?	[Sale Compliance]
Yes	
I wanted some strawberries but these don't look very ripe	[Sale Enquiry]
Oh they're ripe alright, they're just that colour, a greeny pink	
Mmm I see	
Will they be OK for this evening?	[Sale Enquiry]
Oh yeah they'll be fine. I had some yesterday and they're good, very sweet and fresh	
Oh alright then. I'll take two	[Sale Request]
You'll like them cos they're good	
Will that be all?	[Sale Enquiry]
Yeah thank you	[Sale Compliance]
That'll be two dollars sixty-nine please	[Sale]
I can give you nine cents	[Purchase]
Yeah OK thanks, eighty, a hundred, three dollars	[Purchase Closure]
Come again	[Finis]
See ya	

The point here is that the entire transaction is realized by talk. To understand it, there is no need for any context, or any consideration of nonverbal communication. Shopping in a modern supermarket, on the other hand, does not happen in this way. Every single one of the component activities or "stages" of the shopping transaction analyzed by Hasan will occur, but instead of asking about the quality of the products, they will be visually inspected and handled silently. The checkout queue, too, will form silently, and the products will be silently taken from the trolley and placed on the conveyor belt, although the checkout assistant will perhaps still say the total amount out loud and mumble a "thank you." In other words, it has become a multimodal structure. Some of the stages are realized verbally, others through action, or through writing and visual communication (looking at the price tags on the shelves, reading the sell-by date and the ingredients on the package). The same applies to getting cash from an automatic teller machine. The directives issued by the machine are realized visually or verbally, the responses are mechanical actions. If, in studying interactions of this kind, we were to transcribe only the speech, our transcription would make little sense. In a study of children watching a video and interacting with a computer, Sigrid Norris makes the same point, concluding that the linguistic utterances in such interactions "at best seem to be related through repetition and prosody, and at worst seem bare, fragmented and lacking coherence" (2002:117).

Here is one more example, taken from Paddy Chayevsky's 1953 television play script *Printer's Measure* (1994). Note how some of the communicative acts, some of the microevents that constitute this "apprenticeship episode," are realized by speech, others by actions such as looking up, scurrying down the shop, and pulling out a letterhead. Remember also that the individual stages, whether dominated by speech or action, are all in themselves also multimodal, as pointed out in the previous section: Mr. Healey's summons ("Hey! Come here!"), once performed by an actor, is just as multimodal as Kitchener's call to arms in the poster.

MR. HEALEY:	Hey! Come here!	[Call to attention]
The boy looks up and comes scurrying down the shop, dodging the poking arm of the Kluege press, and comes to Mr. Healey.		
Mr. Healey pulls out a letterhead, points to a line of print.		[Demonstration]
MR. HEALEY:	What kind of type is that?	[Quizzing]
BOY:	Twelve point Clearface.	
MR. HEALEY:	How do you know?	[Probing]
BOY:	It's lighter than Goudy, and the lower case "e" goes up.	
MR. HEALEY:	Clearface is a delicate type. It's clean, it's clear. It's got line and grace. Remember that.	[Instruction]
	Beat it.	[Dismissal]

The boy hurries back to the front of the shop to finish his cleaning.

All this applies not just to face-to-face interaction. The stages of written genres, too, may be realized either verbally or visually. In print advertisements with a "problem-solution" approach, for instance, the "problem" may be represented verbally, as in an advertisement for hearing aids that opens with the line "Want to hear clearly?"; or visually, as in an advertisement for headache tablets that shows a picture of a sufferer with a contorted face.

Hence my next two points:

II. Genres of speech and writing are in fact multimodal: speech genres combine language and action in an integrated whole, written genres combine language, image, and graphics in an integrated whole. Speech genres should therefore be renamed "performed" genres and written genres "inscribed" genres. Various combinations of performance and inscription are of course possible.

III. The communicative acts that define the stages of "performed" genres may or may not include speech, just as the communicative acts that define the stages of genres of "inscribed" communication may or may not include writing.

▒ The boundaries between communicative episodes (groups of stages), are often realized by actions, for instance changes in posture (see Scheflen 1963). The transcript below is an extract from the dialogue of an *X-Files* movie titled *Colony.* Without the nonverbal action, the dialogue appears continuous. But in fact Agent Mulder stands up abruptly as he says "Your guess?" After this the exchange continues, but in a different, more confrontational mode. In other words, the dialogue continues unbroken, with a classic "dialogue hook" (". . .my guess" —"Your guess?"), but the posture change signals the boundary with a new stage in the interaction.

MULDER: What are they?
KURZWEIL: What do you think?
MULDER: Transportation systems. Transgenic crop, the pollen genetically altered to carry a virus.
KURZWEIL: That would be my guess.
MULDER: Your guess? What do you mean your guess? You told me you had the answer.
KURZWEIL: Yeah.

The same applies to written language. In a Spanish language textbook (Martin and Ellis 2001:59), the different parts of the text are given a graphic identity. "Activities" (*'forma frases con* ***es*** *o* ***está****'*) are signaled by a purple logo-number and an icon. The authentic language examples to be studied are printed in cream-colored boxes, and individually framed as well, with different colors for classified advertisements and "proverbs," and new bits of vocabulary and/or grammatical information are enclosed in blue boxes.

Of course, in some genres transitions are still predominantly constructed through language, just as there are still many genres of spoken interaction in which the stages and their boundaries are for the most part realized linguistically. But overall, the relation between language and other semiotic modes is changing in complex ways. As we have seen, in service encounters the increasing importance of "self-service" creates a much greater role for visual communication and bodily action. At the same time, the increased use of distance communication has caused many "manual" actions and transactions to become "dialogized," for instance instructions (e.g., computer help screens and help lines) or medical checkups (telemedicine). Again, although visual structuring is replacing linguistic structuring in many types of print media, new types of screen genres (e.g., websites) make much greater use of written language than older screen media such as film and television. To understand such changes, and their products, the study of speech and writing needs to be integrated fully with the study of other semiotic modes.

So:

IV. The boundaries between the elements or stages of both performed and inscribed genres are often signaled visually.

In a still recent past, the dominant relation between the words and images in written text was what Roland Barthes called "anchorage" (Barthes 1977:38): the text restated the message of the picture, but in a more precise way, distilling just one from the many possible meanings the image might have. In newspapers the captions of news photographs anchored the meaning of images in this way, answering the unspoken question "What (who, where) is it?" In advertisements, visual puns were paralleled by verbal puns, just in case the point was missed. Less common, said Barthes, is the "relay" relation, in which text and image are complementary. It occurs mostly in dialogue (e.g., comic strips), where speaker and context will be represented visually, and the dialogue itself verbally.

Today "relay" is much more common, and not restricted to dialogue. Even at the level of the single "proposition," the visual and the verbal may be integrated into a single syntagm. An advertisement for cat food (see figure 2.3) shows a fluffy grey kitten lying on a soft sheet. A linguistic analysis of the text, with its tender typography, usually reserved for creams, lotions, soaps, and soft tissues, will make little sense. There is only the "spoilt, spoilt, spoilt, spoilt." But together with the picture, the words form something like an attributive clause (Halliday 1985:113) in which the "Carrier" of the attribute (the cat) is realized visually and the attribute verbally ("spoilt, spoilt, spoilt, spoilt"), while the relational process is also realized visually, by visual cohesion and composition.

In diagrams, language is often reduced to lexis, whereas the visual provides the syntax, identifying the participants by, for example, enclosing them in boxes, and

Figure 2.3. Cat Food Advertisement (*Vogue*, November 2001).

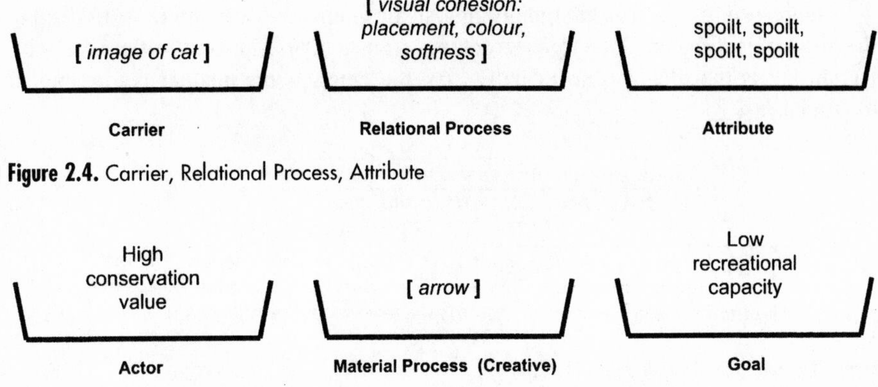

Figure 2.4. Carrier, Relational Process, Attribute

Figure 2.5. Actor, Material Process, Goal

realizing the "process," for example, by means of an arrow, rather than a verb such as "leads to" or "causes" or "results in" (see figure 2.6, which might be analyzed as follows):

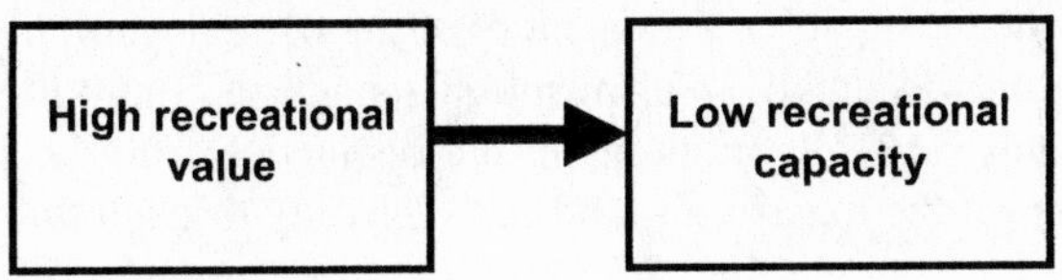

Figure 2.6. High Recreational Value—Low Recreational Capacity

The influential London typographer Jonathan Barnbrook uses this principle in many of his designs for television commercials (figure 2.7): the participants (whether images, text, or graphics) are first identified visually by putting them in various kinds of boxes and giving them distinct typographic identities and colors, and then linked together by lines or arrows.

Figure 2.7. Vicks Commercial (Barnbrook 1996).

Interestingly, this is what many linguists have also done, in attempts to display the structure of clauses or larger structures (figure 2.8). The only difference with Barnbrook is that they do not usually give the components distinct typographical identities:

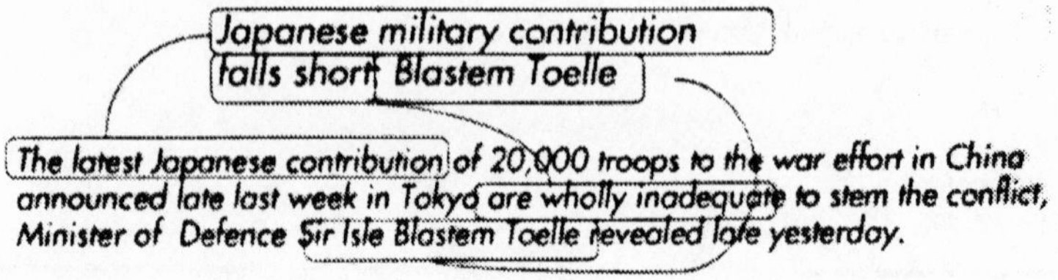

Japanese military contribution
falls short Blastem Toelle

The latest Japanese contribution of 20,000 troops to the war effort in China announced late last week in Tokyo are wholly inadequate to stem the conflict, Minister of Defence Sir Isle Blastem Toelle revealed late yesterday.

Figure 2.8. Diagram from Iedema (1993:142).

So:

V. Even at the level of the single "proposition," the visual and the verbal can be integrated into a single syntagmatic unit.

Typography is an increasingly important branch of visual communication. Formerly it saw itself for the most part as a transmitter of the written word, but today it is becoming a communicative mode in its own right—and itself multimodal. It no longer communicates only through variations in the distinctive features that allow us to identify and connect the letterforms, and not even only through the connotations of particular fonts, for example the association of Park Avenue script with formality and high status, but also through modes which it shares with other types of visual communication—color, texture, and movement. Shown in figure 2.9, for instance, is the logo of an avant-garde arts magazine, hand-knitted by the mother of Enzo Cucchi, the designer. Through its texture it makes a statement against the slick commercial logo and connotes the values of handcrafted art and design.

Figure 2.9. Parkett Logo (Cucchi 1984).

Such uses of typography no longer only occur in the work of professional designers. They can, for instance, also be found in children's schoolwork, as has been demonstrated by Ormerod and Ivanic (2002).

So:

VI. Typography and handwriting are no longer just vehicles for linguistic meaning, but semiotic modes in their own right.

Visual communication is particularly important for critical discourse analysis (CDA). Nowhere near enough attention has been paid to it in CDA, with most critical discourse analysts analyzing transcripts of only the words of political speeches, or newspaper articles taken out of their visual context (for a recent exception, see Fairclough 2000).

Let me demonstrate the point with a simple example relating to racist discourse, an issue of central concern to many critical discourse analysts (see Wodak and Reisigl 2000 for a recent collection). A text like the following, from Anthony Trollope's account of the West Indies in 1858 (quoted in Nederveen Pieterse 1992:199) is now completely unacceptable:

> The Negro is idle, unambitious as to worldly position, sensual and content with little. He lies under the mango-tree and eats the luscious fruit in the sun. He lies on the grass surrounded by oranges, bananas and pine-apples.

But, as Nederveen Pieterse has shown in his book *White on Black* (1992), such racist views were also expressed visually and continue to be expressed to this day, especially in comic strips, advertisements, tourism brochures, and the like. Racist imagery has in fact a much more tenacious life than racist language, maybe because the idea is still widespread that the meaning of images is more subjective than the meaning of words, more "in the eye of the beholder," and maybe also because so many of these images are found in entertainment-oriented texts which often escape critical scrutiny, including critical scrutiny by critical discourse analysts, but may in fact be much more important carriers of political and ideological meanings in contemporary society than parliamentary speeches, newspaper editorials, and BBC radio interviews (see Van Leeuwen 2001).

So:

VII. Critical discourse analysis needs to take account of nonverbal as well as verbally realized discourses and aspects of discourse, and of image as well as text, because these often realize quite different, sometimes even contrasting meanings.

Multimodal analysis must work with concepts and methods that are not specific to language, or indeed to any other mode, but can be applied cross-modally. Such concepts will necessarily center on the communicative *functions* that can be fulfilled by several or all semiotic modes. A few of these have already been mentioned: boundary marking, attributing qualities to entities, calling to attention, and so on. In many cases the concepts clearly are already there, but perhaps without having been thought of as multimodal.

One such concept is modality. It has moved from being uniquely associated with a certain linguistic form class, the modal auxiliaries, to being associated with the communicative function of expressing the truth value of propositions (Hodge and Kress 1988). Once this move was made, it could be seen not only that there are different *kinds* of modality, even within language (Halliday 1985:85, 332), for instance, subjective modality, realized through mental process verbs and nouns, and frequency, realized through frequency adverbs such as "sometimes," "often," and "always"; but also that every semiotic mode that is capable of realizing representations has the means of expressing modality, of expressing the truth or validity of the representations it can realize.

Wherever it is possible to argue about whether something is "true" or "real," there will also be *signifiers* for "truth" and "reality." And just as language allows different degrees and kinds of truth to be expressed, so do other semiotic modes. We can, for instance, say "This is true bread" or "This is real bread"—and if we do, we will do so from the point of view of a particular truth or validity criterion, for instance that of the natural, the "organic." In that case we will look for certain signifiers, the color brown, pictures of sheaves of wheat, the word "organic," seeds baked into the crust of bread. And there will, on the supermarket shelves, be loaves that display some of these signifiers to some degree, but are not quite as hard, heavy, and clunky as bread that is semiotically maximally organic. Needless to say, this does not necessarily mean that it is in fact produced in the most organic way, just as the use of high modality linguistic items such as "definitely" and "certainly" and "absolutely" does not necessarily mean that the propositions they endorse are actually true.

There is not the space here to explain in full the account of visual modality that Gunther Kress and I developed in our book *Reading Images* (1996:159ff). But that there is such a thing as visual modality can be suggested by a simple example. In newspapers, photographs tend to have high modality. They purport to show the facts as they were, and their present electronic manipulability therefore leads to much concern (Ritchen 1990). Drawings, on the other hand, have traditionally been associated with opinion and comment. It is perhaps for this reason that concern about violence in media products targeted at or accessible to children is the greater the higher the modality of these images. What is allowed in children's comic strips would never be allowed in photographic images or movies for children. Drawings, on the other hand, are considered lower in modality, more in the realm of "fantasy" than in the realm of "fact."

So:

VIII. Many of the concepts developed in the study of grammar and text are not specific to language. In some cases, for instance narrative, this has been known for a long time; in others (e.g., transitivity, modality, cohesion) it is only just starting to be realized.

▩ If has often been said that language is unique in its stratal configuration, having the three layers of phonology, lexicogrammar, and discourse, to use the systemic-functional version of the theory (see Martin 1992).

Imagine my surprise when, having organized a seminar on the semiotics of smell and invited an aromatherapist to speak at one of the sessions, I learned that there are fifty basic smells, which combine into fragrances according to a syntax of "head," "body," and "base" in which smells have to have particular qualities to be able to function as head, body, or base, for instance in terms of volatility. These fragrances then in turn combine into a limitless number of possible aromas (scientists, incidentally, have other ways of discerning "elementary smells"). Most of us think of smell as a collection of irreducible, unique experiences that would defy any attempt at systematization and stratification. But apparently any semiotic mode, even smell, can be conceived of as a loose collection of individual signs, a kind of lexicon, or a stratified system of rules that allow a limited number of elements to generate an infinite number of messages. Even language: supported by large-scale language corpora, there are now new linguistic discourses emerging in which language itself is no longer seen as an economic rule-governed system, but as a vast storehouse of short phrases and formulas, and in which linguistic structure is essentially reduced to lexical structure. According to Halliday (see Kress, Hasan, and Martin 1992:184), Chinese linguistics, which goes back to the second or third century B.C., never developed the notion of grammar and had two layers only, a "very abstract phonological tradition" and a "lexicographical and encyclopedic tradition." On the other hand, in our own work Gunther Kress and I have devised grammars in fields that were previously not thought of as having a grammar, such as visual communication (Kress and Van Leeuwen 1996, 2001).

This leads to a further point. The way a semiotic mode is organized relates to what we want to do with it. As I argued earlier, visual communication increasingly fulfils a syntactic role, at least in some highly visible and socially significant genres of writing, while language is increasingly reduced to a lexical role. Is it a wonder that the interest in visual syntax is on the rise, and the interest in linguistic syntax on the wane?

What I have said here about the structure of language as a semiotic resource would also apply to the structure of communicative events. In our recent work on multimodal discourse (Kress and Van Leeuwen 2001) we have in essence adapted Goffman's theory of footing (1981) and argued that the roles of "principal," "author," and "animator" can be applied not just to talk, but also to other semiotic modes (we added a further role, the technological role of preserving and/or disseminating the message, a role Goffman mentions but does not give a name to).

In the terminology used in our book, there is, first of all, a "discourse," a particular way of conceiving of some aspect of the world, say, family life. In Amsterdam such a discourse was developed in the early twentieth century by Wibaut, a councilor who was concerned about the circumstances in which the workers lived in Amsterdam (Roegholt 1976). So Wibaut, and more generally the city of Amsterdam, was the *principal* of this discourse, which included great stress on the values of the family unit, on hygiene, on brightness and light, and much more.

Second, there is "design": the architects of the Amsterdam School were called upon to design family homes for the workers that would realize the discourse (which can itself also be realized in other semiotic modes, for instance in language). These architects were therefore the *authors*. To realize the stress on the family home as a fortress against the outside world, they made apartment blocks that looked like veritable fortresses, and to make sure people would turn inward and sit around the cozy stove rather than hang out of the windows and shout at the neighbors across the road, they made the windows so high that you could not hang out of them unless you stood on a chair.

Finally, there is "production": builders built the fortresses and so acted as the *animators* of this semiotic production.

And just as is the case in talk, such roles may either be combined in one person (e.g., someone building his or her own house to fit a particular view of how families should live), or form the basis of specific divisions of labor.

In short:

IX. The concepts that have been used to describe the structure of language as a resource and the "footing" of talk can also be applied multimodally.

I have tried to put forward some arguments as to why linguists should pay attention to visual communication. Or, to put it more positively, why multimodal communication is an exciting new area for linguistic research, an area in which many projects are just waiting to be done, and many treasures just waiting to be discovered.

But the opposite also applies. Students of visual communication should also pay attention to linguistics. As I have tried to suggest, the skills and experience of the linguist are just what is needed to understand the shape that visual communication is taking today and the ways in which language is integrated with other semiotic modes in contemporary communication.

X. Students of visual communication should also pay attention to linguists, as many linguistic concepts and methods are directly applicable to, and highly productive for, the study of visual communication.

REFERENCES

Barthes, R. 1977. *Image, music, text.* London: Fontana.

Chayevsky, P. 1994. *The collected works of Paddy Chayevsky: The television plays.* New York: Applause Theatre and Cinema Books.

Fairclough, N. 2000. *New labour, new language.* London: Routledge.

Goffman, E. 1981. *Forms of talk.* Oxford: Blackwell.

Halliday, M. A. K. 1985. *An introduction to functional grammar.* London: Arnold.

Hasan, R. 1979. On the notion of text. In J. S. Petöfi, ed., *Text vs. sentence: Basic questions of text linguistics,* vol. II, 369–90. Hamburg: Helmut Buske.

Hodge, R., and G. Kress. 1988. *Social semiotics.* Cambridge: Polity.

Iedema, R. 1993. *Media literacy report.* Sydney: Disadvantaged Schools Project.

Kress, G., and T. Van Leeuwen. 1996. *Reading images: The grammar of visual design.* London: Routledge.

——. 2001. *Multimodal discourse: The modes and media of contemporary communication.* London: Arnold.

Kress, G., R. Hasan, and J. Martin. 1992. An interview with M. A. K. Halliday. *Social Semiotics* 2(1): 176–96.

Martin, J. R. 1992. *English text: System and structure.* Amsterdam: Benjamins.

Martin, R. M., and M. Ellis. 2001. *Pasos: A first course in Spanish*, vol. 1. London: Hodder & Stoughton.

Nederveen Pieterse, J. 1992. *White on black: Images of Africa and blacks in western popular culture.* New Haven: Yale University Press.

Norris, S. 2002. The implication of visual research for discourse analysis: transcription beyond language. *Visual Communication* 1(1): 97–121.

Ormerod, F., and R. Ivanic. 2002. Materiality in children's meaning-making practices. *Visual Communication* 1(1): 65–91.

Ritchen, F. 1990. Photojournalism in the age of computers. In C. Squiers, ed., *The Critical Image,* 28–37. Seattle: Bay Press.

Roegholt, R. 1976. *Amsterdam in de 20e eeuw.* Utrecht: Uitgeverij Het Spectrum.

Scheflen, A. E. 1963. The significance of posture in communication systems. *Psychiatry* 27:316–31.

Van Leeuwen, T. 2001. Visual racism. In R. Wodak and M. Reisigl, eds., *The semiotics of racism,* 333–50. Vienna: Passagen Verlag.

Wodak, R., and M. Reisigl. 2000. *The semiotics of racism.* Vienna: Passagen Verlag.

The Problem of Context in Computer-Mediated Communication

RODNEY H. JONES
City University of Hong Kong

IT IS AN OPEN SECRET in my freshman composition class at City University of Hong Kong that most of the conversations taking place in the computer-equipped classroom are with people who are not present and about topics totally irrelevant to English composition. It is not that the students are not listening to me or completing the tasks I assign to them. But, as they work on in-class writing and peer-editing exercises, conduct searches for reference materials, download notes from the course webpage, and listen to me lecture them about the features of academic writing style, they are at the same time chatting with friends, classmates, and sometimes strangers using the popular chat and instant-messaging software ICQ. As I make my way down the aisles of the classroom, searching for students in need of assistance, I catch glimpses of message windows flickering open and closed and ICQ "contact lists" expanding and collapsing on the sides of screens. At first I found this practice rather disturbing, a clear indication that the students were not paying attention to what they should be paying attention to. When I confronted them with my concern, however, not only did they fail to offer the kind of contrition one might expect of students who have been "caught in the act," but they also expressed confusion as to why I would object to such a practice. They didn't understand how their side involvement with ICQ could in any way be seen as competing with the academic activities taking place, and some of them even wondered out loud how I could expect them to operate a computer *without* having their ICQ contact lists open.

I have since learned to tolerate this practice, resigned to the fact that I cannot police every computer screen in the room. Still, I often find myself wondering what my students are "doing" when they are gazing at their computer terminals—are they chatting on ICQ *while* they are studying English writing, or are they studying English writing *while* they are chatting on ICQ? In other words, is my lesson for them the "text," or is it merely the "context" for other (more important?) activities. It is these questions that have led me to the issues I will be addressing in this paper, issues around the status of *context* in the study of computer mediated communication (CMC).

Despite the importance accorded to the role of *context* in linguistics in recent years (see Goodwin and Duranti 1992; Halliday and Hasan 1985; Tracy 1998), linguistic studies of computer mediated communication have often conveniently avoided addressing the environments (both virtual and "actual") in which such communication takes place, restricting themselves for the most part to the analysis of decontextualized chat logs, email messages, or Usenet postings (Hine 2000; Jones

2001; Kendall 1999; see Collot and Belmore 1996; Davis and Brewer 1997; Rintel and Pittam 1997). Reading many academic accounts of computer-mediated communication, in fact, leaves one with the impression that such interaction takes place in a kind of virtual vacuum with little connection to the material worlds of the people sitting in front of computer screens and producing the words that analysts spend so much time dissecting and interpreting.

As the preceding story demonstrates, however, the physical circumstances in which computer-mediated communication takes place can have important effects on how such interaction is conducted, and the conduct of computer-mediated interaction can have important effects on how physical activities in the material world play out. The problem, however, in integrating discussions of context into the study of computer-mediated communication is that, from the point of view of the analyst, it is often difficult to put one's finger on exactly what aspects of the situation ought to count as context and sometimes even more difficult for the analyst to gain access to those aspects of the communication, especially when they involve the "private" actions of people sitting alone in front of their computer screens.

The purpose of this paper is to explore ways in which approaches to context developed for the study of written texts and face-to-face interaction might need to be revised if they are to be successfully applied to the study of computer mediated communication. The data for my discussion come from a participatory ethnographic study of the use of CMC by university students in Hong Kong, which involved the collection of data in a variety of different modes and from a variety of different perspectives, including interview and focus group data, online participant observation, reflective diaries, and "screen movies" of participants' computer use (Jones 2001). Results of the study suggest that traditional sociolinguistic conceptualizations of the terms of interaction and the contexts in which it takes place may need to be radically rethought in light of new communication technologies (Katriel 1999). In what follows I will suggest some of the lines along which I believe this rethinking ought to take place. More specifically, I will suggest that understanding the contexts of communication involving new media technologies will require that we challenge the *dichotomies* upon which some of our most basic assumptions about CMC in particular, and communication in general, rest: dichotomies that separate the "virtual" from the "real," the "sender" from the "receiver," the "public" from the "private," the "figure" from the "ground," and, finally, the "text" from the "context."

Perspectives on Context

> Utterance and situation are bound up inextricably with each other and the context of situation is indispensable for the understanding of the words. . . . A word without linguistic context is a mere figment that stands for nothing by itself; so in the reality of a spoken living tongue, the utterance has no meaning except in the context of situation.
>
> —Malinowski, *The Meaning of Meaning*

Ever since Malinowski, in his seminal paper "The problem of meaning in primitive languages" (1947), coined the term *context of situation,* linguists, anthropologists, and other social scientists have accepted as a given that meaning is situated and contingent on a whole host of factors beyond linguistic structures. Previous notions of context had defined it as the text directly preceding and directly following the particular bit of text (sentence, phrase, word) an analyst was interested in. Malinowski, however, insisted that the notion of context must "burst the bonds of mere linguistics and be carried over to the analysis of the general conditions under which a language is spoken" (306). This insistence marked a turning point in the field of linguistic anthropology, and today, according to Goodwin and Duranti (1992:32), "The notion of context stands at the cutting edge of much contemporary research into the relationship between language, culture, and social organization, as well as into the study of how language is structured in the way that it is."

Although nearly all linguists are in agreement as to the importance of "taking context into account," there is substantial disagreement as to what should be counted as context and how it should be analyzed, resulting in heated debates between students of language who maintain that only those aspects of context which are invoked in the text (or interaction) itself should be considered (Schegloff 1997) and those who insist that, to be meaningful, the notion of context must include broader social structures and the exercise of power and domination through social institutions and ideologies (Fairclough 1992; Van Dijk 1997). Some have worried that many analysts seem to approach context merely as a static "theater-stage backdrop" for the primary "performance" of the text (Goodwin and Duranti 1992), while others have claimed that multiple and murky definitions of context have transformed it into a "conceptual garbage can" into which analysts toss anything that lies outside of their immediate analytical (or disciplinary) focus (Clark and Carlson 1981).

Perhaps the most common approach to the problem of context has been to attempt to divide it up into its component parts. Firth (1957), for example, divided context into three components: the relevant features of participants, persons, personalities, the relevant objects in the situation, and the effect of the verbal action. Later, anthropologist Dell Hymes (1974, 1986) further refined Firth's categories in his model for the *ethnography of speaking,* which divides context into eight components: setting and scene, participants, ends, act sequence, key, instrumentalities, norms, and genre. Still later, Halliday, in considering context as a resource for meaning making and understanding, returned to a three-part division, but one very different from Firth's. He divided context into *field,* referring to the nature of the social action taking place, *tenor,* referring to the participants, their roles and relationships, and *mode,* referring to the symbolic or rhetorical channel and the role which language plays in the situation (Halliday and Hasan 1985:12).

The most important thing about all of these perspectives is that what counts as context is not limited to the physical reality surrounding the text. Instead the focus is on the "models" that people build up in their minds (and in their interaction) of the situation, and how they use these models to make predictions about the kinds of meanings that are likely to be foregrounded (Halliday and Hasan 1985:28) and the kinds of behaviors that will show them to be "competent" members of particular communities (Hymes 1986). At the same time, however, such approaches run the risk of focusing so much on the "parts" of context that they fail to capture the ways these various dimensions interact and affect one another. They also run the risk of portraying context as a rather static entity that remains relatively unchanged throughout a given speech event, thus failing to address the contingent, negotiated, and ever-changing character of context in social interaction.

From the point of view of computer-mediated communication, what makes such models problematic is their underlying assumptions that communication takes place in the form of focused social interactions that occur in particular physical spaces and involve easily identifiable participants with clearly defined roles and relationships, assumptions that do not hold in the face of new temporal, spatial, and social flexibilities introduced by technologically mediated contexts (Fernback 1999; Katriel 1999; Kendall 1999).

Other scholars have concerned themselves less with context as something communication "exists in," and more as something that interactants create as they go along. Perhaps the most influential approach of this kind is based on Goffman's (1974) notion of "framing"(see Gumperz 1992; Tannen 1993; Tannen and Wallat 1983), which he defines as the moment-by-moment shifts of "alignment" participants bring to interaction to signal "what they are doing" and "who they are being." For Goffman, context is not a simple, static thing that can be dissected and defined, but rather consists of multiple and complex *layers* of reality and deceit through which implicature and inference are managed. This view of context has been particularly influential in the fields of interactional sociolinguistics, with its concern with how people use particular conventions to signal their understandings of context (Gumperz 1992), and conversation analysis, with its concern with "micro-level" or "proximate" context, the ways context is created and managed through the sequential organization of talk (Schegloff 1991, 1997).

The most important way these approaches inform the study of computer-mediated communication is by reminding us that context is a function of interaction and negotiation, bound up with communicative intentions and purposes and dependent on the ways people enact *social presence* and become aware of and interpret the enactment of *social presence* by others. The "social situation," according to Goffman (1964:134), is, in its most fundamental definition, "an environment of *mutual monitoring possibilities,* anywhere within which an individual will find himself accessible to the naked senses of all others who are present, and similarly find them accessible to him" (emphasis mine).

It is this point that, as I will argue, lies at the heart of the inadequacies of models that were developed for written and face-to-face communication to deal with the question of context in computer-mediated communication. What makes communicating with new technologies different from face-to-face communication is not so much, as others have suggested, the "despatialization" of communication (Katriel 1999) or the loss of contextualization cues (Dubrovsky 1985; Dubrovsky et al. 1991; Sproull and Kiesler 1986), but rather the different sets of "mutual monitoring possibilities" that these technologies make available, the different ways in which they allow us to be *present* to one another and to be aware of other peoples' *presence.*

Places, Practices, and People

Despite their disagreements, analysts in nearly all the traditions discussed above have concerned themselves with three basic dimensions of context: the physical dimension, or "setting" (including both the physical environment in which communication takes place and the various channels for communication available in this environment), the dimension of the "activity" being engaged in (what participants are doing when they come together in particular settings), and the dimension of "participants" (including not just those immediately involved in the interaction but also other whose presence may affect it) (Murray 1988). Using Goffman's terminology, we would call these three dimensions *the social situation, the social occasion,* and *the social gathering.* In what follows I will briefly consider these three dimensions and the *dichotomies* that underlie them and suggest how they might be revised to both better accommodate the new terms of interaction introduced by computer-mediated communication and to help us see more traditional modes of interaction in new potentially more useful ways.

Setting: The virtual situation

> There is no longer an elsewhere.
>
> —de Certeau, *The Practice of Everyday Life*

Perhaps the biggest barrier to a useful understanding of the context in which computer-mediated interaction occurs is the tendency for the attention of analysts of CMC to stop at the screen's edge, for people to regard "virtual realties" and "material realities" as separate things. Part of this tendency stems from "media scripts" (Sannicolas 1997) about the Internet and academic perspectives on it that display a kind of utopian attachment to the "transcendent" nature of computer-mediated communication, seen to take place in the rarified realm of "cyberspace," populated by futuristic beings called "cyborgs" who are unencumbered by the concerns of mundane material reality (Haraway 1991; Negroponte 1995). Others have put forth less optimistic versions of the same "virtual"/"actual" dichotomy (Hamman 1998; Kendall 1999) expressing concern that the development of online communities threatens the maintenance of offline communities and social networks as users turn their backs on friends and relatives and "isolate" themselves in front of their computer terminals (Kraut et al. 1998; Kroker and Weinstein 1994). What has been lacking in discussions and research on "cyberspace" has been an exploration of its relationship to ordinary, occasioned practices in the material world of users (Hine 2000).

Nearly all research that has looked in detail at this relationship has found that the vast majority of people who engage in computer-mediated communication regard it as an extension (McLuhan 1994) of their "real-life" social interactions rather than as separate from them, that, far from propelling users into "cyberspace," the effect of CMC is more often to ground them more firmly within their existing material communities and circumstances. The participants in my study in Hong Kong, for example, used computer-mediated communication (ICQ chat and email) primarily to communicate with friends and classmates from their offline social networks rather than strangers. Several of the participants, in fact, were quite adamant in rejecting the traditional dichotomy of "actual" and "virtual" reality, insisting that computer-mediated communication is as "real" as anything else ("as real as a telephone call"). Similarly, Hamman (1998, 1999), in his study of a hundred AOL (America Online) users, found that, contrary to most media portrayals of "virtual communities," nearly all of the participants used the service to communicate via computer with people they already knew offline rather than to meet new people online, and the effect of such communication was, rather than social isolation and a weakening of "real-life" relationships, the strengthening of existing social networks.

Rather than creating new and separate "settings" for communication, then, what new media technology primarily does is alter and enhance the communicative possibilities of already existing physical settings, and it is to these settings, to real-world environments beyond the screen, that we need to look to discover the context of computer-mediated communication (Jones 2001).

While CMC does to some degree "problematize the spatial-contextual dimension of communication," it does not, as Katriel (1999:97) suggests, result in a "despatialization of communication." In fact, physical spaces and the activities that take place in them are often central to the interpretation of online language. An example of this can be seen in the following diary entry by one of the participants in my study:

> I like to play on-line games when I am using ICQ. But this time, the difference is the number of participants. I have Iris and Jackie sitting next to me. But instead of playing the games with me, they chatted with my ICQ friend! (Without my permission!! :)) We all have gone crazy because Iris tried to type "I love. . . . " I was so surprised and wanted to stop her from sending the whole thing out. It would be very embarrassing if my friend received this ridiculous message from ME.

What is evident from this example is not a splitting of virtual and actual realities, but rather a situation made up of *layers* of various realities overlapping and interacting with one another.

Furthermore, just as material reality plays an important contextualization role in online communication, online communication itself plays an important role in constructing the contexts of offline interactions, dramatically expanding our access to people, information, and "objects" (like documents, music files, and mail-order goods) and altering our basic expectations about and practices around communication (Katriel 1999; Jones 2001).

Under these circumstances, the term "setting" is too static and material to capture adequately the dynamic, contingent, and expansive interaction of material and virtual realities involved in computer mediated communication. A better term would be *Umwelt,* the German word for "surround" adopted by Goffman (1971) (from Jacob von Uexküll) to capture how social actors perceive and manage their settings when interacting in public places. Goffman (252) defines it as "the region around an individual from which signs of alarm can come." For my purposes, I will define it slightly more broadly as an individual's environment of communicative possibilities. The sources of potential communication that go to make up a typical computer user's *Umwelt* include not just the multiple communicative possibilities offered through the computer screen, but also possibilities offered by other communication technologies that might be at hand (telephones, pagers, televisions, radios, PA systems, and so forth) as well as those offered by other physically co-present individuals.

Just as the *Umwelt* of an animal in the wild is not solely determined by the lay of the land, but is chiefly a matter of an animal's abilities, experience, and skill, so is a person's *Umwelt* determined not just by the communication technologies surrounding him or her, but also his or her skill in making use of these technologies, and sometimes in juggling several at one time. If I am unable to operate a computer, for example, even if there is one switched on right next to me, it cannot count as part of my *Umwelt* (though it might be seen as part of the physical "setting" in a more traditional sense of the word). Similarly, a teenager sitting in a flat in front of her computer experiences a very different *Umwelt* than her mother or grandmother sitting in the very same room.

There is, then, a paradoxical nature to this "technological surround": while CMC can expand the computer user's accessibility to people who are not physically co-present, it can also restrict accessibility of people who are physically co-present (such as teachers, parents, or bosses) to users' online interactions (as well as restricting accessibility of on-line interlocutors to other online interactions occurring simultaneously). It does this by allowing users to erect "involvement screens" (Goffman 1964) between themselves and other participants by exploiting the "muting" of various modes of interaction that is a feature of CMC. The "muting" of the visual mode, for example, allows users to engage in a wide range of physical activities that are inaccessible to their online interlocutors, and the "muting" of the aural mode allows them to carry on online conversations which are inaccessible to others who are physically co-present. In other words, part of the power of new technologies to accommodate these intersecting and overlapping layers of reality lies in their power simultaneously to expand and constrain interactants' "mutual monitoring possibilities," giving to actors far greater control over developing the "definition of the situation" (Sannicolas 1997). Objects, spaces, and barriers move in and out of interactional prominence as participants negotiate physical alignments and levels of involvement.

"What ru doin?": Polyfocality and the virtual social occasion

> Jenny: What ru doin?
> Piggy: hih ar i just sing a song check email and see TV

Just as new technologies force us to reconsider our previous definitions of social setting, leading us to exchange the notion of "setting" for the more flexible concept of *Umwelt* or "surround," they also lead us to question the utility of the simple binary distinction between *figure* and *ground* that has been central to most previous approaches to context. According to Goodwin and Duranti (1992:3), the notion of context involves "a fundamental juxtaposition of two entities: (1) a focal event; and (2) a field of action within which that event is embedded." From this perspective, communication is seen to involve a process of selection on the part of interactants as to what is to be treated as "focal" and what is to be treated as "background" (Kendon 1992), and the legitimacy of linguistic analysis primarily rests on the analyst's ability to accurately discern this process of selection.

In computer-mediated communication, however, it is often difficult for the analyst to determine which actions constitute users' *primary involvement* and which constitute *secondary involvements* (Goffman 1963), or even to know where to look when attempting to separate out the "text" from the "context." One particularly dramatic example of this is a common practice of my participants, which they referred to as "playing info" (Jones 2001), the practice of using one's "personal information" window to communicate with friends rather than the chat or instant messaging windows. One participant described it this way:

> Actually, it is the special function, that is, we communicate and correspond with each other through personal info. These words here are the reply to his info where he wrote "long time no see. How is it going?" I could send a message, but I am fond of playing info.

In such situations, the "text" is actually situated within what most analysts would unproblematically define as the "context."

What makes defining *figure* and *ground* even more difficult is the fact that participants seldom appear to have a single "primary involvement." Rather, they most often appear to be simultaneously engaged with *multiple figures* against the backdrop of *multiple grounds*. In one of the "screen movies" taken by my participants, for example, within a time span of only five minutes, the user involves herself in reading and answering emails, surfing the Internet and downloading MP3 files, listening to an Internet radio station, chatting with a classmate about a homework assignment and conducting another messaging session in which she comforts a friend whose uncle has recently been diagnosed with cancer (not to mention the various offline involvements that might have gone on, such as eating, referring to printed texts, or speaking to others present in the same room, which the "screen movie" does not capture).

Indeed, the most striking feature of my participants' use of computers is that they almost never use them to do only one thing at one time, and one of the apparent attractions of new communications technologies for them is that they allow them to do more things at one time. A typical beginning to an ICQ chat or messaging session is "What ru doin?"—a question with the built-in implication that the interlocutor is always going to be doing something (or many things) in addition to chatting with me.

These practices and the ethos that has grown up around them force us to rethink our assumption that communication is something that takes place within what Goffman (1963) calls "focused engagements" involving clear and discernable primary involvements. In the "digital surround" created by new communications technologies, communication is more *polyfocal* (Scollon et al. 1999); it skips among multiple "attentional tracks" (Goffman 1963), which sometimes intertwine and sometimes do not. *Polyfocality* seems, in fact, to be part of the very *ethos* of new communication technologies—celebrated in advertisements for computers, mobile phones, and PDAs (Lupton 2000) and bragged about by users. Part of the "fun" of "playing ICQ," admitted some of my participants, was in attempting to involve as many people as possible in apparently "focused engagements" and keeping all of these different involvements straight in one's mind.

This is not to say that *polyfocality* is a phenomenon new to computer-mediated communication. All interaction typically involves interactants doing several things at one time. In fact, the term was developed by Scollon and his colleagues to describe the behavior of participants very like those in my study (Hong Kong university students) at a period *before* computer-mediated communication became so popular. They write, "Perhaps the most striking thing about our students' attention is that it is polyfocal. That is, very rarely do they direct their attention in a focal, concentrated way to any single text or medium. When they watch television, they also listen to music and read or carry on conversations; traveling on the bus or Mass Transit Railway they read and listen to music—most commonly they 'read' while chatting, watching television and listening to music on CD" (1999:35). What changes with the introduction of new communication technologies is that *polyfocality* becomes easier to "pull off."

What is crucial here, as was in our discussion of the "technological surround," is the changes in "mutual monitoring possibilities" that new technologies make available. If I am having a face-to-face conversation with you about your uncle's cancer, for instance, although I may be able to think about a lot of other things and even engage in a number of side involvements like smoking or eating, I would not be able to listen to music on my Walkman, read a magazine, write a letter, or engage in a totally unrelated conversation with someone unknown to you and at the same time sustain the appropriate *display* of involvement warranted by the situation. New communication technologies, on the other hand, allow users to display "primary involvement" along a number of attentional tracks at once and not risk offending anybody. Because CMC simultaneously expands and constrains "mutual monitoring possibilities," users are able to take *polyfocality* to new levels.

In this regard, perhaps the biggest mistake in dealing with the concept of *focus* is to treat it as primarily a cognitive phenomenon. What these changes in social behavior brought about by new technologies point to is the fact that *focus* is as much a social as it is an individual construct. *Attention* is not just something going on in people's heads; it is a kind of *social transaction* (thus, we *pay attention, get* someone's *attention,* and so on).

Rather than sift through the polyfocal and polyvocal web of CMC in order to locate a *figure* and stake out a *ground,* what analysts should be paying attention to is the *attentional choreography* through which users manage multiple interactions and activities and move in and out of "synch" with different interlocutors.

"Add me please~": The virtual social gathering

Just as CMC alters our sense of place and our sense of focal activity, it also alters what we mean by and how we experience "participation." First of all, from the point of view of the user, the most important "interaction" occurring at any given moment may not be that *between* a "sender and receiver" (Shannon and Weaver 1949) but rather that occurring *among* multiple users with varying participation statuses (some physical, some virtual, some online and some offline). One of the main ways new communication technologies alter context is by creating a new kind of *interactional accessibility* involving new ways of being *present* and monitoring others' *presence.*

In these circumstances, as Katriel (1999:97) suggests, "rather than talking about separate interactions, we might talk about an "interactional field" that may encompass both focused interactions and secondary involvements of various kinds."

At the center of this new kind of interactional accessibility for users of ICQ is what is known as one's "contact list," an interface that displays the names of those one regularly interacts with along with information about their status (online, offline,

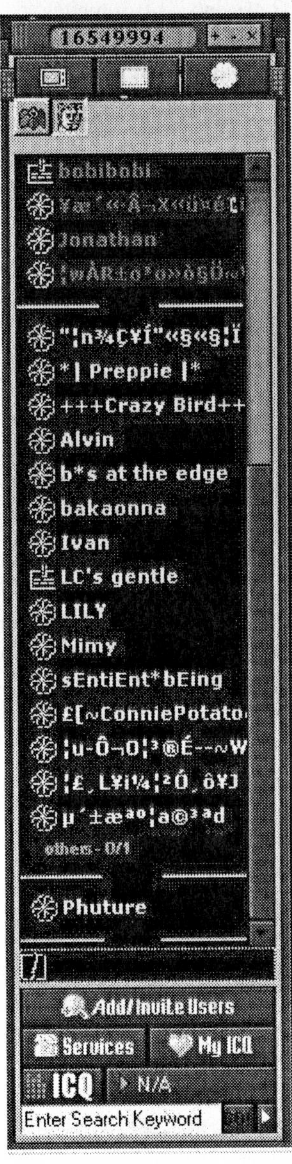

Figure 3.1. ICQ Contact List.

busy, away, available for chat, etc.). The contact list constitutes a kind of "customized community" that users build up over time (and that is never the same for any two users). It also constitutes an "instant" *social gathering* (Goffman 1963) that materializes every time a user switches on his or her computer (and is never exactly the same from one time to the next). At the same time, going "online" means becoming part of multiple and varied other *social gatherings* that are appearing on other computer screens far removed geographically from one another.

In this situation, the line between what it means to be a "participant" and what it means to be a "nonparticipant" blurs. Even those who are not "virtually co-present" (online) cannot escape participation in the social gathering I have made, for I can still interact with them by sending them an offline (asynchronous) message or by accessing their personal information windows, and their presence on my contact list "gives off" information about their physical whereabouts.

This practice of populating one's computer screen with friends and classmates and the multiparticipation status (Scollon et al. 1999) that it inevitably entails is, from the point of view of my participants, young people in the technological urban milieu of Hong Kong, perhaps not unusual, mirroring as it does their everyday interactions in the crowded and "wired" environments in which they live. As Scollon and his colleagues earlier observed regarding this population, they are "virtually never alone. Whether at home or at the university—for many of them even in transit—they do what they do together with others. . . . There are virtually no private spaces available. Students find that the only way they experience something like individual privacy is to stay up very late until all of the other members of the family have gone to sleep" (Scollon et al. 1999:35). Oddly enough, what most of these students do alone in their tiny flats after their family members have gone to sleep is to turn on their computers and populate their privacy with the people on their ICQ contact lists.

Given the argument I have presented thus far, this notion of *populated privacy* is actually not the contradiction that it first seems to be, particularly if one defines privacy not necessarily as "being alone," but rather as achieving a certain level of control over how and by whom one's involvements can be monitored. CMC affords users new ways to control and manipulate their participation statuses with others and new ways to control the ways others monitor their presence that physical spaces do not afford. It also provides ways to be privately present to certain people in ways that might be impractical or inappropriate in the physical world.

Another change in the ways participants can be *present* to one another is in the levels of intimacy they can achieve. One of the many paradoxes of CMC is that its "muting" of visual and aural modes and privileging of the textual mode does not, as one might expect and some have predicted (Sproull and Kiesler 1986; Culnan and Markus 1987), result in a kind of compromised or "abbreviated" social presence, but rather in heightened degrees of intimacy which Walther (1996) has called "hyperpersonal" communication, interaction that "surpasses the level of affection and emotion of parallel (face-to-face) interaction" (17). Many of my participants reported that their ICQ conversations were generally more intimate than their face-to-face interactions, and one even said, "I feel my self on ICQ is more like my real self than that in daily life." Part of the reason for people's increased intimacy online might be that the various involvement screens CMC makes available also act as emotional buffers. As another participant insisted, "It's easier to type an emotion." Thus, the absence of many of the contextualization cues used in face-to-face communication in CMC does not result in an impoverished context, but rather one fraught with greater possibilities.

At the same time, however, the "reduced cues" of computer-mediated contexts also make available new ways of participation on the other extreme of the personal-impersonal scale wherein users participate as impersonal "agents" (Jones 2001), dropping bits of information into one another's computers with a minimum of interactional intimacy (Biocca and Levy 1995).

Rather than think in terms of "participants," students of context, at least those of computer-mediated contexts, need to think in terms of how people simultaneously manage multiple ways of being present and multiple levels of presence within multiple fields of interaction.

Conclusion: Taking the "Text" Out of "Context"

New communication technologies are forcing linguists to examine the ways in which their "professional vision" (Goodwin 1994) is constrained by the terminological screens of their discipline. One of the main constraints has been our tendency to privilege written and spoken texts above all other phenomena, and to consider objects, actions, and people as simply making up "the environment in which the text comes to life" (Halliday 1975:25; Peng 1986).

The aspects of context I have pointed out here that are made salient through new communication technologies are actually part of offline interactions as well, and the inadequacies of our present notions of context not only make it difficult for us to deal with CMC, but also present barriers to our fully understanding what is going on in more traditional kinds of interaction.

In some ways, asking linguists to pay less attention to texts seems an unusual request. It is, however, only through breaking down the traditional hierarchical separation of "text" and "context" and moving our focus onto the *social actions* and *social identities* that texts make possible that we will achieve a true grasp of exactly how important texts are and how they fit into the web of places, practices, and communities that human beings inhabit.

To capture truly the dynamic display of involvement and identity in which text and context are continually negotiated in interaction, analysts themselves need to adopt a polyfocal perspective. They need to "burst the bonds of mere linguistics" (Malinowski 1947:306), to experiment with new "ways of seeing" (Goodwin 1994) social interaction, ways that encompass multiple modes and make use of multiple methods, ways that begin not with texts but with people's actions and experiences around texts. Through this wider perspective we might finally come to understand what we have always "known," that text and context are "aspects of the same process" (Halliday and Hasan 1985:5).

REFERENCES

Biocca, F., and M. R. Levy. 1995. Communication application of virtual reality. In F. Biocca and M. R. Levy, eds., *Communication in the age of virtual reality*, 127–58. Hillsdale, NJ: Erlbaum.

Clark, H., and T. Carlson. 1981. Context for comprehension. In J. Long and A. Baddeley, eds., *Attention and performance IX*, 313–30. Hillsdale, NJ: Erlbaum.

Collot, M., and N. Belmore. 1996. Electronic language: A new variety of English. In S. Herring, ed., *Computer-mediated communication: Linguistic, social and cross-cultural perspectives*, 13–28. Amsterdam: John Benjamins.

Culnan, M. J., and M. L. Markus. 1987. Information technologies. In F. M. Jablin et al., eds., *Handbook of organizational communication: An interdisciplinary perspective*, 420–43. Newbury Park, CA: Sage.

Davis, B. H., and J. P. Brewer. 1997. *Electronic discourse: Linguistic individuals in virtual space*. Albany: State University of New York Press.

de Certeau, M. 1984. *The practice of everyday life*. Trans. S. Rendell. Berkeley: University of California Press.

Dubrovsky, V. J. 1985. Real-time computer conferencing versus electronic mail. In *Proceedings of the human factor society*, vol. 29, 380–84. Santa Monica, CA: Human Factors Society.

Dubrovsky, V. J., S. Kiesler, and B. N. Sethna. 1991. The equalization of phenomenon: Status effects in computer-mediated and face-to-face decision making groups. *Human Computer Interaction* 6(1): 19–146.

Fairclough, N. 1992. *Discourse and social change*. Cambridge: Polity Press.

Fernback, J. 1999. There is a there there: Notes towards a definition of cybercommunity. In S. Jones, ed., *Doing Internet research: Critical issues and methods for examining the net*, 203–220. Thousand Oaks, CA: Sage.

Firth, J. R. 1957. *Papers in linguistics 1934–1951*. London: Oxford University Press.

Goffman, E. 1963. *Behavior in public places*. New York: Free Press.

——. 1964. The neglected situation. *American Anthropologist* 66:133–36.

——. 1971. *Relations in public*. New York: Harper & Row.

——. 1974. *Frame analysis: An essay on the organization of experience*. New York: Harper & Row.

Goodwin, C. 1994. Professional vision. *American Anthropologist* 96(3): 606–33.

Goodwin, C., and A. Duranti. 1992. Rethinking context: An introduction. In A. Duranti and C. Goodwin, eds., *Rethinking context: Language as an interactive phenomenon*, 191–227. Cambridge: Cambridge University Press.

Gumperz, J. 1992. Contextualization and understanding. In A. Duranti and C. Goodwin, eds., *Rethinking context: Language as an interactive phenomenon*, 229–52. Cambridge: Cambridge University Press.

Halliday, M. A. K. 1975. Language as social semiotic: Towards a general sociolinguistic theory. In A. Makkai and V. Makkai, eds., *The first LACUS Forum 1974*, 17–46. Columbia, SC: Hornbeam.

Halliday, M. A. K., and R. Hasan. 1985. *Language, context and text: Aspects of language in a social semiotic perspective*. Oxford: Oxford University Press.

Hamman, R. B. 1998. The online/offline dichotomy: Debunking some myths about AOL users and the effects of their being online upon offline friendships and offline community. M.Phil. thesis, University of Liverpool.

——. 1999. Computer networks linking network communities: A study of the effects of computer network use upon pre-existing communities. www.socio.demon.co.uk/cybersociety.

Haraway, D. 1991. *Simians, cyborgs and women: The reinvention of nature*. New York: Routledge.

Hine, C. 2000. *Virtual ethnography*. London: Sage.

Hymes, D. 1974. *Foundations of sociolinguistics: An ethnographic approach*. Philadelphia: University of Pennsylvania Press.

——. 1986. Models of interaction of language and social life. In J. Gumperz and D. Hymes, eds., *Directions in sociolinguistics: The ethnography of communication*, 35–71. Oxford: Blackwell.

Jones, R. 2001. Beyond the screen: A participatory study of computer mediated communication among Hong Kong youth. Paper presented at the Annual Meeting of the American Anthropological Association, Washington, DC.

Katriel, T. 1999. Rethinking the terms of social interaction. *Research on Language and Social Interaction* 32:95–101.

Kendall, L. 1999. Recontextualizing "cyberspace": Methodological considerations for on-line research. In S. Jones, ed., *Doing Internet research: Critical issues and methods for examining the net,* 57–74. Thousand Oaks, CA: Sage.

Kendon, A. 1992. The negotiation of context in face-to-face interaction. In A. Duranti and C. Goodwin, eds., *Rethinking context: Language as an interactive phenomenon,* 323–34. Cambridge: Cambridge University Press.

Kraut, R., M. Patterson, V. Lundmark, S. Kiesler, T. Mukophadhyay, and W. Scherlis. 1998. Internet paradox: A social technology that reduces social involvement and psychological well-being? *American Psychologist* 51(9): 1017–31.

Kroker, A., and M. A. Weinstein. 1994. *Data trash: The theory of the virtual class.* New York: St. Martin's.

Lupton, D. 2000. The embodied computer user. In D. Bell and B. M. Kennedy, eds., *The cybercultures reader,* 477–87. London: Routledge.

Malinowski, B. 1947. The problem of meaning in primitive languages. In C. K. Ogden and I. A. Richards, eds., *The meaning of meaning,* 296–336. London: Harcourt-Brace.

McLuhan, M. 1994. *Understanding media: The extensions of man.* Cambridge: MIT Press.

Murray, D. E. 1988. The context of oral and written language: A framework for mode and medium switching. *Language and Society* 17:351–73.

Negroponte, N. 1995. *Being digital.* London: Hodder and Stoughton.

Peng, F. C. C. 1986. On the context of situation. *International Journal of the Sociology of Language* 58:91–105.

Rintel, F. S., and J. Pittam. 1997. Strangers in a strange land: Interaction management on Internet relay chat. *Human Communication Research* 23(4): 507–34.

Sannicolas, N. 1997. Erving Goffman, dramaturgy and on-line relationships. www.cybersoc.com/magazine/1/is1nikki.html.

Schegloff, E. 1991. In another context. In A. Duranti and C. Goodwin, eds., *Rethinking context: Language as an interactive phenomenon,* 191–227. Cambridge: Cambridge University Press.

——. 1997. Whose text? Whose context? *Discourse and Society* 8:165–87.

Scollon, R., V. Bhatia, D. Li, and V. Yung. 1999. Blurred genres and fuzzy identities in Hong Kong public discourse: Foundational ethnographic issues in the study of reading. *Applied Linguistics* 20(1): 22–43.

Shannon, C., and W. Weaver. 1949. *Mathematical theory of communication.* Urbana: University of Illinois Press.

Sproull, L., and Kiesler, S. 1986. Reducing social context cues: Electronic mail in organizational communication. *Management Science* 32:1492–1512.

Tannen, D. 1993. What's in a frame? In D. Tannen, ed., *Framing in discourse,* 14–56. New York: Oxford University Press.

Tannen, D., and C. Wallat. 1983. Doctor/mother/child communication: Linguistic analysis of a paediatric interaction. In S. Fisher and A. D. Todd, eds., *The social organization of doctor-patient communication,* 203–19. Washington, DC: Center for Applied Linguistics.

Tracy, K. 1998. Analyzing context: Framing the discussion. *Research on Language in Social Interaction* 31(1): 1–28.

Van Dijk, T. 1997. Discourse as interaction in society. In T. A. Van Dijk, ed., *Discourse as Social Interaction,* 1–37. London: Sage.

Walther, J. B. 1996. Computer-mediated communication: Impersonal, interpersonal and hyperpersonal interaction. *Communication Research* 23(1): 3–43.

"The Way to Write a Phone Call": Multimodality in Novices' Use and Perceptions of Interactive Written Discourse (IWD)

ANGELA GODDARD
Manchester Metropolitan University

INTERACTIVE WRITTEN DISCOURSE (IWD) is normally classified as an aspect of computer-mediated communication (CMC). The latter is defined here, after Herring (1996:1), as "communication that takes place between human beings via the instrumentality of computers." IWD is often distinguished from other types of CMC by its synchronicity (Werry 1996).

This is a report on the nature of IWD as produced and experienced by a particular group of users. Specifically, my focus is on the multimodality of IWD with reference to speech and writing.

Participants

Sixty beginning undergraduates studying human communication during 1999 at a university in the United Kingdom received their language module online. The students were initially strangers to each other as well as to their new study context.

A "chat" facility formed part of a suite of communication tools on the course. In questionnaires, 60 percent of the students classified themselves as never having worked online before, or having worked online a long time ago and with little memory of it ("online" being defined as using webpages as well as bulletin boards and chatrooms). Although the group was relatively inexperienced in this new communication context, none of the participants can be considered novices in terms of their own communication skills; and as students of human communication they were already oriented to the exploration of new communication contexts.

Scrutiny of the IWD use and perceptions of this group, therefore, allows some insight into the ways expert communicators deploy their existing resources of speech and writing in a novel context.

Data

Approximately 30,000 words of IWD data were produced by the students as part of their online course, and collected in the form of chatlogs. The software used was WebCT (see figure 4.1 for a sample screenshot). A precourse questionnaire assessed students' information and communication technology (ICT) competence; and a postcourse questionnaire assessed anonymously how students experienced the "chat" tool. After the course ended, students were also interviewed as a group and given their chatlogs to read.

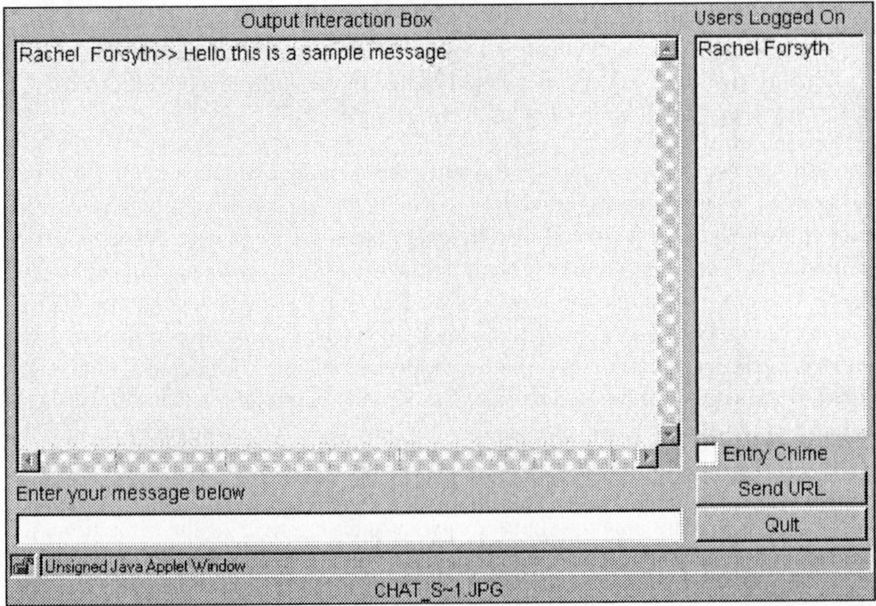

Figure 4.1. WebCT "Chat" Screenshot (© 2002 WebCT, Inc.).

Models of Speech and Writing

It should perhaps not be surprising that speech and writing in general, and common spoken or written genres in particular, have formed a yardstick for the description of new CMC tools. Collot and Belmore (1996) cite Spitzer's (1986) collection of comments by academic colleagues using CMC for the first time: "'Talking in writing,' 'writing letters which are mailed over the telephone,' 'a panel discussion in slow motion,' 'using language as if having a conversation, yet the message must be written'" (Spitzer 1986:19).

These comments parallel the current marketing of new communications by companies such as British Telecom and Mannesman, where hybridity is expressed by disrupting expected collocations:

BT:	E-mail, the new way to write a phone call.
MANNESMAN:	Turn the telephone on, it's time to watch the news.

One of the difficulties when faced with impressionistic accounts such as those above is that although they are engaging in an imaginative sense, they offer little detail about the speaker's model of spoken and written language. Remaining vague about models of language can suit those with certain kinds of vested interest: for BT, for example, there is a useful indeterminacy in describing email as "the new way to write a phone call," allowing appeal both to the phone-phobe and the phone-phile. In other contexts, however, a lack of transparency in thinking about speech and writing can have more obviously deleterious effects. Consider the following (personal notes, November 1998):

> A group of staff who were writing online courses for students discussed the various WebCT communication tools. One colleague remarked that the chat facility (i.e. the IWD system) would enable those students who performed "*better orally than in writing*" to be more successful.

I would suggest that this example illustrates the strongly oral connotations attached to the word "chat" are strong enough to prevail in the speaker's cognitive framework even though he knew very well that the chatroom software runs on Javascript (i.e., written text). It could be argued, in terms of Lakoff's (1987) account of metaphor and conceptual categories, that the speaker was downplaying the sound/symbol distinction between speech and writing, and playing up some other aspect of potential difference, such as synchronicity. Whatever aspect was being considered salient is unclear, as the speaker did not elaborate. But what is very clear is that the speaker's model would have profound implications for how users were assessed.

The preceding discussion is intended to set out some ground and indicate my position on it. I see "speech" and "writing," "spoken" and "written," "oral" and "literate" as terms that are anything but transparently descriptive. At the same time, the connotative power of particular genres, such as "chat," is being harnessed by the communications industry for their own purposes. This situation results in problems for academic description. For example, I prefer to use IWD after Werry (1996) because I want deliberately to problematize the apparently seamless connection that has been made in commercial contexts between a form of electronic discourse and spoken language. This connection also exists in the academic terms "netspeak" (Crystal 2001), "chat system," and "internet relay chat" (see Werry 1996 for discussion).

One of the problems with using speech and writing as apparently transparent categories is that, historically, there have been many changes in how notions of speech and writing have been viewed, resulting in a complex picture. For example, older notions of "the great divide" (see Gee 1990 for discussion) held "that writing makes possible verbatim memory and abstract and sequentially logical thought, and that written discourse is decontextualized or autonomous, whereas nonliterate culture is associated with constructive memory and concrete and rhapsodic thought, and that spoken discourse is context-bound" (Chafe and Tannen 1987:392).

These characterizations have been countered on all fronts: the supposed difference in mindsets (Finnegan 1988); the supposed autonomy of writing (Street 1988); the supposed noncollaborative nature of writing (Heath 1983). Similarly, formal distinctions between speech and writing as systems of communication have been questioned and found wanting. For example, Crystal's summary of distinctions—"Speech is typically time-bound, spontaneous, face-to-face, socially interactive, loosely structured, immediately revisable, and prosodically rich. Writing is typically space-bound, contrived, visually decontextualised, factually communicative, elaborately structured, repeatedly revisable, and graphically rich" (2001:28)—holds only for certain genres of speech and writing. As Tannen (1982) has shown, contrasts such as factuality and interactivity are very much predicated on using casual conversation as the prototype for speech and essayist literacy as the prototype for writing.

If such notions of binary contrast were seen as problematic before the development of new CMC genres, their application to electronic discourse, particularly to IWD, renders them useless. In operating both visually and synchronously, IWD is simultaneously space-bound *and* time-bound. IWD is both spontaneous *and* revisable (Biber's [1988] "interactive" vs. "edited" categories). In considering the "face-to-face" aspect of communication, IWD involves "presence" if not face visibility; and for some scholars in ICT, "presence" is less about physical visibility than impressions of agency or communicative force (Stone 1995). While graphically rich, IWD can also be seen as not entirely without prosodics if the focus is on rhythm rather than, say, voice pitch.

Corpus-based work by Biber (1988) on "styles of stance" does avoid the perils of binary contrasts between speech and writing; and this method, where texts are typed by the occurrence of clusters of linguistic features, has been used by some CMC analysts (for example, Collot and Belmore 1996). However, this approach loses sight of the users in all their situated contexts. This is no small omission. For example, Biber (1988) sees the genre of personal letters as expressing more affect (as encoded in lexical and grammatical usage) than face-to-face encounters. Rather than seeing a lack of affect as the result of the behavior of "texts" I would argue that Biber's corpus material, based overwhelmingly on the language of middle-class participants, at best shows the discourse "habitus" (Bourdieu 1991) of certain social groups. Although work in the "stance styles" tradition does escape the problem of seeing speech and writing as discrete systems, then, the approach falls foul of the idea that texts are stable entities regardless of the users.

Mediated Discourse Theory (MDT)

In exploring the multimodality of IWD and other CMC genres, the task is to find a set of principles for discourse analysis that are able to consider the particular constraints and affordances of different communication systems, while also paying attention to the users in their situated contexts—"situated" not just in terms of their physical setting, but also socially and politically. In my view, Mediated Discourse Theory (MDT), envisaged by Scollon (1998, 2001) as a "program of linkages" between historically diverse schools of discourse analysis, may well support such a project. In what follows, I propose to set out some of the tenets of MDT and consider their usefulness in relation to my data.

Scollon sees MDT as based in interactional sociolinguistics, which has as its raison d'être: "The ways in which people in communication with each other mutually construct the situations they are in and their identities in those situations through discourse" (Scollon 1998:147). Focusing on language-as-action rather than language-as-text, MDT shares the approach of pragmatics-based theories to see language as a form of social behavior, as *mediated action.* However, Scollon's concept of MDT ensures that texts remain seen as the actions of real communicators rather than as the embodiments of a priori classifications. The importance of this can be seen, for example, in his notion of *sites of engagement,* highlighting as it does the "windows" in space and time whereby texts are appropriated for use. The complex network of relations that exist for individuals as they appropriate different texts for action and therefore negotiate their participation in social events is characterized by Scollon as a nexus *of practice.* And finally, the principle of *texts as mediational means* establishes texts as the means by which sociocultural practice becomes instantiated in human action. A key issue here is the idea of polyvocality:

> Communication . . . must make use of the language, the texts, of others and because of that, those other voices provide both amplification and limitations of our own voices. A text which is appropriated for use in mediated action brings with it the conventionalizations of the social practices of its history of use. We say not only what we want to say but also what the text must inevitably say for us. At the same time, our use of texts in mediated actions changes those texts and in turn alters the discursive practices (Scollon 1998:15).

Within the tenet of *texts as mediational means,* a crucial question then concerns the way in which the indeterminacy suggested above is used by participants to position themselves and others.

Data and Analysis

Scollon's notion of *sites of engagement* seems to have a particular resonance for IWD in general, and for my IWD data in particular. All genres of course involve issues of "where" participants are, but parameters of indexicality are reconfigured in CMC genres, where Stone (1995) claims we face "the architecture of elsewhere"—a reality that cannot be tied to any stable location. IWD's "architecture" combines synchronicity with apparently disembodied visual symbol: one can see the contributions of invisible remote others arriving on the screen as if by some process of fairy magic. IWD users therefore have to find ways to understand and exploit these new points of reference.

My participants explore a number of different orientations or "laminations" (Goffman 1974) in their framing of location: geographical region of origin; university site where they are logged in; and where they are logged in on the same site, the area of the computer room they are occupying. These dimensions are illustrated in the two data samples that follow. Note, as well, how some of the students in Sample 2 playfully resist their course tutor's more profound questions about identity by constructing a deliberately banal characterization of themselves as "Joe from Joeville":

Sample 1

Natalie>> yeak

Natalie>> sorry yea

Simon>> why yeah

Rachael>> where are you Natalie Hale so I know who I;m talking to?

Natalie>> i dont mean it like yeah man i mean it like yeay

Simon>> what is the difference

Natalie>> i'm at john dalton

Rachael>> OK

Natalie>> it's happier and less cheesy

Simon>> and that is worthy of a yehah

Sample 2

RyanW>> hello

Simon>> are right joe

RyanW>> not bad yourself?

Natalie>> joe?

Simon>> everyone is going, yes joe

Andrew>> Joe is a great guy

RyanW>> manchester thing

Simon>> manchester thing

Natalie>> echo?

Andrew>> liverpool thing

Simon>> everyine must love joe

RyanW>> joe is sound

Natalie>> not a nottingham thing then

Sorcha>> I don't have a clue who anyone is, no smart comments Andrew!

Andrew>> where is everyone from?

RyanW>> no probably not

Natalie>> Theres a question. Who are you/

Simon>> I dont know you tell us

Natalie>> [lecturer's name] asked us yesterday how the hell are you supposed to answer that?

RyanW>> joe town

Simon>> Joeville, Manchester

Simon>> [lecturer's name] asked us what

Natalie>> who are you?

Simon>> Philosophically?

Natalie>> annoyingly?

The group interview data provided further insights that relate very directly to Scollon's notion of sites of engagement. One idea that was voiced by many of the participants was that it was difficult to remember what was going on, in order to make sense of the chatlog. When I pursued this idea, it transpired that participants were often in the same room, enabling the IWD to be integrated with face-to-face chat. Students talked about actively seeking out others visually. Language use that attempts to locate others physically is therefore regularly seen in this data: for example, in Sample 1 above. At other times, participants specifically mention being physically proximate. For example:

Sample 3

Janine>> I feel silly sitting next to you and having a conversation like this

Although a popular notion of the "chatroom" is of a text-only tool where participants are anonymous and remote, a more frequent use of such tools is likely to lead to many different types of situations, each with its own configurations as different communication modes are grouped together and appropriated in particular ways. For example, these same students have gone on to use Microsoft Netmeeting where they communicated with students in Sweden via the simultaneous use of "chat" tools, videocam, and sound, with groups of students sharing one computer. In the Netmeeting output, as here with WebCT, the nature of the written language that was produced was highly shaped by its multimodal situation, not just in terms of which channel is taken up at a specific moment, but also in the reference points contained within the writing itself. For example, the participants in Sample 3 engage in extensive play involving mutual teasing. This results in utterances such as the following:

Sample 4

Janine>> You speak like this—jhfiuefcjk jfhfudvj aqwkeojew
fjd awoeirj vuhtr urthre;

Whatever spoken language was exchanged between these students is lost; but the fact that they could hear each other is important when considering the force of the utterance above, where the joke relies heavily on the disruption of expectations following the use of the verb "speak."

When the students talk about the difficulty of understanding the chatlogs as written text, they are clearly referring to the more "embodied" way in which their IWD worked. This includes examples such as the previous one, where participants were physically proximate, but there are further ways in which embodiment was realized in the original IWD output, even where participants were working in isolation. For example, consider the following extract, where students are discussing the connotations of color:

Sample 5

Lucy>> does anyone know what a blue joke is?
RyanS>> no
Lindsay>> no
RyanS>> blue movie
Andrew>> dirty, rude isn't it?
Lindsay>> r u gonna tell us?
Lucy>> blue movie what's that?
RyanS>> mmmmmm. . . . naked
Andrew>> dirty, rude isn't it?
RyanS>> rude
RyanS>> dirty

Lucy>> it was on the colour article
RyanS>> isn't it
Lucy>> I think it must be
Lindsay>> wey hey

Andrew's playful repetition of "dirty, rude isn't it," picked up in turn by Ryan in a three-line reiteration—"rude," "dirty," and "isn't it"—strikes the eye as a form of visual patterning when looking at the chatlog as written data. However, it must also have been experienced as a temporal phenomenon by the participants: the real-time nature of IWD foregrounds rhythm—normally included within speech prosodics—as well as the spatial dimensions usually associated with writing. Samples 4 and 5 are typical of the way participants in my IWD data use multimodality in playful and creative ways to position themselves and others.

The slightly risqué nature of the interaction in Sample 5 invokes a further aspect of sites of engagement. Scollon pays tribute to Critical Discourse Analysis in his development of MDT, locating one of the strengths of CDA as its focus on the idea of texts as discourses of power (Fairclough 1995). Although MDT's concept of sites of engagement focuses principally on the appropriation of texts for use in social interactional contexts, the work of CDA scholars reminds us that texts are always situated sociopolitically and that conflict should be expected as bids for power meet resistance. This is taking the idea of sites of engagement towards a more conflict-oriented model. The fact that my students were ejected from the university library at one point simply for using my course IWD tool (there is a university ban on the use of chatrooms) forced me to think about the tensions inherent in using these texts in educational spaces; and the enforced compromise, which was to replace my IWD icon (a pair of chatting lips) with our very dull university logo, gave me pause for thought about public signifiers of "serious" and "frivolous" language use.

If the notion of sites of engagement is a usefully plastic concept allowing consideration of the situated nature of the participants, MDT's interest in polyvocality, after the work of Goffman (1974, 1981) and Bakhtin (1981, 1986), proves a creative tool for thinking about how participants shape their IWD contributions as they draw on previously known genres and reconfigure those texts for a new communication context. In Tannen's (1993) terms, this involves a new kind of "frame" as participants redraw their space with new items foregrounded; for Kristeva, a new set of "enunciative positionalities" (cited in Moi 1986). For example, there are clear examples in my IWD data of the type of opening, preclosing, and closing routines quarried in detail by researchers in the CA tradition (see summary in Hopper 1992). In this IWD context, there are ways in which some of these expressions are reconfigured in order to exploit the affordances of the medium. For example, in what I have elsewhere called "broadcast messages" (Gillen and Goddard 2000), chatroom incomers entering multiparty conversations often exploit the mass-communication aspect of the IWD situation by using group greetings such as "hello guys" or "hello people." At the same time, the fact that an early entrant can write up a greeting that doesn't "degrade" sets the IWD context very much apart from the phone call genre. In the case of the early entrant, then, the lone participant who is expecting others to arrive can have a "hello" firmly inscribed, not just to greet incomers but to register his or her own presence in perhaps a more existential sense.

Although in the preceding cases greetings more familiar from spoken contexts are given a new visual and more permanent form, other intertextual reshapings involve the manipulation of written texts in an attempt to represent the subtle nuances of speech noises: see Sample 1, where participants focus on some different interjections—"yea," "yeah," "yeay," and "yehah," or Sample 5, where a participant uses "wey hey." These examples illustrate what Goffman (1981) terms "response cries," conventionalized blurtings that are expressive forms of language often conveying reactions to unexpected events. Goffman refers to the complexity of such interjections, noting the doubly symbolic nature of some of them: for example, in saying "tut-tut," we use a speech form based on a written expression where the latter is supposedly imitative of a speech form.

The intertextuality that is at the heart of MDT's principle of *texts as mediational means* clearly functions in my IWD data as a strategy for the participants' identity work. The nature of this intertextuality is often an adaptation of others' contributions, so that what emerges is a collaborative structure that has both a set of internal relationships and a set of external reference points to other texts and voices. For example, in the following:

Sample 6

Nadia>>	Andie can you stop your twitching please
Glyn>>	thanks
Andrew>>	~I don't
RyanS>>	simon?
Glyn>>	your name has been added to the list you will not see another sunrise andrew
RyanS>>	the blair twitch project
Alexandra>>	So your a twitcher then Andy
RyanS>>	smack my twitch up
RyanW>>	the wicked twitch of the west
RyanW>>	or wirral
Nadia>>	Whos going to America next season in our course
RyanS>>	i might pop in
Andrew>>	I would but if your going. . . . . Perhaps not

Students use intertextuality at a number of different linguistic levels simultaneously: via phonological and graphological patterns, via lexical adaptations, and via reference to particular cultural artifacts—the *Blair Witch Project,* the rap lyric "Smack My Bitch Up," and *The Wizard of Oz.* In constructing these references, the participants can be seen as claiming for themselves a kind of group membership via their shared cultural knowledge. This is understandably important in this context where participants are engaged in forming relationships and working out what it means to be part of the student community. But the themes that are played on can also be seen as significant, in that they construct representations of the online medium. All these references connote a kind of menace—the horror of the *Blair Witch Project,* the violence of the rap song, the wicked witch of the *Oz* film. It may be that being online with relative strangers stimulates particular themes—in this case, ideas of embodiment/disembodiment and the unknown intentions of "invisible" others—which are then explored as subject matter in the ideational sense (Halliday 1985). But even with a menacing theme, play is not so far away: Ryan Walker's "or wirral" (an area near Liverpool) is a wonderful piece of bathos.

There are many further occasions where playing in those spaces afforded by speech-writing relationships allows, simultaneously, both participant-positioning and medium exploration. Although applied in very different ways, the idea of "liminal" spaces as used by Rampton (1997) to explore issues of identity and positioning among UK black adolescents may well have relevance here. Rampton's work suggests that his participants' polyvocality creates a space where they can perform different identities in order to gauge their instrumental power; in my data, participants could be seen as working a liminal space configured by multimodal references in order to do something similar. For example:

Sample 7

Dawn>> get off your high horse young man!
Sorcha>> god andrew what have you started
Simon>> John wants to know how long people are going to be here for
Natalie>> at least the original high horse isn't here
Andrew>> I'm no god, but thanks for the compliment

Dawn's "get off your high horse young man" in the sample above can be seen as a piece of popular idiom which relies for its effect on the idea of a particular kind of speaker—a genteel older lady who is something of a martinet. For British English speakers, this utterance calls up a specific kind of voice—not just female, middle-aged, and middle or upper class, but RP-accented, too, a kind of Lady Bracknell (from Oscar Wilde's *The Importance of Being Earnest*). To this extent, the utterance depends on connections with *spoken* language for its force. And yet, a little further on in the interaction, Natalie seems to be approaching the idea of the "high horse," not as part of a popular spoken exhortation, but as a *visual* image:

Natalie>> at least the original high horse isn't here

It's as if seeing Dawn's utterance written out has given Natalie a form of "schema refreshment" (Cook 2000), whereby the "high horse," embedded for a long time in a well-worn popular saying, has suddenly acquired a new and startling visual representation. Natalie expresses this by using the modifier "original," signaling that, for her, the old cliché has come to life in an interesting new way.

In the same way, the exchange between Sorcha and Andrew relies for its effect on grapho-phonemic relationships: the lack of punctuation allows ambiguity, with two different readings associated with different intonation patterns. Andrew then chooses to read "god" as a modifier rather than an expletive. This allows him to demur on the topic of his godlike status while also pointing it out.

Lone talk (termed "self-talk" by Goffman 1981) is no exception to patterns of polyvocality and positioning. Examples such as 8, below, illustrate Bakhtin's (1981) claim that even monologic utterances are audience-oriented, and, thus, dialogic.

Sample 8

RyanS>> pooo
RyanS>> helo
RyanS>> hello?
RyanS>> oooooоiiiiiiiiiii!!!!!
RyanS>> oi oi oi oi oi oi oi oi oi ioi ioi iooi ioio ioio ioioi
RyanS>> excuse me
RyanS>> are you there
RyanS>> fine
RyanS>> be like that
RyanS>> by then
RyanS>> seeya
RyanS>> oi
RyanS>> hello
RyanS>> youre no fun

Goffman reiterates Bakhtin's view that even solitary talk is social, offering his own examples of speakers "blurting" out a response when surprised or shocked by a turn of events. However, Sample 8 appears to demonstrate a more extensive fantasy construction, something that we might associate more with the egocentric speech of young children (Vygotsky and Luria 1930) than with the IWD output of adults.

The essentially dramatic nature of Sample 8, where a one-sided conversation constructs an identity for two participants, has obvious similarities with literary soliloquy, particularly in the realization of strong attitudes by the participants: Ryan is aggressively pursuing his recalcitrant and stubbornly silent interlocutor, with little success. Ryan's own view of his lone talk on reading his chatlog was that this IWD context afforded an opportunity for the covert expression of resistance to authority. He likened his language use in this situation with the secret signals one sometimes communicates to oneself about another person where that person cannot be openly gainsaid—for example, the rude gesture delivered from the safe distance of concealment behind a book or magazine.

Conclusions

This has been a necessarily brief exploration of the use and perceptions of IWD by a particular group. Generalizations are dangerous, not least because the IWD tool can clearly be used for many purposes, and in different ways by different groups.

However, it does seem possible to review at this stage what avenues are blocked or made possible by certain analytical approaches.

Street (1988) urges us to refrain from the "generalisations of the grandiose sort" that he sees as characterizing attempts to describe whole channels; similarly, Schiffrin (1994) proposes a project of "microlinguistics," where notions of universals are superseded by those of localized instantiations.

Emphasis on the local and particular is also at the core of MDT, where, because texts are seen as mediational means for social action, textual analysis has to encompass users' situations. While corpus-based work such as Biber's research on stance styles tends to remove the nature of the users from the picture, MDT seeks out connections between users, texts and contexts with an expectation of conflict and complexity because of the "ideologically saturated" (Bakhtin 1986) nature of all texts.

Tested against my IWD data, an MDT approach does reveal some important complexities, particularly the nature of participants' simultaneity in their deployment of IWD; and the creative polyvocality in evidence in participants' textual output as they explore the "enunciative positionalities" opened up by this new communication tool. Such findings can act as a useful counterpoint to those public discourses about declining standards and reduced repertoires of language use in young people as a result of their participation in new forms of electronic discourse.

REFERENCES

Bakhtin, M. M. 1981. *The dialogic imagination.* Austin: University of Texas Press.

——. 1986. *Speech genres and other late essays.* Ed. C. Emerson and M. Holquist. Austin: University of Texas Press.

Biber, D. 1988. *Variation across speech and writing.* Cambridge: Cambridge University Press.

Bourdieu, P. 1991. *Language and symbolic power.* Cambridge, MA: Harvard University Press.

Chafe, W., and D. Tannen. 1987. The relation between written and spoken language. *Annual Review of Anthropology* 16:383–407.

Collot, M., and N. Belmore. 1996. Electronic language: A new variety of English. In S. Herring, ed., *Computer-mediated communication: Linguistic, social and cross-cultural perspectives,* 13–28. Amsterdam: John Benjamins.

Cook, G. 2000. *Language play, language learning.* Oxford: Oxford University Press.

Crystal, D. 2001. *Language and the Internet.* Cambridge: Cambridge University Press.

Fairclough, N. 1995. *Critical discourse analysis: The critical study of language.* London: Longman.

Finnegan, R. 1988. *Literacy and orality: Studies in the technology of communication.* Oxford: Basil Blackwell.

Gee, J. P. 1990. *Social linguistics and literacies: Ideology in discourses.* Bristol, PA: Falmer Press.

Gillen, J., and A. Goddard. 2000. Medium management for beginners: The discursive practices of undergraduate and mature novice users of internet relay chat, compared with those of young children using the telephone. Paper presented at the conference of the International Association for Dialogue Analysis, Bologna, Italy.

Goffman, E. 1974. *Frame analysis.* Harmondsworth: Penguin.

——. 1981. *Forms of talk.* Oxford: Blackwell.

Halliday, M. A. K. 1985. *Spoken and written language.* Oxford: Oxford University Press.

Heath, S. B. 1983. *Ways with words: Language, life and words of communities and classrooms.* Cambridge: Cambridge University Press.

Herring, S. 1996. *Computer-mediated communication.* Amsterdam: John Benjamins.

Hopper, R. 1992. *Telephone conversation.* Bloomington: Indiana University Press.

Lakoff, George. 1987. *Women, fire and dangerous things.* Chicago: University of Chicago Press.

Moi, T. 1986. *The Kristeva reader*. New York: Columbia University Press.

Rampton, B. 1997. Sociolinguistics and cultural studies: New ethnicities, liminality and interaction. *Working Papers in Urban Language and Literacies* 4. London: King's College.

Schiffrin, D. 1994. *Approaches to discourse.* Oxford: Blackwell.

Scollon, R. 1998. *Mediated discourse as social interaction.* Harlow, Essex: Longman.

——. 2001. *Mediated discourse: The nexus of practice.* London: Routledge.

Spitzer, M. 1986. Writing style in computer conferences. *IEEE Transactions of Professional Communication* PC-29(1): 19–22.

Stone, A. R. 1995. *The war of desire and technology at the close of the machine age.* Cambridge: MIT Press.

Street, B. 1988. Literacy practices and literacy myths. In Roger Saljo, ed., *The written word: Studies in literate thought and action,* 59–72. Berlin: Springer-Verlag.

Tannen, D. 1982. Oral and literate strategies in spoken and written narratives. *Language* 58(1): 1–21.

——. 1993. *Framing in discourse.* Oxford: Oxford University Press.

Vygotsky, L. S., and A. L. Luria. 1930. The function and fate of egocentric speech. *Proceedings of the 9th International Congress of Psychology.* Princeton: Psychological Review.

Werry, C. 1996. Linguistic and interactional features of internet relay chat. In S. Herring, ed., *Computer-mediated communication: Linguistic, social and cross-cultural perspectives,* 47–63. Amsterdam: John Benjamins.

Trying on Voices: Using Questions to Establish Authority, Identity, and Recipient Design in Electronic Discourse

BOYD DAVIS AND PEYTON MASON
University of North Carolina, Charlotte

THIS DISCUSSION EXAMINES the communicative and ritual functions of rhetorical and leading questions in asynchronous electronic discourse in order to see how people choose and adapt conversational practices to the electronic medium, and how men and women vary in their manipulation of that medium to try on different voices. Our analysis suggests different facets of how people present themselves as they engage in asynchronous interaction, such as in the online conference conducted by university students we review here. One facet is the appropriation of what is perceived to be the suitable "professional" voice. On the surface, the ways men and women handled conflict directly and more especially, indirectly, in a semester-long online conference did not jibe with models for gender-cued dominance and subordination (Yerian 1997). As Tannen comments in her 1993 discussion of gender and dominance, indirect acts are both ambiguous and polysemic. Their interpretation is keyed to setting, status of participants, "and also on the linguistic conventions that are ritualized in the cultural context" (1993:175). In our data, rhetorical and, to a lesser extent, leading questions become first conventionalized and then ritualized in dispute and debate when the participants want to retain some friendliness and perhaps even build solidarity.

People learn the conventions and customs of a particular conference or list while they are engaged in interaction, and they construct conventions in the same way. Without face-to-face social cues such as intonation or Mm-hmms, facial expressions or gestures, people exchanging messages in the new medium draw on their idiosyncratic and creative repertoires of familiar discourse, particularly conversation (Davis and Brewer 1997). They adapt features of their habitual and preferred conversational routines to the new situation and setting, probably from a desire to obtain an immediate or quick reply from others. The easiest text-based technique for letting other participants know that you have read their words is to echo, or paraphrase, or in some other way appropriate part of their message.

Asynchronous electronic text is highly appropriative. People signal they are reading-as-hearing and responding to a particular person's artifactual voice by using that person's words or emulating that person's organization. The record of interaction is a mimetic representation of orality, to borrow Harryette Mullen's explanation of her own poems (Hogue 1999). Electronic discourse feels singulary when one is reading or writing a message, but some of its visual details—the list of subject headers or writers' names, the time or date stamping, the quotations or use of "Re . . . Re"—signal its artifactually multiparty nature and potential. As Edelsky noted long ago, multiparty interaction confuses the notion of who has the floor, who is currently "speaking," and whose turn it might be (Edelsky 1981). The appropriativeness of online text may on the one hand be the writers' way of keeping track where they are at any given time or space of a discussion, while simultaneously crucial to the writer's self-presentation.

Self-presentation on the Internet is more typically discussed in terms of how people design their webpages (Giese 1998; Miller 1995). However, stylistic features have been studied for the last two decades in terms of audience or recipient design, and more recently in connection with referee design (Yaeger-Dror 2001). Rhetorical and leading questions were the most visible stylistic features used to carry on dispute and debate in a semester-long online conference: to frame our discussion of how the use of these questions conveyed self-representation in the sense of speaking in a voice appropriate to dispute and debate in a university setting, we combine approaches from the ethnography of communication and from interactional and variationist sociolinguistics, each of which speaks to different segments of the discussion.

The Local Setting

The semester-long series of disputes in an asynchronous online exchange is embedded in larger settings: first, within the practices for a university class, then within what could be argued as the cultural conventions for dispute on university campuses. The local and mediational setting is also embedded: that is, the specific online conference is part of the wider set of computer-mediated, text-based interactions that are in turn part of the online universe, but expectations for its conventions are explored as the interaction is created. The online setting, or interactional environment, skews time in general, since one time online is as good as another. In asynchronous textual interaction, there is space but no sound, voice but no noise; and though one's voice can be silenced by the lack of a reply or any signal that the voice has been seen/heard, there is no silence in the sense of a pause between sounds.

The "Investigations" conference was seldom quiet in the sense of lacking traffic. It was a student-created, online asynchronous conference intended to extend class discussion for students and professors in an undergraduate honors program seminar. Its fourteen participants saw and talked with each other every week, and used their own names in the online setting. Half of the students, two of the seven men and five of the seven women, were fluent speakers of both American English and either another language (Hindi, German, Italian, Russian) or a geographically distinct variety of World English. We were not part of their regular seminar, which must have been highly stimulating, inasmuch as discussion of controversial speakers, readings, and emerging ethical issues frequently continued in the online conference. Students consented to let us read, archive, study, and report about their conference, provided we disguised their names.

The major theme for the conference was the extent to which new scientific research in biological areas, particularly as implemented through technology, could be seen as morally or ethically justifiable. Disagreement among the students was frequent and pungent, and on multiple occasions moved into a debate format: here, a student would present both an argument and an opponent's counterargument, before marshalling the evidence supporting his or her claim. And it is that specific format that first attracted our attention: students were not signaling disagreement by "flaming" in the sense of offering short bursts of exaggerated opinion, generally without factual comment, delivered in or accompanied by inflammatory, crude, suggestive, or obscene phrases. Instead, the debate was managed by questions. The question-cued interactions revealed intersections of cultural contact and emerging professional voices.

Questions in Electronic Discourse

Questions are seldom innocent. Rhetorical questions, which are presented as questions and purport to call for answers, actually anticipate no answer given out loud from their recipients. Instead, the questioner either answers the question, as if on behalf of the recipients, or expects the recipients to ponder with the questioner the response directed by the question. The rhetorical question can actually have the force of a prediction, an assertion, a request, a directive, or any of a number of direct and indirect speech acts (Davis and Brewer 1997:141–42; see Ilie 1994). In online discourse, the rhetorical question is intimately connected to issues of readership, or recipient design. In effect, it establishes a dialogue in ways similar to the use of questions in written medical American English or in other areas of scientific discourse.

The questions in medical texts can be used to create interaction, claims Russell-Pinson (2002), by setting up a mental dialogue for the reader. The medical writer can assume the role of the projected reader with the presentation of general information, and then assume the role of a counselor by posing more specific questions. These questions foreshadow the projected reader's response and ask the real reader to consider her or his own circumstances from a different or more explicit position. When the students used rhetorical and leading questions in their online debate, they positioned themselves in dual roles as well: the projected reader and the debater, as illustrated in this example:

> R___, your point is well taken. However, I will remind you of your comments in class today complaining. . . . Are you now saying that it's okay for things to just spontaneously come into being? If man cannot just "happen," then how can that be the case for morality? Is it just an innate characteristic of man that came in the blueprints from which God was working? Apparently, He didn't do a very good job considering the fruit tree.

The questions insinuated a layer of dialogism in that they functioned as an invitation to the recipient to respond, just as if they had been sincere requests for information or clarification.

What the rhetorical question provides is a "space" for the recipient in the sense of an opportunity to reply. The recipient can reply to the issue or content of the rhetorical question on an "as if" basis, and agree or even disagree without negative consequences, as long as the disagreement is not inflammatory. That is because the recipient can self-position as reacting to content, not to the writer. The rhetorical questions in our corpus are one of the ways students handled disagreement and agreement. They were often used as a way to suggest personal opinion or experience, but they were seldom directly addressed to anybody by name. We suspect that is because the affective force of a rhetorical question might conflict with emerging norms of surface politeness. Leading questions were also used to introduce the potential for a dialogue offering disputation. However, the words of leading questions were less frequently appropriated in successive responses, so the leading question less frequently aligned the questioner with previous positions in prior messages. The leading question proposes a specific answer and asks the recipient to verify it by embedding the suggested answer. In sum, a questioner claims authority by posing a rhetorical question, and releases some of that authority by positioning others as valid responders able to claim the same point of view as the questioner, by means of their unspoken/unwritten but presumed assent. Leading questions set up a slightly different sequence of events: in oral conversation, the posing of the leading question presumes a second event in which the questioner validates the answer elicited from the respondent, and thus the questioner does not surrender control or authority as validator.

Questions and Recipient Design

Arundale (1999) has recently reemphasized the hearer—who becomes the reader in electronic communications—with his model of recipient design. His Recipient Design Principle outlines the processes by which he claims communication is co-constituted: speakers **frame** utterances using expectations from interpreting a prior utterance and "recipient interpretings yet to be formulated"; they **attribute** knowledge about the future to the recipient; they **project** how the recipient will interpret; they **produce** the utterance, they **presume** they will be held accountable by the recipients (paraphrased to include Arundale's boldface, 1999:134).

In oral discourse, the speaker using leading and rhetorical questions seems to have the recipient clearly in mind, especially in terms of projecting the recipient's interpretation. In electronic discourse, projection by means of a rhetorical or leading question is dialogic in effect, because it simulates joint production and attracts responses.

Whether keyed to Bell's model for audience design (1984, 1999), language accommodation theory advanced by Giles and Coupland (recently summarized in Williams and Nussbaum 2001), Arundale's model for recipient design, or Harré and Van Lagenhove's positioning theory (1998), a sizeable amount of current research on language interaction assumes that speakers design conversation or narrative for their recipients, and that language interaction is a joint production. Analysis of the interaction in computer-mediated online discourse, however, is temporarily constrained by certain inherent features. Each entry is saved to the conference as a time-stamped entity, and there is no turn-taking, overlap, backchannel, or interruption in the conventional sense of oral conversation. Such interaction is simulated by dialogism. In electronic discourse, particularly in conferences or lists with a feeling of community or communal purpose, people may choose to announce something or to shut off discussion by verbal abuse, but generally, they write in order to attract replies. Using rhetorical and leading questions is a strategic choice; combining them while appropriating other people's words is part of a participant's recipient design. Whenever an online message in our corpus used questions to enable dual roles for the reader-respondent, or other stylistic features suggesting the possibility of two voices or two sides to an argument, then that message typically attracted response, resulting in an actual dialogue.

Appropriating as Recipient Design

Messages in online conferences are typically repetitive, in patterned ways enjoined by situation, topic, and participants constructing meanings around the topic. Messages in the "Investigations" conference fell into three kinds: Announcements, Attractors, and Responses. We named all messages "Attractors" that attracted two or more responses; those responses almost always echo, repeat, mark (with punctuation) quotation, paraphrase, allude, emulate or in other ways appropriate from the Attractor text. At utterance level, Attractor entries presented dialog first with reported speech in the form of quotation or attribution or by emulation of organization, and then either explicitly by sketching two sides of a position or implicitly, by following the attribution with questions that allowed the reader to infer another side to the position. Responses signaled agreement and disagreement through appropriation, as seen in figure 5.1.

We used the software program Code-A-Text to look at each Attractor message to see what co-occurred in the neighborhood of rhetorical and leading questions. We used the SPSS program AnswerTree (1998) to detect significant interactions among

* Certainty, Machinery & Motivation - Mark 9/27/99
  attributes with reported speech; RQ; I ~ we; presents both sides; all-caps for emphasis
  - o Re: Certainty, Machinery & Motivation – Brett 9/28/99
    quotes Mark-text, uses quotation marks for emphasis; RQ; quotes Doris Day
    - + Re: Re: Certainty, Machinery & Motivation – Lolla 9/28/99
      quotes -text, alludes to Doris Day; presents both sides; all-caps for emphasis
      - + Re: Re: Re: Certainty, Machinery & Motivation -Meg 9/28/99
        quotes Lolla-text, quotes Mark-text; presents both sides; all-caps for emphasis
        - + the how and why of the world - Cait 9/30/99
          quotes Meg-text; RQ; all-caps for emphasis
          - + Re: the how and why of the world - Magda 10/01/99
            quotes herself [reported speech] from class, directed to Cait's proposition; RQ
            - + Re: Re: the how and why of the world - Lolla 10/01/99
              quotes Magda-text, gives both sides
    - + Re: Re: Certainty, Machinery & Motivation – Sally 9/29/99
      quotes Brett-text, RQ, series of "I cannot understand" references to his points
      - + Re: Re: Re: Certainty, Machinery & Motivation – Brett 9/30/99
        appropriates Sally-text order to answer her points; RQ; quot marks for emphasis
        - + Re: Re: Re: Re: Certainty, Machinery & Motivation - Rina 9/30/99
          quotes single-words, appropriates order of Brett-text; RQ
    - + Let's try this again... – Brett 9/30/99
      appropriates from Rina-text; presents both sides; RQ; quot marks for emphasis
  - o Re: Certainty, Machinery & Motivation – Aaron 9/29/99
    appropriates, quotes single words from Mark, RQ

Figure 5.1. Appropriation in Threaded Discourse.

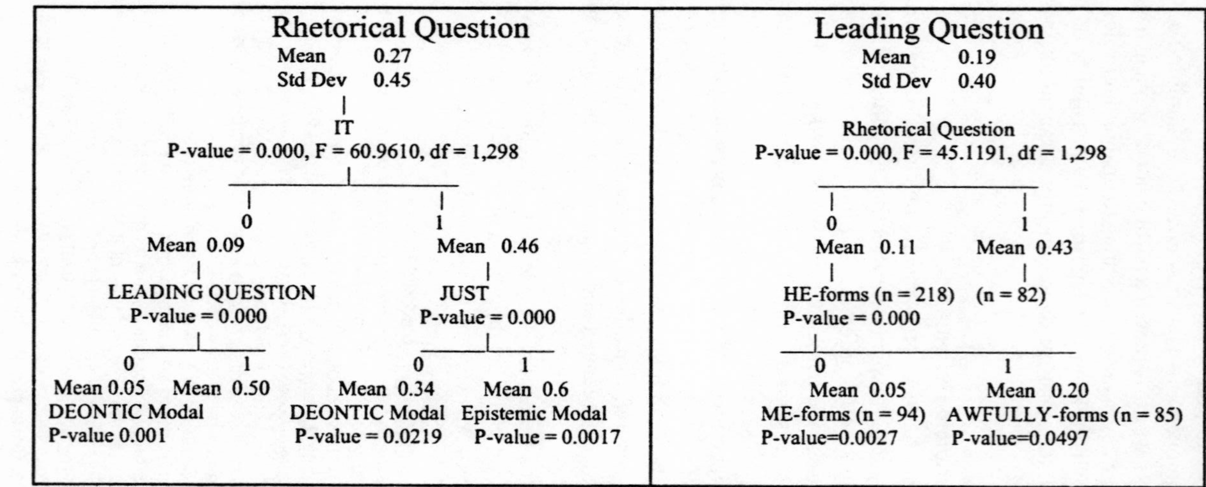

Figure 5.2. Significant Interactions for Rhetorical and Leading Questions.

question types, modals, stance adverbs, and intensifiers in both the full text of the conference and the subset of Attractors. AnswerTree searches data for the first significant segmentation and forces successive segmentations. These are relatively reliable for the initial significant interactions, but as the numbers within a cohort begin to shrink, the significance becomes more forced and less reliable.

The sketch below captures the Rhetorical Question, and the spaces it provides for the interlocutor to enter the dialogue. If *it*—whether anaphoric or cataphoric—occurs in a segment, the writer moves to choose whether or not to employ *just,* and if *just* is present, the writer typically selects an epistemic modal such as "can" or "might."

If there is no *it*-clause in the segment, the writer usually moves to employ a leading question, and ends the segment with a phrase containing a deontic modal. Typically, an it-clause precedes the rhetorical question, establishing distance; the rhetorical question narrows the distance: this is the Push me–Pull you of dialogism.

Rhetorical questions are frequently accompanied by the *it* of rapid writing and the *it* of pseudo-cleft constructions, which foreground information, qualify the information with *just*—as opposed to other kinds of intensifiers—and then give a third chance for the reader to find an alternative entrance, with the epistemic modal. Leading questions, however, as seen in the diagram below, do not give the writer as many ways to enter into dialogue, if they do not presage a rhetorical question.

Intensifiers also differ in the ways they create openings for readers to chime in as writers without losing face. *Just,* for example, typically collocates with clefts and anaphoric references, rhetorical questions and epistemic modals, while other modals collocate more immediately with private verbs of thinking and perceiving and move rather rapidly to interpersonal engagement.

Interactions of Gender and Disagreement

Earlier, we suggested that leading questions were less likely to attract response, keyed to their lower presence in messages that attracted two or more entries. A number of researchers, such as Herring, have suggested that online interactions, at least in Internet groups, replicate the male-dominated, gender-cued behavior of everyday

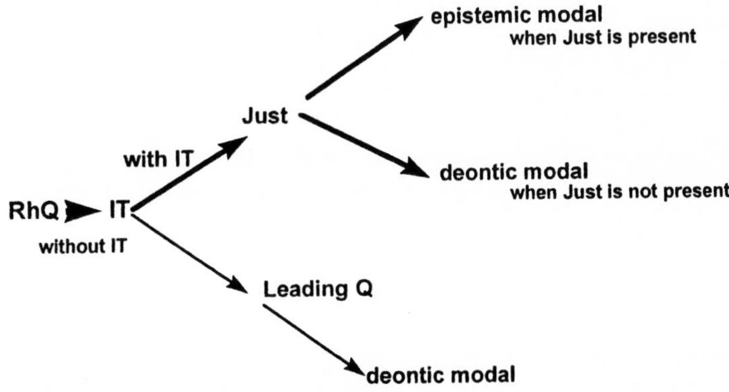

Figure 5.3. Choices Triggered by Rhetorical Questions.

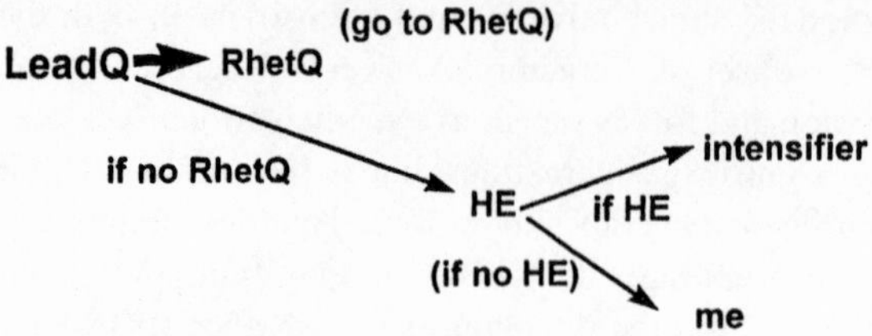

Figure 5.4. Choices Triggered by Leading Questions.

conversation (Herring 1993, 2000). King summarizes Herring's studies over the last decade with a comparison between women's and men's language in public online interactions: for example, women present attenuated assertions, apologies, and personal orientation, whereas men present strong assertions, self-promotion, and authoritative orientation. King finds slightly different interactional patterns in online communities that are "women-friendly," noting that such gender-based differences fade in settings that support interactions for common goals among revealed users, that is, those who are neither anonymous nor masked by ambiguous screen names (King 2000).

In the next part of this discussion, we look at when and how gender may have come into play, given conventional or even stereotypical expectations for gender-cued behavior, and we begin with conventional tabulations before returning to look at function, convention, and style. Who wrote more, men or women students? Who wrote more frequently? Initiated more discussions? Sparked controversy? Whose writings attracted more responses? How was disagreement handled? Who used rhetorical questions?

The number of participants in the conference was equally balanced. Women wrote more entries: 58 percent of the 232 postings. They initiated discussion more frequently by writing 18 of the initial messages heading the 25 multiple-response topics. Ten of these topics, with a total of 131 messages, presented strong, hot disagreement: of the 10 "hot" threads, women students initiated 7, and wrote the plurality of entries: 82 of the 131, or 62 percent.

In terms of frequency of postings, the women more than held their own. However, there were differences in the ways in which disagreements were signaled (see Rees-Miller 2000 for a review of classroom disagreements). In the "Investigations" conference, students debated issues in topic after topic, thread after thread, all semester long, using primarily the features of softened and aggravated disagreement. Nobody ever said "I disagree" and stopped there. Moreover, in a single message, which was typically three or more sentences long, a writer might mix features of both mitigated, or softened disagreement and intensified, or aggravated disagreement. And in fact, that is what the student writers in the "Investigations" conference did: they mingled features of both softened and aggravated disagreement using modals and adverbs for the former and intensifiers for the latter, and they did so both in their initial messages which opened topics and in their responses to each other. (Mixing modes—such as casual and formal, or guarded and verbose, or softened and aggravated disagreement—may be a characteristic of registers across the genre of electronic discourse regardless of the age of the writer; see Zyngier and Seidl de Moura [1997] on Brazilian elementary school students). Rhetorical and leading questions were not only abundant, they were not an exclusively "male" strategy in terms of frequency of use by both men and women students, though they may be so considered when issues of self-presentation and identity are examined.

The features of what Rees-Miller calls softened disagreement are what Scollon and Scollon (2000) call Strategies of Involvement, in which the writer/speaker primarily uses positive politeness. Such features include colloquial speech, inclusive pronouns, and modals. We examined *we* and *could* as tokens suggesting these strategies. We chose *but* and *just* to illustrate features used for Scollon and Scollon's Strategies of Independence, which typically present negative politeness. *Just* can be used either to intensify or to tone down a statement; its concordance showed that in this conference, *just* is most frequently used for the latter purpose, making it a Strategy of Independence. In both the full conference and the Attractor subset, women students barely edged out men in inviting affiliation with more tokens of inclusive *we* and the mitigating *could.* Women students used significantly more tokens of *but* as a way to slide into disagreement; *just,* however, was fairly evenly distributed. The women students, then, used slightly more tokens suggesting positive and negative politeness than the men and could also be said to present more softened disagreement, whether in the full conference or in the Attractor subset.

Investigative and clarificative questions are often associated with female style; rhetorical questions have often been more strongly associated with male style, with challenge and controversy, negative politeness, and aggravated disagreement. Yet, both rhetorical questions and leading questions were used throughout the conference by both genders, and women students, who were half of the participants, wrote more than half (62 percent) of the entries that combined both kinds. We think that disagreement in this conference was one way of creating solidarity (Tannen 1993). That is, using questions as a signal of the power to disagree, or as the potential to be disagreed *with,* was a signal of self-presentation and self-authorization.

Questions and Authority: The Emergent Professional Voice

When Galegher and Sproull examined ways that members of online support and hobby groups established legitimacy and authority, they noted a crucial difference in where and how this was accomplished. Support group members construct and convey authority from reports of their personal experience, keyed to their projection of which experiences match what group members are interested in discussing. Hobbyists also present questions, but their interactions generally take the form of problem-diagnosis-solution (Galegher and Sproull 1998). In "Investigations," participants chose to derive or construct authority externally, from professional credentials. Although all were students, the women claimed the authority of "professions." Can we assume that they wrote in the style they projected as matching professional styles, particularly in the sciences? That would suggest that they were in the process of creating professional identities for themselves and wrote out of those identities. As university honors students, most of whom were in the sciences and intent on graduate work in research, law, or medicine, it would be surprising if they were *not* involved in such as process. Lemke (2002), in a discussion of how people learn registers and identities in the sciences, comments that "identities can be conceptualized . . . as being constituted by the orientational stances we take, toward others and toward the contents and effects of our own utterances, in enacting roles within specialized subcultures by speaking and writing in the appropriate registers and genres" (2002:68).

Questioning is encouraged as a necessary part of hypothesis-formation and scientific inquiry beginning in elementary and secondary school. Rhetorical questions and, to some extent, leading questions are part of the working register for argumentation and debate in philosophy and logic, the legal profession and the sciences, at least on television, in the movies, and in classroom lectures. Whether learning to talk the talk and manipulate these question-types is indeed both an implicit and necessary part of becoming socialized into the discourse of professional scientists, philosophers, and lawyers is not the point (though we think it is true). Rather, the fact that (1) some of the students—the women—overtly claimed professional affiliation as part of establishing their authority, following these claims with questions as stylistic, interactional strategies, and that (2) both men and women students saw those strategies emulated or appropriated by other students, and reused those strategies in their responses to the responses, strongly suggests that such actions are seen by students as being an important part of being novice scientists.

Authority, Questions, and Self-Presentation

In the "Investigations" conference, the women claimed the authority of professions and hence the professional styles of law and science, self-identifying "as a biologist," "as a biology major," "as a philosophy major," as a researcher who conducts "research to discover, not to control," and claiming group membership: "as scientists, we . . ." None of the men students overtly identified themselves in the conference as writers/researchers affiliated with a particular professional stance; although they may, of course, have done so in face-to-face discussions, none of the writings in the conference specifically addressed or presented any male student in terms of such a claim. Instead, the style spoke.

Perhaps it never occurred to any of the male students that such self-identification was needed. Men students as well as women students appealed to external authority in the form of quotations from or allusions to well-known scholars; to each other (temporarily raising their group and individual status); to classroom readings, citations of articles, and postings of websites. All but one of the women students consistently used the strategy of asking rhetorical and leading questions, particularly in responses. The only person who did not position herself as a professional, either externally by appealing to professional research or internally by using one or both kinds of questions in a consistent manner, met with aggravated disagreement in two successive discussions that pitted arguments for "Faith" against arguments for "Science." She argued that she did not have—and did not want—strategies with which to combat the positions of her peers: "I can't really argue my point with hard evidence because my ideas are based on faith," an argument that the other students were unwilling to accept because, as one response stated, it was perfectly possible to draw on empirical positions to argue for faith.

As the "Faith vs. Science" arguments began to wind down, the interaction in the conference began to dissipate, as seen in the lessening success of Attractor-entries to attract embedded discussion, and a much less frequent participation by half of the original participants, including the L2–American English men and the L1–American English women. Part of this diminution can be seen as the typical cycle of an online conference, which ebbs and flows. However, perhaps the "Faith vs. Science" debate triggered issues around boundaries, in the sense of Petronio et al. (1998). That is, the debate, extending over two long, embedded, topically threaded discussions, and establishing a clear demarcation between "winner" and "loser," may have blurred the boundary signals of what was and was not proper argument style, topic, or content for the participants. With boundaries blurred or uneven, the delicate system of the conference, comprised of successive conference interactions and their recipient design, could have become unstable, so that some participants felt it possible or even advantageous to withdraw.

The participants in the "Investigations" conference were, in the heat of discussion, exploiting a questioning style that is an interactional norm for formal oral debate, if not for ordinary conversation. The style is one that in oral classroom situations characterizes an aggravated disagreement, but in this particular online conference seems to have been thought a professionalizing register whose use conferred authority upon its speakers by virtue of its characteristics of appraisal and evaluation, and which presented dialogism by virtue of its alternation with presentation of both sides of an issue. The women participants in the conference used the majority of positive and negative politeness tokens in their remarks to present softened disagreement with their peers, presumably to maintain collaborative and social relationships. At the same time, most of them overtly claimed professional roles historically filled by males, taking on the register as well. We would not claim that either cohort of men or women displayed more power or claimed more authority in this conference: for one thing, issues of socialization for first and second language variety may have come into play. More important, their shared assumptions about and appropriation of a professional voice by both genders, from multiple language backgrounds, complicates any notion of singularity in their constructions of identity or self-presentation in online electronic discourse.

REFERENCES

AnswerTree 1.0. Users Guide. 1998. Chicago: SPSS Inc.

Arundale, R. 1999. An alternative model and ideology of communication for an alternative to politeness theory. *Pragmatics* 9:119–54.

Bell, A. 1984. Language style as audience design. *Language in Society* 13:145–204.

———. 1999. Styling the other to define the self: A study in New Zealand identity making. *Journal of Sociolinguistics* 3:523–41.

Davis, B., and J. Brewer. 1997. *Electronic discourse: Linguistic individuals in virtual space.* Albany: State University of New York Press.

Edelsky, C. 1981. Who's got the floor? *Language in Society* 10: 383–421.

Galegher, J., and L. Sproull. 1998. Legitimacy, authority and community in electronic support groups. *Written Communication* 15:493–531.

Giese, M. 1998. Self without body: Textual self-representation in an electronic community. *FirstMonday*. www.firstmonday.dk/issues/issue3_4/giese.

Harré, R., and L. Van Langenhove. 1998. *Positioning theory: Moral contexts of international action*. Oxford: Blackwell.

Herring, S. 1993. Gender and democracy in computer-mediated communication. *Electronic Journal of Communication* 3. www.cios.org/www/ejc/v3n293.htm.

——. 2000. Gender differences in CMC: findings and implications. *CPSR Newsletter* 18. www.cpsr.org/publications/newsletters/issues/2000/Winter2000/herring.html.

Hogue, C. 1999. Interview with Harryette Mullen. *PostModern Culture* 9. www.iath.Virginia.edu/pmc/text-only/issue.199/9.2hogue.txt.

Ilie, C. 1994. *What else can I tell you?: A pragmatic study of English rhetorical questions as discursive and argumentative acts*. Stockholm: Almqvist and Wiksell International.

King, L. 2000. Gender issues in online communities. *CPSR Newsletter* 18. www.cpsr.org/publications/newsletters/issues/2000/Winter2000/king.html.

Lemke, J. M. 2002. Learning academic language identities: Multiple timescales in the social ecology of education. In C. Kramsch, ed., *Language acquisition and language socialization: Ecological perspectives*, 68–87. London: Continuum.

Miller, H. 1995. The presentation of self in electronic life: Goffman on the Internet. Paper presented at Conference on Embodied Knowledge and Virtual Space, University of London.

Petronio, S., N. Ellemers, H. Giles, and C. Gallois. 1998. (Mis)communicating across boundaries: Interpersonal and intergroup considerations. *Communication Research* 25:571–96.

Rees-Miller, J. 2000. Power, severity and context in disagreement. *Journal of Pragmatics* 32:1087–11.

Russell-Pinson, L. 2002. Grammatical and extratextual variation in medical English texts: A comparative genre analysis. Ph.D. diss., Georgetown University.

Scollon, R., and S. Scollon. 2000. *Intercultural communication*. 2d ed. Oxford: Blackwell.

Tannen, D. 1993. The relativity of linguistic strategies: Rethinking power and solidarity in gender and dominance. In D. Tannen, ed., *Gender and conversational interaction*, 165–88. New York: Oxford University Press.

Williams, A., and J. Nussbaum. 2001. *Intergenerational communication across the life span*. Mahwah, NJ: Erlbaum.

Yaeger-Dror, M. 2001. Primitives of a system for "style" and "register." In P. Eckert and J. Rickford, eds., *Style and sociolinguistic variation*, 170–84. Cambridge: Cambridge University Press.

Yerian, K. 1997. From stereotypes of gender differences to stereotypes of theory: A response to Hayley Davis' review of Deborah Tannen's Gender and Discourse. *Language and Communication* 17:165–76.

Zyngier, S., and M. Seidl de Moura. 1997. Pragmatic aspects of spontaneous electronic communication in a school setting. *Text* 17:127–55.

Mock Taiwanese-Accented Mandarin in the Internet Community in Taiwan: The Interaction between Technology, Linguistic Practice, and Language Ideologies

HSI-YAO SU
University of Texas at Austin

IN THE PAST DECADE OR SO, the prevalence of computer technology and the growing population of Internet users have given rise to a new arena for the investigation of discourse, linguistic style, and identity. In the realm of the Internet, the participants in any type of communication do not have to be bound by physical territory. Dialogue can take place between spatially distant interlocutors. In addition, the anonymous nature of the Internet can sometimes downplay the importance of social categories frequently evoked in face-to-face communication, such as gender, socioeconomic status, and age, and offer opportunities for playing with them. The relationship between language use on the Internet and factors often adopted by sociolinguists to account for language variation may not be as salient as that in face-to-face communication.

However, the lack of salience does not imply that the study of language on the Internet and the identity of Internet users cannot be fruitful. On the contrary, the Internet provides an opportunity to examine the ways identities can be formed in a deterritorialized and depersonalized realm. It may also shed light on the relationships among emerging on-line language practices, the larger social context, and dominant ideologies of languages. In this paper I focus on a particular linguistic practice that is believed to have originated on the Internet in Taiwan, which I term "Written Mock Taiwanese-Accented Mandarin" (hereafter MTM), following Hill (1999) in naming Anglo Americans' incorporation of Spanish-language materials into English "Mock Spanish." Taiwanese Internet users draw on the stereotypical linkage between Taiwanese-accented Mandarin in speech and the multiple social meanings associated with such an accent to create a new form of language play, which serves as a tool for identity construction among Internet users.

The research questions I attempt to answer are:

1. How is discourse influenced by technology? How do speakers or Internet users make use of the linguistic resources at their disposal to create new language styles when the mode of communication changes? What characteristics of the Internet foster the emergence of such a practice?
2. How are identities formed on the Internet, where personal information is easily concealed?

3. What are the linguistic elements and social factors that contribute to the humorous effects of such a type of language play? How can the practice of MTM shed light on dominant language ideologies in Taiwanese society?

Although all three groups of questions are discussed in this article, the focus is on the first, while the next two are covered in less detail.

The Chinese Writing System and MTM

The practice of MTM makes use of the characteristics of the Chinese writing system to mimic Mandarin as spoken by speakers who have a strong Taiwanese accent, which is stereotypically associated with members of older generations or less educated rural residents. The Chinese writing system is logographic, that is, each character represents one morpheme, which has an inherent meaning, and is associated with a phonological structure. In the production of MTM, characters that represent sounds similar to the accent are adopted, regardless of their original meanings. Thus, when one is reading such a sentence, the effect is what sounds like the mimicry of an intelligible Mandarin sentence heavily influenced by Taiwanese phonology, while the strings of characters present an anomaly in meaning. The discrepancy between the recovered meaning of the sentence, the sound effect of the sentence, and the meaning inherent in each character is exactly the source of the parodic effect of the language play. Two examples are given in (1). Each example provides a comparison between a case of MTM and its intended meaning. MTM is indicated by an arrow. Pinyin, a subsidiary system of writing Mandarin with a modified Roman alphabet, is also presented to show the contrast in sound structure.

(1)a. *The intended meaning:*

Character	很	多	人	去	考
Pinyin	**hen**	duo	ren	**qu**	kao
Gloss	*very*	*many people go*		*take-exam*	

"Many people took the exam."

The actual production in MTM:

→	Character	混	多	人	企	考
	Pinyin	**hun**	duo	ren	**qi**	kao
	Gloss	*mix*	*many people business*		*take-exam*	

b. *The intended meaning:*

Character	是	個	帥	哥
Pinyin	shi	ge	shuai	**ge**
Glos	*is*	*CL*[1]	*handsome*	*brother*

"(He) is a good-looking guy."

[1] [CL = classifiers]

The actual production in MTM

→	Character	是	個	帥	鍋
	Pinyin	shi	ge	shuai	**guo**
	Gloss	*is*	*CL*	*handsome*	*pot*

I believe that MTM is both a product of the culture of the Internet and a reflection of and reaction to the sociolinguistic situation in Taiwan, especially the dominant language attitudes toward Mandarin and Taiwanese and the relationships between ethnic groups. The emergence of this practice is related to the dependence on writing as the sole means of communication on the Internet and the personas Internet users jointly construct—young, lively, congenial, and witty—which, in turn, are associated with access to computer technology and education. To investigate the meanings attached to such a practice, it is necessary to understand the social context that gives rise to this form of language play.

The Sociolinguistic Situation in Taiwan and MTM

The better-known part of the history of Taiwan begins with the Chinese settlement established by immigrants from coastal areas of the Chinese mainland in the seventeenth and eighteenth centuries. The majority of the immigrants came from Fujian Province and spoke dialects of Southern Min, which became the dominant language in Taiwan. The dialect of Southern Min spoken in Taiwan today is referred to as *Taiwanese.* In 1949 the Chinese Nationalist government lost the civil war with Chinese Communists and retreated to Taiwan, which created another wave of immigration. The immigrants who moved to Taiwan during this period and their descendants are called *mainlanders.* The central government of the Nationalists was reestablished in Taipei, and mainlanders became the dominant group in terms of its political power. Mandarin was promoted as the official and the only legitimate language. Since then, the influence of Taiwanese has been declining, although it is still the native language of up to 70 percent of Taiwanese people. For two decades now, the ban on ethnic languages other than Mandarin has been lifted, and an increasing number of politicians who speak Taiwanese as their first language have become influential, including the current president, Chen Shui-Bian. The status of Taiwanese has risen, but Mandarin is still considered a more overtly prestigious language than Taiwanese.

Two salient factors should not be neglected in understanding language use in Taiwan today, namely, language shift between generations and differences in language use between rural and urban areas (Huang 1993; Su 2000). In rural areas, the use of Taiwanese prevails. It is the language of daily life, which is spoken within the family and among friends, and is used in local institutions. Members of the younger generation learn Mandarin at school, but maintain fluent Taiwanese ability. In contrast, in urban areas where the majority of mainlanders reside, the use of Mandarin has penetrated many informal settings. Language shift between generations is particularly salient in urban areas, where many members of younger generations of

Southern Min heritage have limited ability in their parents' native language and speak predominantly Mandarin.

One result of the interaction between age and region is that Mandarin spoken with heavy influence from Taiwanese phonology is more common among older generations and among members of younger generations who grow up outside of urban areas. Hence, in the spirit of Ochs (1992), who demonstrates that the relation between language and cultural contexts (such as social identities) is constituted and mediated by the relation of language to particular stances and social acts, the degree of the influence of Taiwanese phonology in Mandarin directly indexes age and region. Furthermore, because rurality and older age often indicate a lack of adequate educational access or facilities, a Taiwanese accent when speaking Mandarin is indirectly linked with undesired qualities such as ignorance or outdatedness. On the other hand, similar to many other regional varieties reported in different societies, the accent has local prestige and is associated with friendliness, congeniality, and local color. Recently, owing to the hostile relationship between China and Taiwan and the rise of a Taiwanese identity (as opposed to a Mainland Chinese-based identity), the accent, though often considered unsophisticated, is appreciated more for its uniqueness, that is to say, the fact that it belongs only to Taiwanese society.

It is within this social context that I investigate MTM on the Internet in Taiwan. The data I present in the study come from a variety of sources. The actual examples of the practice are collected mainly from chatrooms in 1998 in two campus bulletin boards in Taiwan, those of the National Taiwan University and Taipei Municipal First Girls' High School. The other part of my data comes from interviews in which Taiwanese were asked to comment on the practice of Mock Taiwanese-accented Mandarin. I interviewed nine Taiwanese students at the University of Texas at Austin informally either in a one-on-one interview or in a group interview. All of them showed familiarity with Mock Taiwanese-accented Mandarin and the culture of the Internet in Taiwan.

Phonological Features of MTM

The perception that age and regional factors are related to Taiwanese-accented Mandarin might be factual, but the idea that there is a single Taiwanese accent is stereotypical. In reality, speakers with diverse backgrounds manage to speak Mandarin in different ways, yet the accent captured by MTM seems to focus on the stereotypical images held by the general public. Thus, it is worth exploring the features that Internet users associate with "the accent." From the data I collected, it appears that all contrasts made in written Mock Taiwanese-accented Mandarin are related to two phonological features: roundedness and retroflexness. Table 6.1 shows some of the instances of MTM from my data.

In contrast to that of Mandarin, the sound inventory of Taiwanese does not include retroflex consonants, a fact captured in the lack of retroflex sounds in MTM. However, the origin of the contrast of roundedness and unroundedness is unclear. Both Mandarin and Taiwanese have rounded and unrounded vowels, and the use of this feature seems to be less consistent.

Table 6.1
Phonological features of MTM

Mandarin counterpart			Mock Taiwanese-accented Mandarin		
Characters	Meaning	Features	Characters	Meaning	Features
我 wo	I/me	[+round]	偶 ou	even number	[−round]
去 qu	to go	[+round]	企 qi	business	[−round]
哥 ge	brother	[−round]	鍋 guo	pot	[+round]
人 ren	people	[−round] [+retroflex]	倫 lun	order	[+round] [−retroflex]
誰 shei	who	[−round] [+retroflex]	髓 sui	marrow	[+round] [−retroflex]
兒 er	son	[+retroflex]	鵝 e	goose	[−retroflex]
是 shi	to be	[−round] [+retroflex]	素 su	plain; simple	[+round] [−retroflex]

The Function of MTM and the Community of Practice

MTM is currently used in a variety of domains, from the Internet to traditional print media such as comic books and romance novels, and from the public domain to the private domain, such as chatrooms, forwarded mass emails, personal email messages, and written notes to friends in daily life. However, it appears that the Internet is most likely the origin of this practice, or at least the realm where the practice is popularized. My interviewees, when asked the question, "Where have you seen such a practice?" all mentioned the Internet. If such is the case, what are the functions of MTM in the Internet environment? What characteristics of Internet chatrooms fostered the emergence of such a practice?

From a functional point of view, forms of computer-mediated communication, although resembling face-to-face conversations to a certain degree, have physical constraints on the display of contextualization cues (Gumperz 1992) such as prosody, gesture, and addressitivity. As the link between speakers and listeners is weakened, speakers have to add variety in the written discourse to compete for attention (Werry 1996). Indeed MTM is simply one practice of language play among many others on the Internet. Some of the other practices include mixing between Chinese characters, National Phonetic Symbols *(zhuyin)*, and the English alphabet, the extensive use of punctuation marks, and use of space to create visual images.

The functional need may account for the emergence of the unique communication style on the Internet, but the characteristics of the Internet medium do not give us a full picture of the complexity of the Internet culture. The need to catch attention and the loose coherence of Internet chat may invite humorous play (Herring 1999), yet humorous performance can further be used to create group solidarity and identity among the Internet users (Baym 1995), as illustrated by the comment from an interview in example (2). The comment from the interviewee is highlighted. HY refers to the interviewer.

(2) HY: *. . ..Na ni zheyang xie huoshi ni kandao bieren zheyang xie ni juede, ta de gongneng shi shenme? Haishi keyi dadao shenme xiaoguo ma?*

. . . when you write like this or when you see someone writes like this, what do you think the function is? Or what kind of effect can one get?

WL: ***Chuncui youqu haowan la.***

It's simply for fun.

HY: *Hm-hmm.*

WL: ***Dui a. Yinggai ye keyi shuo you yidian, jiusuan shi na zhong, e, jiaozuo, en, zhe ge jiao shenme, liuxing ba.***

Yeah, maybe also a little, uh, I am not sure how to say it, maybe trendy?

HY: *Hm-hmm.*

WL: ***Jiushi yinwei haoxiang, turan zhijian haoxiang wanglu shang zhe zhong yuyan henduo.***

Because all of a sudden, there are so many such usages on the Internet.

HY: *Hm-hmm.*

WL: ***Ranhou yeshi gen zhe dajia liuxing, ranhou, ziji ye, ye wei le hao wan ranhou ye gen zhe dajia zheyang yong zhe zhong yuyan zhe yang.***

So I just follow the trend, and I myself follow everyone and use this kind of usage for fun.

The Internet in Taiwan can be analyzed as a community of practice (Lave and Wenger 1991; Wenger 1998), defined by Eckert as "an aggregate of people who come together around some enterprise. United by this common enterprise, people come to develop and share ways of doing things, ways of talking, beliefs, values—in short, practices—as a function of their joint engagement in activity" (2000:35).

Whether the members of the Internet community have shared speech norms is unknown, but members participate in a common endeavor to create a unique Internet environment and jointly construct relations through the development of a common view toward the community and its participants. The pursuit of online communication brings Internet users together, and through mutual engagement they negotiate the meanings of their experiences on the Internet and develop routines and styles of communication as a result of their shared history of learning and exploring. A community of practice, thus, is not defined simply by the purpose of the joint engagement: it is simultaneously defined by its memberships and a repertoire of negotiable resources accumulated over time. Internet users develop a shared body of knowledge on what to do and what not to do. Language practices on the Internet are highly stylized such that a new user needs to undergo socialization to learn to be a fully competent participant in the community. On the Internet, it appears that the exploration and the extensive use of various forms of language play are highly encouraged. MTM's humorous nature thus suits well the playful atmosphere of the Internet chat room. However, it is important to recognize that the playful effect of MTM does not come solely from the form of language play itself, but also from the negotiated meaning attached to the practice as funny and friendly in the community. Example (3) contains two excerpts in which interviewees comment on the effects MTM produces.

(3)a. *WL:* ***. . .. . .Dang wo kan dao ta yong zhe zhong yuyan zai biaoda ta de xiangfa huo shi zai xie dong xi de shihou,***

. . . . .When I see someone using this kind of usage to express his/her thoughts,

HY: *Hm-hmm,*

WL: ***Wo hui hen zhijue de renwei zhe ge ren yinggai shi, jiushi hui you zhe zhong gexing jiushi hen xihuan wannao. Ranhou yinggai shi hen rongyi gen renjia da cheng yipian, qinjin de gexing.***

I would intuitively think that this person is probably, this person probably loves crowds. He/she must be very out-going and easy-going.

b. (When asked what kind of effect MTM produces)

YH: ***Bijiao qinqie ba.***

It's friendlier.

HY: *Bijiao qinqie.*

Friendlier.

YH: ***Dui, bijiao pingyi jinren yidian.***

Right, more easygoing.

HY: *Hm-hmm.*

WS: ***Wo juede tamen jiushi keyi zai gaoxiao.***

I think they are just trying to be funny.

Having discussed the factors that encourage the emergence of language play, I now turn to a discussion of why MTM is received as humorous. More specifically, (1) what linguistic or sociolinguistic factors make the Mock Taiwanese accent funny? And this question is inevitably related to another question: (2) what types of identity are indexed with the use of MTM on the Internet in Taiwan?

The Multiple Functionality of MTM on the Linguistic Level

Roman Jakobson, in his article "Closing Statement: Linguistics and Poetics" (1960: 353), proposes a schema that includes factors inalienably involved in verbal communications:

(4)

	Context	
Addresser	Message	Addressee
	Contact	
	Code	

Each of these six factors determines a different function of language: addresser—emotive; addressee—conative; context—referential; message—poetic; contact—phatic; and code—metalingual. According to Jakobson's model, the use of MTM fulfills at least three functions simultaneously: the referential function, which orients toward the context; the poetic function, which directs attention to the form of the message; and the metalingual function, which calls for knowledge of language. In the production and interpretation of MTM, on the level of referential function, the intended sentential meaning is conveyed, and attention is also directed to the sociolinguistic situation (see the following section) that gives rise to the mimicry of such an accent. On the level of poetic function, attention is directed to the discrepancy between the intended meaning of the sentence and the anomaly in meaning of the string of words containing MTM. Furthermore, metalinguistic ability is required to be able to produce and to interpret instances of MTM. The complexity and multiple functions involved illustrate that MTM is a form of language play that has aesthetic value. Part of the funny, jocular effect created by such a practice comes from its inherently functional multiplicity.

A linguistic analysis alone, however, does not fully account for the effect MTM produces. One key aspect of the language play lies in the parodic juxtaposition of the representation of an accent that is often associated with a lack of education and one's intellectual ability to analyze the accent and to manipulate the writing system. In order to investigate this aspect, it is necessary to examine the relationship between the stylized Mock Taiwanese accent practice and the identities and images the members of the Internet community wish to project.

Identity, Crossing, and the Practice of MTM in the Internet Community

Although Internet users' personal identities outside of the Internet are impossible to trace, members do share some characteristics: all of them have access to computers and the Internet, have the ability to use computers, and can not only write but also have the metalinguistic ability to reflect on a certain type of accent with wordplay. All these abilities require a certain amount of education and access to modern technology, although the degree of education and access may vary among members. Better access to education and technology is often associated with younger generations, metropolitan residents, and modernity. My intention here is not to claim that Internet users necessarily have these qualities. In contrast, I believe that attention should be paid to the image and the identity Internet users jointly construct. According to the interviewees and my own observations, it does appear that the characteristics of being young, outgoing, and modern are often associated with the Internet community. In other words, these qualities are the preferred image shared by many, if not all, Internet users. To a certain degree, the Internet thus represents an imagined community (Anderson 1983), where members do not necessarily have concrete relationships with each other and the images users project do not necessarily match their identity in daily life. However, the style of the Internet discourse and the persona members jointly construct are real in important senses.

On the Internet, members of the community constantly explore means of language play to project an energetic and modern image. The desired image on the

Internet stands in opposition to characteristics such as uneducated, outdated, aged, or rural. Interestingly, the undesired features are stereotypically associated with the speakers whose Mandarin has strong influences from Taiwanese phonology. In other words, the practice of MTM on the Internet creates a sense of modernity and urbanity by imitating the speech of the group of speakers whom the Internet users may not wish to identify with completely.

I suggest that MTM on the Internet is a practice of *crossing,* which Rampton defines as "a range of ways in which people use language and dialect in discursive practice to appropriate, explore, reproduce or challenge influential images and stereotypes of groups that they *don't* themselves (straightforwardly) belong to" (1999:421). Members of the Internet communities clearly present themselves as belonging to the educated younger generations that are linked to an urban lifestyle. Speakers of this social category are not recognized as speakers of Taiwanese-accented Mandarin according to local ideologies. Hence, MTM on the Internet can be considered a type of crossing.

In his theorizing of crossing, Rampton (1995, 1999) raises Bakhtin's notion of "double-voicing" (1981, 1984) as an important analytical tool. Rampton states that "within single stretches of speech, stereotypic elements from elsewhere mingle with habitual speech patterns, and in the process, they generate symbolically condensed dialogues between self and other" (1999:422). Bakhtin (1984) further characterizes several kinds of double-voicing. With unidirectional double-voicing, the speaker employs someone else's discourse "in the direction of its own particular aspirations" (193). In contrast, with varidirectional double-voicing, "the author again speaks in someone else's discourse, but . . . introduces into that discourse a semantic intention directly opposed to the original one" (193).

Within the context of Taiwanese society, the act of crossing in MTM evokes multiple conflicting voices. On the one hand, in each expression with MTM, the author's voice is there. The recovered sentential meaning expresses the core referential content of the sentence the writer attempts to convey. On the other hand, MTM evokes the voice of speakers with a Taiwanese accent, yet in a twisted way. The familiar, congenial persona associated with the accent is integrated into the practice of MTM. On this level, the voicing is unidirectional: the author aligns himself or herself with the indexical values associated with the accent and its local prestige. However, the transformation from a spoken accent to written wordplay, which implies the ability to manipulate language, filters out the negative connotation of backwardness often linked with the accent. On this level, the act of crossing is varidirectional: the author positions himself or herself away from the negative representations of speakers with the accent. Hence, by using MTM, the Internet users simultaneously associate themselves with and dissociate themselves from the different levels of connotations of such an accent. This form of language play manifests the complex nature of linguistic practice and speaker/writer agency in the negotiation of meaning with the symbolic resources available at hand.

In a more global context, however, MTM may not be recognized as an act of crossing. Taiwanese-accented Mandarin is a unique linguistic variety spoken only in Taiwan, and language play based on the accent is a linguistic product that belongs solely to a society in which members are familiar with both the Chinese writing system and the accent. This particular linguistic style, originated in Taiwan, thus has its importance in the ideologizing of social differentiations: it distinguishes Taiwanese society from other Chinese-speaking/writing world. As Irvine (2001) suggests, styles can be recognized as a part of a social semiosis of distinctiveness. With an ambivalent relationship between China and Taiwan and the emergence of a Taiwanese identity, the use of MTM can be considered a way in which Internet users understand the social meanings attached to salient social groups and negotiate their positions within a system of distinctions. The existence of various ideologies at both a global and a local level, therefore, makes it possible for authors of MTM to display multiple positionalities with regard to self and other. The dynamic nature of linguistic practice is clearly manifested in each instance of MTM, which presents an ongoing interaction between dominant and local ideologies.

It is through the multiple functionality at the linguistic level and the multiple evocation of social categories and ideologies at the sociolinguistic level that MTM is able to produce its humorous and playful effect. Popularized on the Internet, MTM has now spread to other domains which take younger readers as their target. With the increasing visibility of the practice in public domains and the positive, jocular image associated with the practice, the next question worth exploring is whether this practice challenges the hierarchy of languages in Taiwan in any way.

I believe the answer is no. A symbolic transgression does not necessarily indicate identifying with a particular group. In her study of use of African American Vernacular English (AAVE) by middle-class European American boys, Bucholtz (1999) argues that language crossing to AAVE and other discursive strategies in narratives actually preserve the existing racial hierarchy. In her study of Mock Spanish used by Anglo Americans, Hill (1999) suggests that Mock Spanish is indirectly indexed with covert racist image, and that only the powerful group (whites) can afford to transgress boundaries without losing identity. I believe that MTM presents a similar example. In the practice of MTM, the Internet users gain profits from symbolically negating the hierarchy of the languages without disrupting it (Bourdieu 1991). As mentioned earlier, although the accent is adopted in public, the very act of transforming the accent to a written medium reinforces the separation between the accent and its speakers, on the one hand, and language play and Internet users, on the other. Their ability to play with words and their access to modern technology ensure the recognition that the practice of crossing is simply a symbolic transgression, not an actual one.

Another effect of the transformation from a spoken accent to a written form of language play lies in the dichotomy between the standard and the stigmatized implied in the written form. In speech, Mandarin speakers in Taiwan display a range of variation with regard to the degree of influence from Taiwanese phonology in their speech. The various accents form a continuum, in which one end is standard Taiwanese Mandarin while the other end is the most stigmatized variety of Taiwanese-accented Mandarin. In MTM, however, a dichotomy is created between the standard Chinese writing and the mockery of the stereotypical accent. The dichotomy-making is a process of erasure (Irvine 2001), in which an ideology simplifies the sociolinguistic field, ignoring some phenomena while rendering others distinctive.

The transformation from spoken to written context disregards internal variations in the continuum and reproduces the ideology that the standard variety is further away from the stigmatized accent in the hierarchy of languages in Taiwan than it often is.

Conclusion

In this paper, I have investigated the practice of MTM on the Internet in Taiwan. The discussion demonstrates that MTM is a product of the meaning-making process of Internet community in Taiwan. The unique environment of the Internet and the characteristics of the Chinese writing system foster the birth of this practice, but the meaning attached to MTM can be understood only in light of the context of contemporary Taiwanese society. On both the linguistic and sociolinguistic levels, MTM is characterized by multiplicity. The playful, humorous effect of the practice comes from the multiple linguistic functions, the various levels of positionalities with respect to self and other, and the interaction of dominant and local language ideologies.

NOTE

Special thanks to Keith Walters, Qing Zhang, and Elaine Chun for offering thoughtful comments on earlier drafts of this article. I am also grateful to the interviewees in this study and the participants at GURT 2002, especially Beverly Hong-Fincher, whose suggestions have shaped many of my ideas.

REFERENCES

Anderson, B. 1983. *Imagined communities.* London: Verso.

Bakhtin, M. 1981. *The dialogic imagination.* Austin: University of Texas Press.

——. 1984. *Problems in Dostoevsky's poetics.* Manchester: Manchester University Press.

Baym, N. 1995. The performance of humor in computer-mediated communication. www.jcmc.huji.ac.il//vol1//issue2/byam.html.

Bourdieu, P. 1991. *Language and symbolic power.* Cambridge, MA: Harvard University Press.

Bucholtz, M. 1999. You da man: Narrating the racial other in the production of white masculinity. *Journal of Sociolinguistics* 3(4): 443–60.

Eckert, P. 2000. *Linguistic variation as social practice: The linguistic construction of identity in Belton High.* Oxford: Blackwell.

Gumperz, J. 1992. Contextualization and understanding. In A. Duranti and C. Goodwin, eds., *Rethinking context,* 229–52. Cambridge: Cambridge University Press.

Herring, S. 1999. Interactional coherence in CMC. http://jcmc.hjui.ac.il/vol4/issue4/herring.html#ABSTRACT.

Hill, J. 1999. Language, race, and white public space. *American Anthropologist* 100(3): 680–89.

Huang, S. 1993. *Yuyan, shehui, yu zuqun yishi: Taiwan yuyan shehuixue de yanjiu* [Language, society, and ethnic identity: A sociolinguistic study on Taiwan]. Taipei: Crane.

Irvine, J. 2001. "Style" as distinctiveness: The culture and ideology of linguistic differentiation. In P. Eckert and J. R. Rickford, eds., *Style and sociolinguistic variation,* 21–43. Cambridge: Cambridge University Press.

Jakobson, R. 1960. Closing statement: Linguistics and poetics. In T. A. Sebeok, ed., *Style in language,* 350–77. Cambridge, MA: MIT Press.

Lave, J., and E. Wenger. 1991. *Situated learning: Legitimate peripheral participation.* Cambridge: Cambridge University Press.

Ochs, E. 1992. Indexing gender. In A. Duranti and C. Goodwin, eds., *Rethinking context,* 335–58. Cambridge: Cambridge University Press.

Rampton, B. 1995. *Crossing: Language and ethnicity among adolescents.* London: Longman.

——. 1999. Styling the other: Introduction. *Journal of Sociolinguistics* 3(4): 421–27.

Su, H-Y. 2000. Code-switching between Mandarin and Taiwanese in Taiwan: Conversational interaction and the political economy of language use. M.A. thesis, University of Texas at Austin.

Wenger, E. 1998. *Communities of practice: Learning, meaning and identity.* Cambridge: Cambridge University Press.

Werry, C. 1996. Linguistic and interactional features of Internet Relay Chat. In S. Herring, ed., *Computer-mediated communication,* 47–63. Amsterdam: John Benjamins.

Materiality in Discourse: The Influence of Space and Layout in Making Meaning

INGRID DE SAINT-GEORGES
Georgetown University

THE RELATIONSHIP BETWEEN UTTERANCE and place of enunciation is a perplexing issue. On one hand, discourse is bound to spaces of actions and interactions. There is no discourse, knowledge, or social practice that stands outside of a social, historical, and physical space. On the other hand, discourse is also "about" space (Lefebvre 1991:132). It can formulate it, appropriate it, or participate in its transformation. Because of this dialectic dimension between space and discourse, it remains challenging to draw a map of the linkages between discourse and space. Language takes its significance from spaces of action, but how is this relationship of indexicality concretely realized in situated action? Space affects ongoing interactions, but how do ongoing interactions affect their spaces of action? The subject matter of this article is to examine empirically some interrelations between material and semiotic processes.

Discourse analysis (Conversation Analysis, Interactional Sociolinguistics, Critical Discourse Analysis, Pragmatics) has not traditionally paid attention to the physical and territorial placement of sign and systems of representation in much detail.[1] This absence of interest might be traceable in part to its methodological focus on audiotaped interaction and on verbal material. Research in discourse analysis has mainly focused on discourse types and settings involving a limited number of participants (dyads, triads, or small groups), where interactants are most often co-present and within hearing and speaking distance of each other. The conversations analyzed have also typically involved minimal movement of the participants during the interaction itself and maximal verbal interchange. These conditions have traditionally been considered most useful to facilitate the process of transcription of the interaction, which is often a prerequisite in these approaches to language. As a result, discourse analyses have often centered on activities such as dinner-table conversations, sociolinguistic interviews, gatekeeping encounters, counseling sessions, or classroom discourse. Many common forms of social interactions, however, fall outside of these "ideal" parameters for recording. Many daily interactions are characterized by participants moving across spaces, engaging in interaction with different individuals at a variety of sites, or managing several actions at a time. In these actions, discourse is sometimes little more than a few utterances interspersed in the midst of other nondiscursive actions, an instance of "textualization 'in' action" as Filliettaz (2002:261) puts it. The analysis of these forms of discourse cannot be cut off from reference to the world of action in which they take place without severing them from the meanings they acquire indexically from the embedding world. Because of its focus on verbal data, discourse analysis has thus not been in a position to analyze in much detail the relationship between discourse and its spatial emplacement and to say much about instances of textualization in action.

Recently, however, discourse analysis has started to take a multimodal turn (Kress et al. 2001; Kress and Van Leeuwen 1996, 2001), and a developing body of research has started to investigate the relationship existing between different semiotic systems (gestures, language, actions, physical layout, space, time, images). The multimodal position seeks to develop new concepts and ideas to approach the old issue of communication, a global process that integrates different modes of making meaning, including or excluding language. This body of research seeks to take a fresh stance regarding the role and function of language, to "step outside it and take a satellite view of it" (Kress et al. 2001:8).

Within this multimodal perspective, geosemiotics (Scollon and Scollon 2003) has taken on the task of exploring how the physical and territorial placement of systems of representation contribute to their meaning. It centers on the relationship between semiotic signs, their placement in space, and the actions through which they are appropriated. Geosemiotics thereby examines signs in relation with the "lived spatialities" (Crang and Thrift 2000:4) they ecologically develop, transform, or exist in.

To date, geosemiotically inspired studies (de Saint-Georges and Norris 2000; Pan 1998; Scollon and Pan 1997; Scollon and Scollon 1998, 2000, 2003) have mostly focused on how the discourses of city signs (advertising posters, shop and business signs, road signs) get appropriated by passersby. They have also examined how the "visible arrangements of locomotion" (Lee and Watson 1993)—paths, barriers, lanes, doors, walls—orient individuals' actions in public space (Scollon and Scollon 2003). I believe the concept of geosemiotics is expandable to examining layout and material organization of more private, organizational, spaces. I thus turn my attention in this research to scrutinizing (1) how a space becomes constructed as a space of action, (2) how actions and turns-at-talk are constrained and influenced by spatial layout; and (3) what is the role played by discourse in organizing spaces of action.

Data

The data for this research are drawn from six months of ethnographic fieldwork in a Belgian vocational training center. The center, which I call Horizons, is a registered nonprofit organization providing the unemployed with professional training in various trades. The individuals attending the training typically have little or no professional qualifications, live on social welfare, and have been unemployed for a long period of time. The task of the center is to provide them with appropriate work skills as a means to improve their adaptability in the job market. The data for this paper document the cleaning of the center's attic by the group being trained to become professional cleaners.

The segments examined come from a 16′45″ videotape shot on February 7, 2000. It shows Laura, Stéphanie, Corinne, Jean-Philippe, Anabelle, and their monitor, Natasha, at work.[2] The video shows different stages of the work, and the coordinated activities that lead to accomplishing the cleaning of the attic. In my analysis of this data, I examine first how, through anticipatory discourse, the attic is construed as a space of activity. Next, I turn to show how the spatial layout and architectural design of the attic have a structuring effect on the discourse and actions produced. I next examine briefly how under the action of the participants, the space is being progressively transformed. Following that, I examine in more detail the role played by discourse in space transformation.

Emergence and Creation of an Eventful Space

The first issue I would like to explore concerns how the attic passes from being a perceptible but unnoticed aspect of the architectural design of Horizons' building to becoming an element active in the training of the cleaner's group. In other words, I am interested in examining how the space of the attic becomes constructed as an "eventful space" (Crang and Thrift 2000:6), a socially produced space for purposeful and motivated actions. I would like to show that the attic is not just the given setting within which the cleaning occurs. Rather, there is a dynamic, real-time creation of the attic as part of the practices of the group observed.

One such practice for the cleaners' group is to have daily morning briefing sessions. In these sessions, the activities for the day are announced and various practical issues are settled. These sessions can be considered instances of what Scollon and Scollon (2000) term *anticipatory discourse.* Through this concept, Scollon and Scollon highlight that our actions usually "begin as preparation for action" (Scollon 2001b) and that one can understand the significance of an action in a sequence of action steps only by analyzing what motivations or course of actions have led to its accomplishment. Anticipatory discourses provide the "meta-discursive or reflective structure" (Scollon 2001b) that participates in lending meaning to actions.

Methodologically, anticipatory discourses are difficult to capture. By definition, because they occur outside and prior to action, they are spatially and temporally remote from the site and time of action. It is thus often difficult for the researcher to be present not only to capture the preparatory discourse that anticipates actions but also the corresponding performance of the action itself. As a result, capturing anticipatory discourses is often akin to archaeological reconstruction. I do not have a recording of the briefing session that introduced the attic as a space of action on February 7; however, several recordings of other briefing sessions display typical features of this activity. Fieldwork suggests that the following extract, recorded on February 2, is a representative case. This extract provides clues as to how a space first becomes available for further appropriation through action and discourse within the practices of the group observed.[3]

(1)

[Head]:

1. So, today e:r

2. [. . .]

4. For the cleaners, there is [Elton] and [CRS].

5. So you share the work in the morning and Corinne is not here today okay

6. [Elton] and [CRS]

7. And then e:r [Chief Cook] e:r

8. You're done with [Chief Cook] around 12, 12:30?
[Monitor 1]: 9. no, no we start at 12 =
[Monitor 2]: 10. we start at 12:30.
[Monitor 1]: 11. = when the shop is closed.
[Head]: 12. Oh. Oh. Yes.
13. And- and in the afternoon [Smith]
14. But I thought it went the other way around, I forgot.
15. Okay. [Smith].
16. [. . .]

The briefing session that forms a prelude for the action serves to conjure up a space of action. The production of space and the process of signification thus begin outside of the sensory and experiential space of the working site and prior to physically engaging in transforming it. Anticipatory discourse's role is thus to make spaces of action relevant to the activities of the group. In the excerpt above, it appears that this relevance is constructed following two strands of logic: a logic of temporalization and a logic of spatialization (Weiss 2001).

The discourse first provides a periodizing of the activities of the participants. A line is drawn between morning and afternoon activities. The morning activities are further sequentially and chronologically organized: the cleaners will start with [Elton] and [CRS]/ *And then* e:r [Chief Cook] e:r.; and *in the afternoon* [Smith]. Through scheduling, anticipatory discourse thus organizes the social world according to various temporally ordered "units of work" (Kress 1998:65–66) that provide a time frame for the activities. Spaces of activities are bound to times of activities.

The anticipatory discourse, moreover, summons in trainees' minds places of activities. It is the second logic: the logic of spatialization or territorialization (Weiss 2001). The existential construction ("there is") introduces new referents in the discourse, which are also known names of contractors ([Elton] and [CRS]). For the trainees who have already spent some time at Horizons, those referents are in a state of "semi-active" consciousness (Chafe 1994), since they correspond to regular working sites. The evocation of these spaces of activities makes them referentially salient as well as cognitively activates associated domains of performative knowledge for its users (the site's location, the equipment that should be brought for work, the set of tasks to be performed on site). Because the briefing session refers to practices habitual to the members of the group, it is enough for the head to call into focus spaces of action and times of action, without further specifying what sets of actions are expected to be performed by the trainees at each site. Anticipatory discourse thus participates in scheduling actions to come by relying on the specific cluster of practices routinely enacted by the participants.

Space begins in this case as a cognitive and discursive representation (an act of imagination), caught within the practices, representations, and aims of a social group. By bringing spaces and times of action into focus, anticipatory discourse makes them available for cognitive and discursive appropriation. For the space to be available for transformation, however, there also needs to be the emergence of a "practico-sensory" space (Lefebvre 1991:16). There needs to be a move from the textual space of anticipatory discourse to the physico-concrete space of situated actions. Filliettaz calls the emergence of a physical or perceptual space enabling an encounter "incursion." In his definition, the incursion is bracketed by opening and closing rituals, parenthesizing the encounter, and it is characterized by agents' readiness to engage in goal-directed activities (Filliettaz 2002; Goffman 1974). Beyond the incursion, agents will exert their agency within the space of action in an attempt to accomplish the tasks they recognize are expected from them. Their sense of purpose will organize and lend meaning to their actions and lead them to engage with various dimensions of the space at what we may call "sites of engagement," which can be defined as "real time window[s] that [are] opened through an intersection of social practices . . . and that make [an] action the focal point of attention of the relevant participants" (Scollon 2001a:3–4).

In the next section I examine sites of engagement and the structuring effect of the spatial layout and the spatial positions of the participants on the discourse produced at these sites.

Structuring Effects of Spatial Layout on Discourse

In the course of time, a variety of objects and documents are accumulated by an organization that threatens to clutter office space. The attic's raison d'être is to hold residual material that might still be of use. It is a place of dumping and archival memory, which, for lack of regular use, displays traces of abandonment. The space's layout, the objects accumulated and their arrangement, contribute to the unique atmosphere and material codification of the space (Ruesch and Kees 1956:89–147). The task of the cleaner is to shape these surroundings through inducing order and cleanliness. While doing so, the disposition of objects in space can be shown to affect their actions and discourse.

The overall setting plays a significant part in communication, providing not only topics for discussion but also positions for interaction (who may speak to whom at what point given the natural boundaries of the space). A rough map locating the attic within the Center's building and displaying sites relevant to the action of its cleaning will illustrate my upcoming argument (figure 7.1):

I have tried to show how a physical space is produced within the practices of a group. It obtains its signification and relevance from the motivations and purpose of the social actors entering the space. Their social practices structure routes, paths, and networks linking places for action in patterns unique to the goals sought to be accomplished. In the present case, the task of the group leads to the articulation of a nexus of scenes (areas of focal attention) including the following five interdependent regions. Together they are actively produced as the space of action:

1. Area 1: the attic. Under the roof, the attic can only be reached through climbing up on a ladder.
2. Area 2: the ladder. The ladder constitutes a temporary and mobile motion path to reach the attic from the hallway.

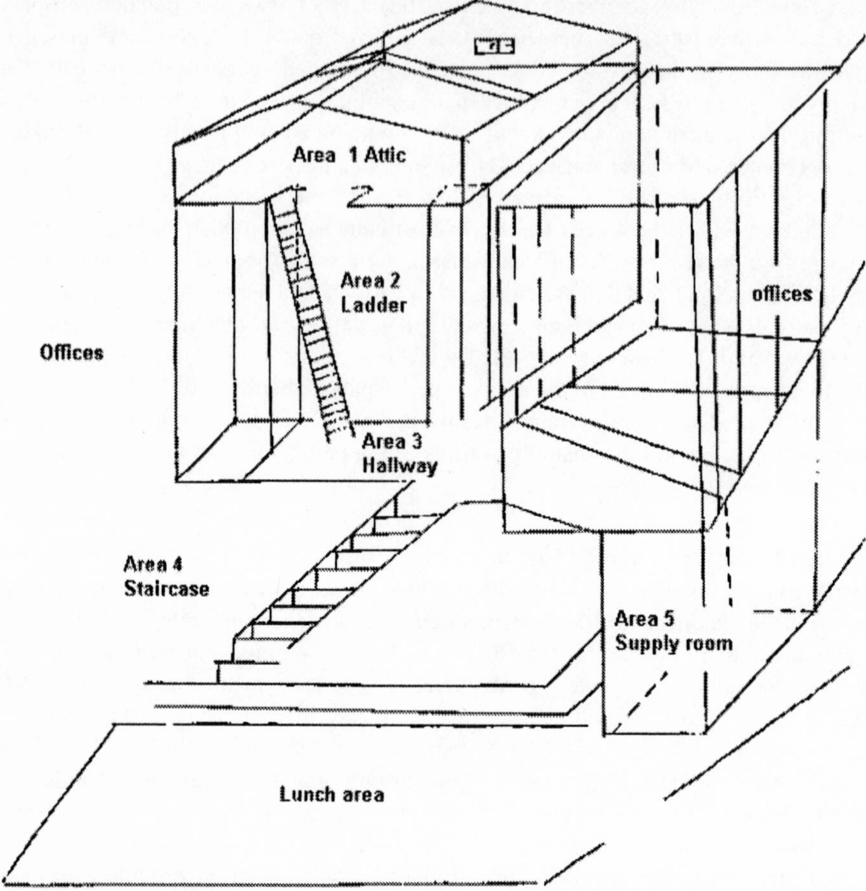

Figure 7.1. Map of the Attic.

3. Area 3: the hallway. A passage-way between offices on the first floor as well as a connecting trail between the ladder and the staircase for the purpose of the cleaning action.
4. Area 4: the staircase. A permanent junction linking the hallway to the ground floor.
5. Area 5: the supply room. In this room cleaning supplies and material are stored.

Cleaning the attic is a complex activity that involves the engagement and coordination of actions at various sites of engagement distributed across these different regions (areas 1 through 5). Some areas are continuous visually (e.g., through the open door of area 1 one can see areas 2, 3, and 4, but not area 5). Others are continuous acoustically (through adjusting one's voice volume and intonation contours it is possible to be heard from area 1 through area 2, 3, or 4). If relays are set, participants can echo information to convey information to acoustically and visually remote participants. This spatial setup is not simply a juxtaposition of independent scenes. Rather, linked together, these scenes define the "communicative situation."

The examination of a 20″ sequence of interaction can be used to illustrate how the topographical configuration of the attic can affect the discourse and actions produced.[4] In excerpt (2), Anabelle has just started climbing down the ladder [1], when her monitor, Natasha, through the aperture of the door, requests some detergent ("Go and fetch me the Comet, please") [2]. Natasha then moves away from the door's aperture and starts scrutinizing the door's surface on both sides to evaluate its state of cleanliness [3]. In the meantime, Stéphanie, who was previously busy sweeping the floor, gets done with the broom and hands it to Anabelle [4] ("here it is"). She reiterates the request for detergent with the directive "the Comet!" Natasha, who by then has evaluated that the door needs cleaning, adds "and a sponge." Because the door's aperture is small and obstructed by Stéphanie's presence, it renders Natasha's direct interaction with Anabelle difficult. She could raise her voice but chooses instead to position Stéphanie as a relay for the interaction. Stéphanie takes on the role of "animator" (in Goffman's sense) to voice to Anabelle Natasha's subsequent requests (for a sponge, and a cloth). Laura behaves as a ratified hearer of the scene who manifests her engagement at the site through eye gaze and body hexis. The repetition rapidly appears comical to Natasha, and she turns away from the door laughing [5] (the interaction is transcribed below the visual representation of the scene).

Photo 7.1.

Photo 7.2.

Photo 7.3.

Photo 7.4.

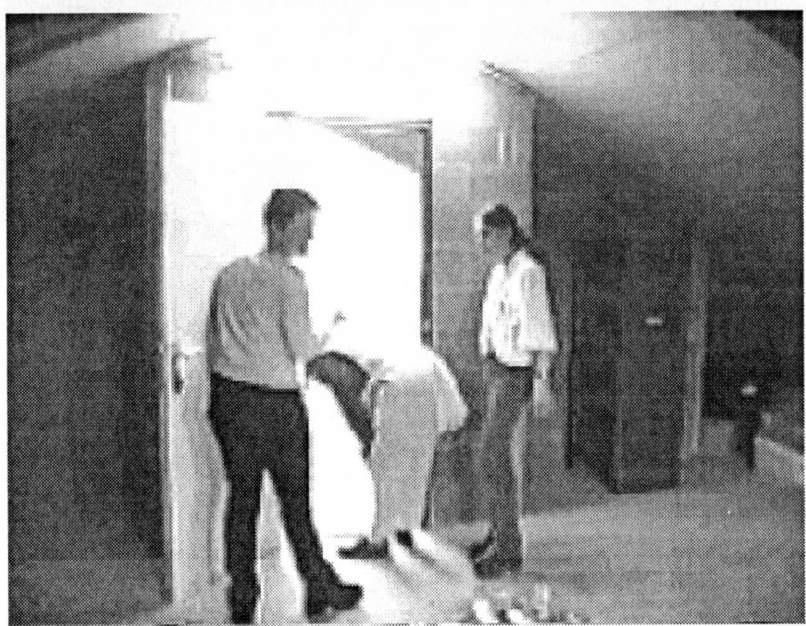

Photo 7.5.

(2)

Transcription[5]

<table>
<tr><th>Through the door</th><th>On the ladder</th></tr>
<tr><td>N [→ LOOKS TOWARD THE DOOR OPENING</td><td>←] A</td></tr>
<tr><td>N [→ “Go and fetch me the ‘Comet,’ Anabelle, please”</td><td>←] A</td></tr>
<tr><td>N | → MOVES AWAY FROM DOOR OPENING</td><td></td></tr>
<tr><td>N | → LOOKS AT THE DOOR'S SURFACE</td><td></td></tr>
</table>

<table>
<tr><th>By the door</th><th>Through the door</th><th>On the ladder Toward the door</th></tr>
<tr><td></td><td></td><td>L | → WIPES HER FACE WITH HER SLEEVE</td></tr>
<tr><td></td><td>S [→ LOOKS AT A ON THE LADDER ←] A</td><td></td></tr>
<tr><td>N | → SWINGS THE DOOR</td><td>S[→ “The ‘Comet’!” ←]A</td><td>L[→ WATCHES TOWARD THE DOOR ←] S/A</td></tr>
<tr><td></td><td>S [→ GIVES BROOM TO A</td><td>←]A</td></tr>
<tr><td></td><td>S [→ “here it is”</td><td>←]A</td></tr>
<tr><td>LOOK AT DOOR ←| N</td><td></td><td></td></tr>
<tr><td>[→ “and a sponge”</td><td>←]S[→ A TAKES BROOM FROM S</td><td>←]A</td></tr>
<tr><td></td><td>S[→ “and a sponge”</td><td>←]A</td></tr>
<tr><td>N[→ “and a cloth”@@@</td><td>←]S[→ LOOK AT A</td><td>←]A</td></tr>
<tr><td></td><td>S[→ “and a cloth”</td><td>←]A</td></tr>
<tr><td>N| → MOVES AWAY FROM DOOR</td><td>S| → STANDS UP AND MOVES AWAY FROM DOOR</td><td>L| → LOOKS THROUGH DOOR</td></tr>
</table>

The repetitions are in this case a direct result of the configuration of the spatial layout (with its visual shields between linked scenes of actions) and of the manner in which the participants are constructing the space (which is to say, are bodily positioned in it and negotiating the participation framework of talk). This construction of interaction rapidly appears awkward to the participants themselves as attested by Natasha's laughing. The discomfort is created by the proxemics of the situation, with the interactants moving within a very small region. Although invisible, Anabelle is at a potential hearing distance from Natasha. The engagement shield is thus only visual and not auditory. The echoing of Natasha's requests consequently sounds like a parroting of her discourse more than a necessary device for ensuring communication.

With this analysis, I do not want to claim too much about the effect of layout on discourse in this excerpt except to emphasize that when observing interactions where talking is not an end in itself but occurs as part of other coordinated action (“textualization ‘in’ action”), the study of language cannot be cut free from reference to these other actions and the material space of their occurrence without cutting it free of its situated meaning. By examining jointly the spaces of action and the construction of interaction, we start to see how the spatial design of the attic participates in facilitating or obstructing certain configurations of interactions and how the boundaries of what would be traditionally called “the setting” is actively constructed around joint or individual sites of engagements. In the next section I examine how, under the actions of the participants, the space is moreover being progressively transformed.

Space as Process

While the structure of the attic (its walls, location on the premises) is relatively stable and could not be modified without considerable alteration to the integrity of the building, space is not, however, just a "practico-inert container of action" (Crang and Thrift 2000:2). Under the actions of the participants and their interaction with its material constituents, the "economy of space" (Ruesch and Kees 1956:136) is being progressively modified. Mobile objects are displaced and reordered. Static constituents are wiped, cleaned, or swept, which contribute to transforming the overall atmosphere of the space. Each transformation has a further constraining effect on what actions can be taken next and what can be said about space.

In figure 7.2, I show the initial, final, and a few selected intermediate moments in the cleaning of the attic. The letters refer to various objects in the room. The representation, however schematic and partial, reveals nevertheless the evolving and emergent organization of space. Space appears "*as process* and *in process* (that is space and time combined in becoming)" (Crang and Thrift 2000:3, emphasis in original). As objects are being wiped, moved, piled, spread, dumped, or aligned and actors work at the maintenance of order (Ruesch and Kees 1956:135), the economy of space is being irreversibly altered.

Regarding the workings of the transformation process, it appears that space is being modified through objects being successively turned into "transactionally

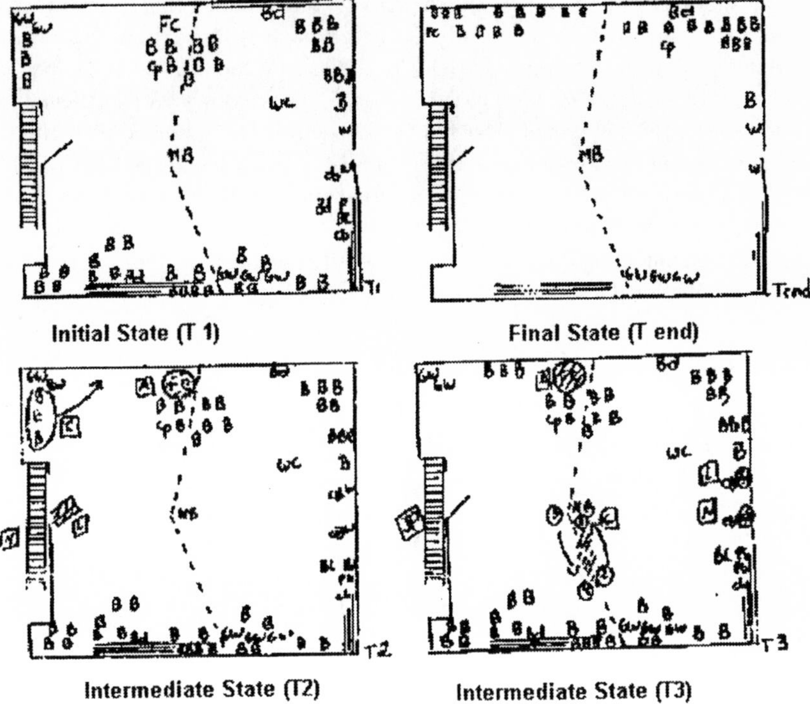

Figure 7.2. Initial, Final, and Two Intermediate States.

Note: B, boxes; Cp, computer; CB, cardboard; Pb, polystyrene board; Bd, polystyrene boards; FC, file cabinet; WC, working clothes; GW, glass wool; W, Window; D, door; C, chair; MB, metallic beam across the room; Bl, linoleum. C, Corinne; L, Laura; JP, Jean-Philippe; S, Stéphanie. Arrows indicate trajectories and hachures engagement with objects and surfaces (floors, etc.).

active objects" (Scollon 2001a:131). They pass from being a perceptible but unnoticed dimension of the space layout (a kind of "wallpaper") (Scollon 1998: 11) to become appropriated for some purpose in action, before returning to their wallpapering function. The shape of objects and the practices of the group dictate the "kinesthetics of usage" (Ruesch and Kees 1956:127)—how each object will be handled, and thus "how" engagement will occur is to some extent predictable. It seems impossible, however, to determine in advance, nor to construct a general theory of, which elements will become relevant and thus activated in action or in discourse at any point in the interaction. All we can say is that at the beginning of the activity, agents have some liberty in choosing and constructing which objects and practices they will engage with first, but as they go on transforming the space around them the set of available options for action grows more and more limited: once all the objects have found their state and place of rest, the overall activity is over. Table 7.1 presents similar data to those shown in figure 7.2, but attempts to highlight this progression in availability, or what could be termed the *chronosemiosis* of the action. For example, at T1, all 6 objects ([B]ox 1, [B]ox 2, [W]orking [C]lothes, [W]indows, [G]lass [W]ool, [F]ile [C]abinet, and [D]oor) constitute a part of the wallpapering of the space. They thus all have the potentiality to become transactionally active objects or not. At T2, B[ox1] is moved from one side of the room to another where it find its resting place. It is not re-engaged with subsequently. At end time, it is thus still in this position. [W]orking [C]lothes, [W]indows, [B]ox2, [G]lass [W]ool, [F]ile [C]abinet, and [D]oor are still available for appropriation. At T3, the windows [W] are cleaned and the file cabinet [FC] is wiped. The file cabinet will be later moved (T9) (thus re-engaged with) but both windows and file cabinet will not be cleaned again. At T8, the roll of glass wool [GW] is thrown in a corner and at T10, the door [D] is cleaned, etc. At end time, all objects that needed to be moved have been moved and cleaned in the appropriate manner ([Bd]: a polystyrene board stayed put all along). The action is considered completed and the goal reached.

Table 7.1.
Evolution of the economy of space: Chronosemiosis of the activity

T1	T2	T3	T4	T5	T6	T7	T8	T9	T10	. . . . . . End *t*
B1	B1									B1T2
WC	WC	WC	WC							WCT4
W	W	W								WT3
B2	B2	B2	B2							B2T4
GW	GW	GW	GW	GW	GW	GW	GW			GWT8
FC	FC	FC						FC		FCT9
D	D	D	D	D	D	D	D	D	D	DT10
Bd	Bd	Bd	Bd	Bd	Bd	Bd	Bd	Bd	Bd	BdT1

Legend: grey = availability; light dots = engagement; white = no further engagement; lighter dots = re-engagement. This is a simplified version of the data for the sake of argument. Only a few times and objects are considered out of the sixty-six time-frames in the original analysis and more than seventy objects appropriated in the overall action.

Because space can be shown to be in process, the next point to establish concerns the relationship between these material processes and discursive processes: to what extent is language linked or pointing to transformative actions? Does it participate in modifying the space of action? If yes, how? If no, what is its role? I attempt to address these questions in the next section.

Discourse and the Economy of Space

Multimodal approaches to discourse point to the fact that utterances are only a moment in the continuous process of communication and that there is no necessary priority of language over other modes of meaning making in social actions (Kress et al. 2001; Kress and Van Leuwen 2001). Therefore, the analysis of language should be initiated only when language appears to play a significant role in the actions examined (Scollon 2001a, b). This proposition reverses what has traditionally been done in discourse analysis. Rather than presuppose that discourse plays a role in social action, it seeks to examine empirically if it does and what role it may have. In this case, because language is integral to the activity of cleaning the attic, it seems important to pay attention to when utterances are deployed and with what effect. In other words, in order to understand what roles it plays (and how directly) in the transformation of the material space, it seems useful to consider how discourse figures in this cleaning action more carefully than has been achieved so far. The first aspect that can be assessed is that turns-at-talk appear to fall within three broad categories in relation to action.[6] There are in the data:

1. *action-preceding discourse and action steering discourse,* which anticipate or funnel action (e.g., *Jean-Philippe, il y a une caisse extrêmement lourde là, tu sais la prendre?* 'Jean-Philippe, there is an extremely heavy box over there, can you take it?'; *Va un peu chercher là un p'tit sac* 'Please, go and get me a small bag now').
2. *action-following discourse,* which evaluate or comment already accomplished actions or the activity as a whole (e.g., *Fais déjà un peu plus propre* 'It's already a bit cleaner'; *J'ai trouvé un paquet de Malboro vide* 'I have found an empty Marlboro pack').
3. *action-accompanying discourse* (e.g., showing traces on the window glass while talking: *Des deux côtés, ça c'est du produit des carreaux* 'On both sides, that thing that's detergent for windows'; e.g., handing an object: *tiens* 'there you go').

Action-following utterances tend to be slightly more frequent than action-preceding ones, as is shown by the distribution of turns in table 7.2. Further examination of the content of these turns reveals that action-preceding turns are most often directives. For example:

- Requests for information: *Qu'est-ce qu'on fait maintenant?* 'What do we do now?'
- Ordering: *Regarde, il y a des toiles d'araignées autour. Faut faire ça.* 'Look, there are spider webs around. That needs to be done.'

Table 7.2.
Distribution of utterances in relation to actions

	No.	%
Action-preceding utterances	163	37
Action-following utterances	191	44
Action-accompanying utterances	33	8
Unintelligible	49	11
TOTAL	436	100

- Warning: *Fais attention à ne pas mouiller les cartons, Anabelle hein* 'Be careful not to wet the boxes, Anabelle, okay'

Action-following discourse is most often expressive (evaluation, assertions) or assertive (justification, explication). For example:

- evaluating: *Ce coin là, euh, on sait pas faire plus, hein* 'This corner there, er, no more can be done, now'
- asserting (after climbing): *Bon moi descendre, j'fais déjà plus* 'Well, going down [the ladder], that's something I won't do no more'
- justifying: *mais c'est parce que c'est noté là en-dessous que je l'ai mis au-dessus* 'but it's because it's written there on the bottom that I have put it on top'

Action-accompanying discourse constitutes a verbalization as the action takes place. Deixis and simultaneous comment on action are examples of action-accompanying discourse:

- *comme ça* 'like this': uttered to oneself while moving a box
- *là* 'there': uttered while pointing at a spider web

The role played by discourse with regard to space transformation seems thus to relate broadly to three levels: instruction, evaluation, and social relationships.

1. Discourse participates in space transformation mainly in that it helps coordinating actions for modifying it. Through discourse, some objects are singled out, their trajectories defined, and the coordination of actions is regulated.

2. Also, discourse participates post hoc to the evaluation of physical actions. If the work is properly done, the objects do not usually come back as topics in discourse. If the work is deemed improperly realized, however, it is in precisely those cases that elements of the physical space become appropriated or reappropriated in discourse.

Discourse thus has a prospective function (calling into focus elements of the setting and turning them into transactionally active objects) and a commentary and evaluation function (critiquing the work after it has been performed). This function of critique might trigger another cycle of actions to improve the work. Discourse is thus capable of vision and retrospection about the state of space.

3. Discourse appears neither necessary (many actions are not accompanied, preceded or followed by discourse) nor completely contingent (there is no discourse which is not somewhat related to the overall activity, and despite some variances between discourse time and action time [Schiffrin 1987:250], topical organization is generally linked to action progression). Discourse is thus not dislocated from space, but neither is it completely constrained by it. If the overwhelming majority of actions in the course of the cleaning are not accompanied by discourse, and if space transformation is really the result of action more than a consequence of discursive moves, what is then ultimately the role of discourse in this activity? Space not only materializes systems of objects of which participants make practical use, but it also materializes social relationships. Evaluating or giving instruction presupposes a dialogic "other" in the space of interaction (instructions are always directed at someone; evaluations are evaluation of someone's work). The utterances thus also point to issues of competence (which expert can claim the knowledge for evaluating others' work) and power (which leader has the authority to command and instruct).

To illustrate this point, let us go back for a moment to example 2, which involved the setting of relays (Natasha to Stéphanie) to convey a message to a visually remote participant (Anabelle on her ladder). At the level of social relationships, the organization of the participant framework with a principal, an animator, and a recipient is an instance of "speaking for another" (Schiffrin 1994:107). Schiffrin shows how "speaking for another" is a discourse strategy that can be interpreted as a way of "taking the role of the other" (131). By delivering her monitor's words and by aligning interactionally with her in requesting Anabelle to perform some task, Stéphanie thus indexes a double social identity: she expresses solidarity and cooperation with Natasha and leadership and expertise in commanding Anabelle. She thus positions herself not only physically but also symbolically at the top of the ladder. In fact, this positioning is very much in line with the self displayed by Stéphanie throughout the cleaning activity. She is the participant who displays most initiative (she never interrupts her work, except to reflect upon it) and is also the most active organizer of the actions of others (after Natasha, the monitor). She thus constructs an authoritative position that goes unchallenged by the other participants who often ask her to instruct them what to do.

The orchestration of change in space and the achievement of the cleaning task as part of the training of the cleaners are thus also dependent on the claims to leadership and expertise made by the various actors and that are expressed in their discourse and their actions. The attic is thus not just a space of action, but also a space for identity claims and construction.

Final Comments

To recapitulate the argument, I have tried to show that diachronically and prior to entering the physical space of action, the role of discourse is to define the event to be situated in that space. At that stage, space is activated within the practices of a group and thus becomes caught within a discourse system through which it enters a process of signification. This anticipatory discourse funnels the course of actions and interactions that will take place within the physical space of action. As space becomes available for action, it becomes apparent that although space is caught within the practices and objectives of the group, its own materiality also defines boundaries and constraints for which actions and turns can be taken within it. Further, although utterances derive their meaning from being situated in this material environment, discourse also plays a role in organizing the modification of the space through coordinating the actions that will transform it. This process of coordination is also a process of identity claims. As participants exert their agency in transforming space, they make claims regarding their expertise and ability to perform the changes, which get ratified or not. Meaning production and interpretation thus seems to arise from (at least) interrelations between agency, discourse, space, and action, and thus from the "coupling of material and semiotic processes." These levels dynamically and dialectically constitute each other within some social semiotic system of interpretation (Lemke 1993).

I have talked a lot about change and transformation. It seems that anyone who wants to be serious about understanding change (even the banal transformation undergone by an attic), and the role played by discourse with regard to this change will need to develop more consequent ethnographic and diachronic studies that will not just presuppose physical or symbolic spaces of action, or examine discourse independent from it, but consider how these are linked. The tools currently developed in geosemiotics, multimodal discourse analysis, and other currents attuned to multimodal data and social actions should help further our understanding of this issue. ▩

NOTES

I wish to thank Cecilia Castillo-Ayometzi, Laurent Filliettaz and Mirjana Nelson-Dedaic for very useful comments on an earlier version of this paper.

1. Exception to this are, for example, Erickson (1990) and Whalen, Whalen, and Henderson (2002).
2. These are pseudonyms.
3. In this excerpt, [Head] is the chief supervisor of the cleaner's group, [Monitor 1] and [Monitor 2] are in charge of the training. All bracketed names (pseudonyms) refer to contractors for the cleaning group. Translations from French are the author's.
4. Pictures have been selected to give the gist of the interaction and to display the material configuration of the space of interaction. No one-to-one correspondence between lines of transcript and images has however been sought. The pictures are stills captured from an analog video film that was transferred onto digital support.
5. Transcription conventions adopt and adapt propositions by Filliettaz (2002, chap. 2).
   - [→ ACTION ←] = "joint actions"; |→ ACTION = "individual actions";
   - SMALL CAPS = 'content of action'; "spoken discourse" = 'utterance';
   - A, S, N, L = Anabelle, Stéphanie, Natasha, Laura; @ = laughter ;
   - , = pausing in discourse ! = exclamation contour ? = interrogation contour

   Reading is line by line, with simultaneous action placed on a same line. Discourse is attributed to the participant situated at the left hand of the brackets.
6. This categorization is built upon Von Cranach (1982:63).

REFERENCES

Chafe, W. 1994. *Discourse, consciousness and time.* Chicago and London: The University of Chicago Press.

Crang, M., and N. Thrift, eds. 2000. *Thinking space.* London: Routledge.

de Saint-Georges, I., and S. Norris. 2000. Nationality and the European Union: Competing identities in the visual design of four European cities. *Visual Sociology* 15:65–78.

Erickson, F. 1990. The social construction of discourse coherence in a family dinner table conversation. In B. Dorval, ed., *Conversational organization and its development,* 207–38. Norwood, NJ: Ablex.

Filliettaz, L. 2002. *La parole en action. Eléments de pragmatique psycho-sociale.* Quebec: Editions Nota.

Goffman, E. 1959. *The presentation of self in everyday life.* New York: Anchor.

——. 1974. *Frame analysis.* New York: Harper & Row.

Kress, G. 1998. Visual and verbal modes of representation in electronically mediated communication: the potentials of new forms of text. In I. Snyder, ed., *Page to screen: Taking literacy into the electronic era,* 53–79. London: Routledge.

Kress, G., C. Jewitt, J. Ogborn, and C. Tsatsarelis. 2001. *Multimodal teaching and learning: The rhetorics of the science classroom.* London and New York: Continuum.

Kress, G., and T. Van Leeuwen. 1996. *Reading images: The grammar of visual design.* London: Routledge.

——. 2001. *Multimodal discourse.* London: Edward Arnold.

Lee, J., and R. Watson. 1993. Regards et habitudes des passants. Les arrangements de visibilité de la locomotion. *Les annales de la recherche urbaine* 57–58: 100–109.

Lefebvre, H. 1991. *The production of space.* Oxford: Basil Blackwell.

Lemke, J. 1993. Discourse, dynamics, and social change. *Cultural Dynamics* 6(1): 243–75.

Pan, Y. 1998. Public literate design and ideological shift: A case study of Mainland China and Hong Kong. Paper presented at the 6th International Conference on Pragmatics, Reims, France.

Ruesch, J., and W. Kees. 1956. *Nonverbal communication: Notes on the visual perception of human relations.* Berkeley: University of California Press.

Schiffrin, D. 1987. *Discourse markers.* Cambridge: Cambridge University Press.

——. 1994. *Approaches to discourse.* Oxford and Cambridge: Blackwell.

Scollon, R. 1998. *Mediated Discourse as social interaction: A study of news discourse.* London and New York: Longman.

——. 2001a. *Mediated discourse: The nexus of practice.* London and New York: Routledge.

——. 2001b. Action and text. Toward an integrated understanding of the place of text in social (inter)action. In R. Wodak and M. Meyer, eds., *Methods in critical discourse analysis,* 139–83. London: Sage.

Scollon, S., and Y. Pan. 1997. Generational and regional readings of the literate face of China. Paper presented at the Second Symposium on Intercultural Communication, Beijing Foreign Studies University.

Scollon, R., and S. W. Scollon. 1998. Literate design in the discourses of revolution, reform, and transition: Hong Kong and China. *Written language and literacy* 1(1): 1–39.

——. 2000. The construction of agency and action in anticipatory discourse: Positioning ourselves against neo-liberalism. Paper presented at the Third Conference for Sociocultural Research, Campinas, São Paulo, Brazil.

——. 2003. *Discourses in place: Language in the material world.* London: Routledge.

Von Cranach, M. 1982. The psychological study of goal-directed action: basic issues. In M. Von Cranach and R. Harré, eds., *The analysis of action: Recent theoretical and empirical advances,* 35–73. Cambridge: Cambridge University Press.

Weiss, G. 2001. European identity and political representation: An analysis of the "new" speculative talk on Europe. Paper presented at the American Anthropology Association annual meeting, Washington, DC.

Whalen, J., M. Whalen, and K. Henderson. 2002. Improvisational choreography in teleservice work. *British Journal of Sociology* 53(2): 239–58.

The Multimodal Negotiation of Service Encounters

LAURENT FILLIETTAZ
University of Geneva

THE SELLING OF GOODS or the provision of a service consists in the performance of a vast array of specific tasks, some of them being mediated by talk or texts. Assuming the position of a shop assistant, for instance, requires an ability to advise clients, facilitate their choices, coordinate with colleagues, make phone calls, locate specific information in catalogues, or provide other various semiotic supports. Usually, most of the "frontstage" or "backstage" activities that assistants engage in are being carried out through communicational means. Nevertheless, service encounters obviously do not come down to such communicational means. As pointed out long ago by Goffman (1981), and as recently stated by linguists such as Streeck (1996a) or Scollon (2001), social interactions taking place in transactional settings are deeply interwoven with physical doings, material objects, or various semiotic practices such as inscriptions or graphic acts (Streeck and Kallmeyer 2001). From this standpoint, public service encounters turn out to be a very relevant domain of investigation for the questions under analysis in this volume, since they obviously call for a multimodal approach to discourse organization.

In this paper I will deal with issues regarding the complex articulation of speech, gesture, action, and material setting. More specifically, I will focus on the impact of *nonverbal behavior* on the construction of service encounters. Drawing on authentic data recently collected in a department store in Geneva, I will argue that a multimodal discourse analytical approach to client-server interaction should account for the fact that a substantial part of the tasks accomplished by the interacting agents are carried out nonverbally.

Within the body of research that has been carried out on nonverbal aspects of social interactions, *talk-accompanying behavior* has undeniably attracted most of the attention of writers for the last couple of decades. By describing how *postures, facial expressions,* or *gesticulations* contribute to the process of utterance formation and interpretation, many authors have oriented their investigations on one particular subtype of nonverbal behavior, namely on what has sometimes been referred to as "communicative gestures" (Cosnier and Vaysse 1997). After more than forty years of systematic inquiry on that topic, many classifications of such communicative gestures have been proposed (iconic gestures, metaphoric gestures, deictic gestures, emblems, beats, etc.). Moreover, as the question of nonlinguistic components of communication progressively came under scrutiny, it gave rise to various controversies among semioticians (Calbris and Porcher 1989; Sonneson 2001), conversation analysts (Schegloff 1984), or psycholinguists (McNeill 1992, 2000) who aimed at defining a conceptual framework that could account for both the linguistic side and the imagistic side of language use.

It is not my purpose here to recall comprehensively the methods, questions, and results of such a wide disciplinary field.[1] Rather, I want to point out that gestures have for the most part been analyzed in the purely expressive realm of conversation. Nevertheless, as recently mentioned by Streeck, it seems important to consider that "the hands, the organs of gesture, are not purely and not primarily expressive organs" (1996b:2). In spite of their obvious expressive function, they are above all powerful instruments for handling, exploring, making things, and changing the universe of reference in which discourse takes place. Consequently, one should consider that the domain of nonverbal behavior should not remain restricted to that of talk-accompanying gestures, but refers to a vast array of complex and heterogeneous empirical realities consisting in physical acts and various communicative practices that are not strictly "affiliated" to speech (Filliettaz 2001d, 2002). In other words, what I would like to argue for in this paper is that a multimodal approach to social interaction should not only aim at describing how speakers are "moving" while talking, nor should it account exclusively for the imagistic side of utterance production; rather, it should also describe how agents "handle things" while interacting, and figure out to what extent joint activities are being mediated by communicational means.

It is this latter and rather broad conception of multimodality that I will briefly sketch in this paper. After presenting the data I worked on for this analysis, I will identify various gestural behaviors attested in one particular service encounter, and present a global theoretical framework that enables a systematic description of such a variety.

The Data

The results I am presenting here are part of a larger research project currently being carried out in the department of linguistics at the University of Geneva, and supported by the Swiss National Science Foundation. This two-year project is devoted to a systematic analysis of service encounters and develops a broad discourse analytical approach for the description of verbal interactions taking place in transactional settings (Filliettaz 2001a–e; Filliettaz and Roulet 2002).

The data used in my analysis are extracted from a large corpus of service encounters that were audio-recorded in a department store in Geneva during the spring of 2001. One of the aims of this data collection was to gather sufficient empirical evidence in order to understand how assistants and clients are coordinating their actions in the context of encounters referring to goods associated with complex technical knowledge. This is the reason why I focused on three specific settings: the sports department, the electronics department, and the do-it yourself and gardening department.

While they interacted with clients, assistants were frequently moving from one place to another, which raised technical constraints for data collection and prevented the use of video cameras. In order to allow place shifting, a light recording device was used, consisting of a pocket-MiniDisc and a microphone fixed on the assistants' shirts. Additional notes resulting from detailed participant observation enabled the researcher to capture nonverbal information and to enrich data collection.

With the consent of the participants, I audio-recorded about 35 hours of assistant-client interaction between May and July 2001, which corresponds to a corpus of more than 350 complete service encounters in French. Each recording session lasted about 75 minutes.

As shown in table 8.1, equal attention was paid to each section of the store, and a plurality of assistants were involved.

I am perfectly aware of the strong methodological limitations associated with the mainly auditory character of these data for a study devoted to nonverbal aspects of face-to-face communication. Nevertheless, I believe that detailed observations during the recording sessions may overcome part of those limitations, as long as the questions under analysis are not restricted to the domain of fine-grained gesticulation. Moreover, I feel that a preliminary theoretical elaboration regarding the various forms and "meanings" of nonverbal behavior remains a necessity, and I consider that audio recordings associated with visual information captured online may be seen as relevant empirical input for carrying out such a theoretical elaboration.

The Role of Nonverbal Behavior in Social Interaction

For this analysis of nonverbal behavior, I will narrow down my focus on a specific transaction recorded in the sports department in April 2001. This three-minute-long interaction takes place between a forty-year-old female client (C), accompanied by her eight-year-old son (B), and a forty-year-old male assistant (A). As the assistant initiates the transaction, the mother is looking for swimming goggles for her son. The young child has just tried on a pair of goggles and complains that they are too tight. In order to help them, the assistant adjusts the goggles to adapt to the child's face and explains to the clients how to use them properly. After a successful second attempt, the child and his mother decide to buy the goggles and the transaction comes to an end.

What makes this transaction particularly interesting from the perspective of multimodal discourse analysis is that language use in this specific context is deeply interwoven with a great variety of nonverbal behaviors that play a prominent role in

Table 8.1
Content of the Geneva-2001 corpus

	No. of MiniDiscs	No. of Assistants	No. of Encounters	Ex. Goods
Sports Department	12	7	100	walking boots, sports clothes, camping material, bikes, skates, running shoes, etc.
Electronic Department	10	4	85	HiFi, computers, household appliances, telephones, etc.
Do-it-yourself + Gardening Department	9	4	170	painting goods, gardening tools, taps, hardware, etc.

the construction of the interactional process. For the reasons mentioned earlier, however, such a variety cannot be described adequately as long as it is conceived exclusively as a semiotic reality. In fact, accounting for the various classes of nonlinguistic components of this service encounter calls for a broad pragmatic framework that specifies how semiotic resources interact with social practices. Before turning to the analysis of concrete examples, I will briefly sketch such a theoretical framework by referring to Jürgen Habermas's *Theory of communicative action* (1984).

Among the various pragmatic models proposed during the last decades, the *Theory of communicative action* constitutes a significant source of new insights for linguistic research, in the sense that it leads to a fine-grained conceptualization of the complex links relating *social action* and *language use.* More specifically, Habermas aimed at accounting for the complex character of communicative actions by describing their twofold organization. He stated, for instance, that discourse-mediated actions should be described both as *teleological* and *semiotic* processes. The teleological level refers to the goal-directed character of the joint activities underlying social interactions (Von Cranach 1982). As for the level of intercomprehension, it refers specifically to language use and to the various semiotic realities that "mediate" these interactions: it is by using language and negotiating the validity of utterances that interactants achieve intercomprehension and that joint projects may be coordinated on the level of goal-directed actions.

Such an articulation between those two levels of analysis has significant epistemological implications for research in discourse analysis. In line with recent currents of thought in language sciences (Bronckart 1997; Clark 1996; Scollon 2001; Van Dijk 1997a, 1997b), the pragmatic model developed by the German philosopher takes the position that talk should be described not only as abstract semiotic forms, but also in terms of the social activities engaged in by specific agents belonging to particular cultural communities. Moreover, by conceiving communicative actions as complex entities, he suggests that discourse realities should be conceived both as *praxeological* processes, namely collective goal-directed actions, and *communicative* processes, namely processes of intercomprehension. In doing so, he certainly contributes to a theory of mediated action in the sense that he captures the "dialectical relationship between a particular discursive event and the situation(s), institution(s) and social structure(s) which frame it" (Wodak 1997:173). On one hand, talk is shaped by a praxeological process in the sense that it is interpreted and described in relation to specific contexts and social actions; on the other hand, it shapes that context by mediating intentions and coordinating joint projects.

It is not my purpose to devote too much space to the presentation of this pragmatic model. Rather, what I would like to argue for is that this theoretical framework and its twofold organization may contribute to a fine-grained analysis of nonverbal behavior in social interaction. Indeed, depending on its intracommunicative or extracommunicative character, hand movements can be assigned various semiotic properties and give rise to various configurations regarding the praxeological and communicative aspects of social interactions. This is what I would like to point out now by identifying and describing some of the gestural behaviors attested in the excerpt of the service encounter under analysis. I will consider in turn four different configurations in which nonlinguistic components can be described successively as

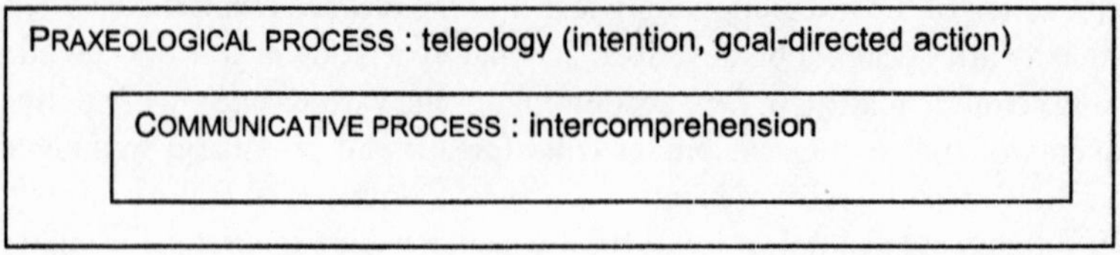

PRAXEOLOGICAL PROCESS : teleology (intention, goal-directed action)

COMMUNICATIVE PROCESS : intercomprehension

Figure 8.1. The Conceptual Framework of Habermas's *Theory of Communicative Action*.

coverbal behaviors, communicative actions, "addressed handling," and, finally, autonomous actions.

Gesture as Coverbal Action

This first sequence takes place at the end of the encounter. After having adjusted the goggles properly, the assistant (A) selects the child (B) as his direct interlocutor and explains to him how to use the goggles.[2]

(1)

A > B : alors . chaque fois que tu les mets avant d'aller à la piscine tu appuies un petit peu dessus d'accord ou avec la paume comme ça [A: lève les mains vers son visage et mime un geste de pression sur l'œil] tu appuies un tout petit coup d'accord? parce que tout l'air qui est dedans il il part un peu . ça les écrase contre les yeux et ça fait l'im: l'imperméabilité

so . every time you put them on before stepping into the water you just press slightly all right or with your hands like this ***[A raises his hands up to his face and imitates the application of fingertip pressure on his eyes]*** *you press just a little bit all right? because the air contained inside goes out . it presses them against the eyes and it makes the whole thing waterproof*

The first point that should be mentioned here is the semiotic heterogeneity of the interaction at hand. As the assistant utters his explanations, he performs body movements that are deeply interwoven with talk. For instance, the gesture of raising his hands and imitating the application of fingertip pressure on his eyes can be seen as an exemplary illustration of what has sometimes been termed "communicative gesture" (Cosnier and Vaysse 1997). Such nonvocal behavior is clearly "affiliated" to talk in the sense that it has the property of being connectable in reasonably clear ways to specific components of the turn-at-talk (Schegloff 1984). In this particular case, an explicit indexical relation can be identified between the gesture and its lexical affiliate (*with your hand like* ***this***). In other words, one should consider that hand movements and speech co-occur, that they present the same meaning, and that they perform the same pragmatic function.[3]

Another interesting property about this particular talk-accompanying behavior is its *iconic* character. Contrary to "emblems," whose meaning is based on social conventions, "iconic gestures" (McNeill 1992:12) are highly idiosyncratic and naturally motivated. The assistant's gesture can be seen as iconic, in that its interpretation results from knowledge about the world rather than relying on language-like conventions. Even though they are abstracted from the physical objects with which the original actions are performed, we understand those gestures because we know what they are doing in the world. In that sense, they can be seen as a "symbolic reenactment" of instrumental acts, to quote Jürgen Streeck's terminology.[4]

Considering the foregoing elements, it is now possible to specify the pragmatic status of this particular instance of nonverbal behavior. Our theoretical framework may help us in that perspective:

Figure 8.2 shows how communicational means contribute to joint activities in this particular transactional episode. It suggests that the interacting agents are engaged in a goal-directed action consisting in sharing knowledge about how to use swimming goggles, and that this praxeological process is mediated by a monological instructional discourse performed by the assistant. As indicated by the shaded surface, the gestures associated with the assistant's explanations do not manifest a teleological dimension on their own. On the contrary, they contribute to a turn-at-talk and function as an integral part of the instructional discourse in which they are embedded. In other terms, they should be considered as internal components of a complex communicative process rather than as an autonomous contribution to a goal-directed action. From that perspective, they can be seen as coverbal gestures.

Gesture as Communicative Action

Gestures and speech arise in a very different configuration in this second example, which takes place in the initial section of the service encounter, at the precise moment when the assistant has to identify why the goggles are hurting the client's son. As we will see, such an identification calls for both verbal and nonverbal contributions. In the following sequence, the assistant (A) asks the child (B) to remove the goggles and indicates how he intends to solve the problem:

(2)

A > B : essaie essaie juste de te les enlever sans . te faire mal d'accord [B enlève les lunettes] voilà je vais te les écarter un peu

try just try to take them off without . hurting yourself all right ***[B removes the goggles]*** *right I will loosen them slightly for you*

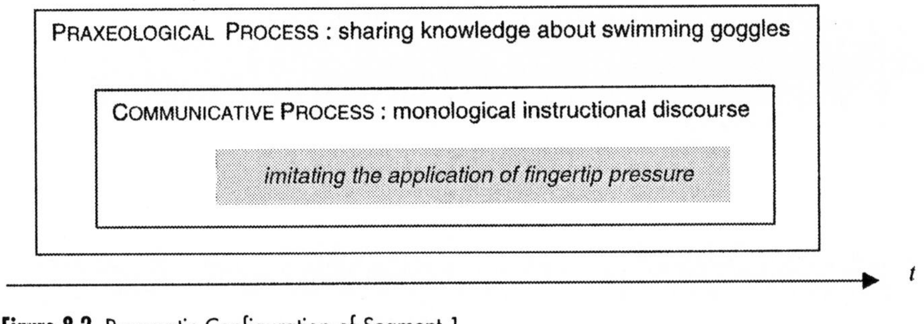

PRAXEOLOGICAL PROCESS : sharing knowledge about swimming goggles

COMMUNICATIVE PROCESS : monological instructional discourse

imitating the application of fingertip pressure

t

Figure 8.2. Pragmatic Configuration of Segment 1.

In this excerpt, the nonlinguistic contributions to the interactional process present specific semiotic properties. For instance, unlike our first example, the nonverbal response to the assistant's request does not metaphorically symbolize an abstract object; it physically involves this material object. Consequently, the act of removing the goggles should not be considered anymore as a "symbolic reenactment" of some physical doing; rather, it *is* a material action on its own. Because these categories of gestures involve physical objects and consist in goal-directed transformations in the real world, they should be interpreted as "praxical gestures" (Cosnier and Vaysse 1997) or "instrumental actions" rather than as talk-accompanying gesticulations.

Nevertheless, assuming the instrumental character of the child's hand movement does not mean that one should deny communicative effects to such nonverbal behavior. Streeck and Kallmeyer (2001) draw our attention to two very interesting properties of graphic acts (i.e., operations such as taking notes, calculating, drawing, etc.) in face-to-face communication. They give evidence for the fact that inscriptions may function as turn-constructional units and that they play a crucial role in the way the interacting agents dramatize their encounter. These observations strongly suggest that categorical distinctions between "instrumental" and "symbolic" acts are clear-cut abstractions that do not account for the variety and complexity of practices found in social interactions.

Coming back to our example, it is noteworthy that the action of handling an object has important communicative implications. By removing the goggles from his face, the child not only transforms the state of affairs in the physical world, but he also "responds" to the assistant's request and "satisfies" the preliminary and essential logical conditions associated with the directive speech act *(try just try to take them off without . hurting yourself all right)*. In doing so, the child "communicates" that he has understood the meaning of the assistant's utterance and takes his turn in the interactional process at hand. There is more, however. The child's nonlinguistic response is discursively ratified by the assistant (*right*) and can therefore be seen as a logical precondition for the interaction to be continued, as attested by the assistant's following turn *(I will loosen them slightly for you)*. Consequently, it seems essential to account for the fact that beyond its instrumental character, the act of removing the goggles is deeply interwoven with a dialogical communicative process.

Figure 8.3 summarizes our analysis and specifies the pragmatic status of this second instance of nonverbal behavior:

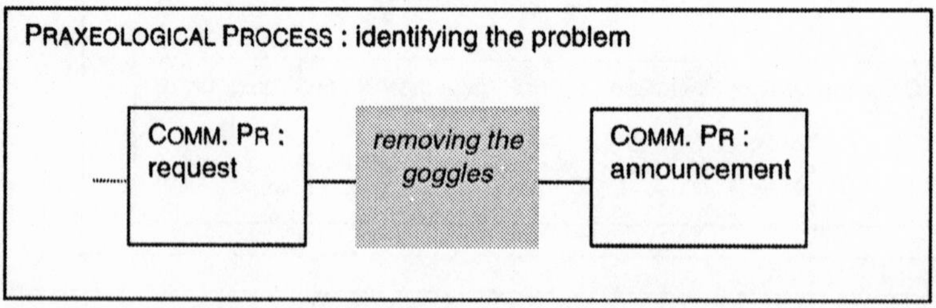

Figure 8.3. Pragmatic Configuration of Segment 2.

It enables us to visualize the complex nature of the action under analysis, and underlies its praxeological and communicative implications. As indicated by the shaded surface, the act of removing the goggles can no longer be seen as strictly "affiliated" to a communicative process. Unlike our first example, it does not co-occur with any linguistic utterance, but consists of a direct instrumental contribution to the praxeological process of identifying the problem. Nevertheless, communicative effects are not absent from the child's response, for it is initiated and ratified by specific speech acts and therefore strongly articulated with discursive contributions. Because these nonverbal empirical units turn out to be both goal-directed and communicative, I will refer to them as "communicative actions."

Speech as Cogestural Communication

The next sequence extracted from our service encounter offers another instance of the fuzzy and shifting character of the boundary between instrumental actions and communication. It immediately follows the excerpt analyzed in the preceding section and shows how the assistant (A) explains to the mother (C) how to adjust the goggles properly:

(3)

A >C:[A prend les lunettes et effectue des réglages pendant toute la séquence] donc pour les écarter vous les ss. sortez ça <C : ah d'accord> vous voyez sur le bord . puis après y a plus qu'à tirer légèrement parce que sinon après y a tout qui vient <C : ouais> . . . voilà je veux pas trop trop tirer d'un côté je vais aussi faire un petit peu de l'autre ..

[A takes the goggles and adjusts them during the whole sequence] *so in order to open them you take this out <C : okay> you see here on the side . and then you just have to pull slightly because otherwise everything will come out <C : yes> . . . right I don't want to pull too much on one side I will pull slightly on the other..*

As we see, speech and gesture co-occur in the example above, but again, the hand movements cannot be interpreted as pure iconic gesticulations. By handling the goggles and adjusting them, the assistant does not perform the "imagistic side" of a global utterance (McNeill 1992:1). On the contrary, he carries on a goal-directed action consisting in an instrumental act.

What makes this example of object handling particularly interesting from the perspective of multimodal discourse analysis, however, is its twofold functioning in the interactional process. By adjusting the goggles, it seems that the assistant achieves in fact two distinct goals. On the one hand, he transforms a state of affairs in the immediate environment and satisfies situational preconditions that determine a successful outcome of the transaction: the goggles should fit the child's face in order to be sold. But on the other hand, he takes this opportunity to explain to the mother how to handle the commodity she is interested in and transforms a situated instrumental action into an extended "lesson." In order to do so, he makes his instrumental action visible and accountable for his interlocutor, and performs what Streeck (1996a:373) would term a "broadcast version" of his handling.

Such a strategy has significant consequences on the communicative level. As indicated in the transcript, the assistant constantly comments on the instrumental actions he is performing. He uses talk as a means to make his nonverbal behavior interpretable by his interactional partner. Indeed, his utterances are explicitly indexical with the instrumental action they focus on, as indicated by the frequent deictic expressions like *to open* ***them;*** *you take* ***this*** *out; you see here on* ***the side,*** etc.

This being said, it seems that a specific connection between action and communication results from the pragmatic status of gesture in this example:

As mentioned in figure 8.4, speech and gestures contribute to a complex praxeological process consisting in an action of adjusting the goggles "in a gestural fashion" (Streeck 1996a:373). But contrary to the configuration described in our first example, it seems inadequate to consider such a nonvocal act as "affiliated" to talk. In this particular case, nonverbal behavior refers directly to the praxeological level, and constitutes the focus of the ongoing interaction. As for the communicative process, it provides local comments that aim at making the action interpretable from the perspective of the client. Interestingly, this multimodal discourse sequence reverses the expected relation between speech and gesture: it is not so much gesture that co-occurs with speech and facilitates its interpretation, but speech that makes an instrumental action jointly accountable. Consequently, rather than considering nonverbal behavior as coverbal in this case, it seems much more adequate to consider speech as cogestural.

Gesture as Autonomous Action

Our last excerpt immediately follows the sequence analyzed above and introduces significant changes in the pragmatic configuration underlying the interactional process. After having completed his "lesson" for the client, the assistant (A) selects the child (B) as his interlocutor and provides some general information about how to use swimming goggles. But during this whole sequence, he goes on handling the goggles and finishes to set them:

(4)

A > B :[A continue de régler les lunettes] donc . . . c'est une lunette de natation . qui est traitée contre la buée et puis sous la longueur du

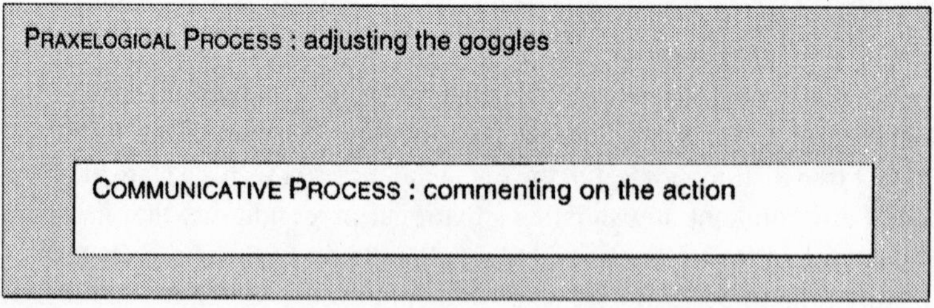

Figure 8.4. Pragmatic Configuration of Segment 3.

temps . elle va revenir la bou la buée . il faut pas:: t'arrêter de nager tu continues . et elle s'en va toute seule t'as compris ? . parce que moi je fais pas mal de natation et . après deux trois cents mètres j'ai un peu de buée je continue de nager puis elle s'en va toute seule . . . mais quand elles seront devenues déjà un petit peu plus vieilles

[A goes on adjusting the goggles] *so . . . those swimming goggles . are specially treated against steam but after some time steam may reappear . you should not stop swimming you should go on and it will disappear automatically do you get it? because I swim a lot and . after two or three hundred meters I get some steam I go on swimming and it disappears . . . but only when they will be a bit older*

[termine le réglage : 11 secondes]

[finishes setting the goggles]

Again, the hand movements performed by the assistant are to be interpreted as instrumental acts and not as communicative symbols. An interesting element that should be mentioned about this episode, however, is that a disjunction seems to occur between this instrumental act and co-occurring talk. Unlike example 3, speech and gestures do not refer to the same entities, and the action of adjusting the goggles does not function as the discourse topic of the utterances performed by the assistant. As shown in the transcript, the explanations provided by the assistant refer to the ways goggles should be used and do not consist any more on local comments on how to adjust them properly.

Moreover, contrary to the "broadcast version" (Streeck 1996a:373) of handling performed previously, the assistant does not aim at making his nonverbal action accountable in this case. The action of setting the goggles remains strictly instrumental and "indicative" in the sense that it cannot be interpreted as the volitional product of an intent to communicate any propositional content (Laver and Beck 2001:17).

Consequently, it appears that the pragmatic configuration specific to this interactional episode is much more heterogeneous than the cases so far:

As indicated in figure 8.5, the interactional process going on in this sequence can no longer be seen as a unified communicative action. On the contrary, it splits into two distinct praxeological processes that are carried out in parallel and that

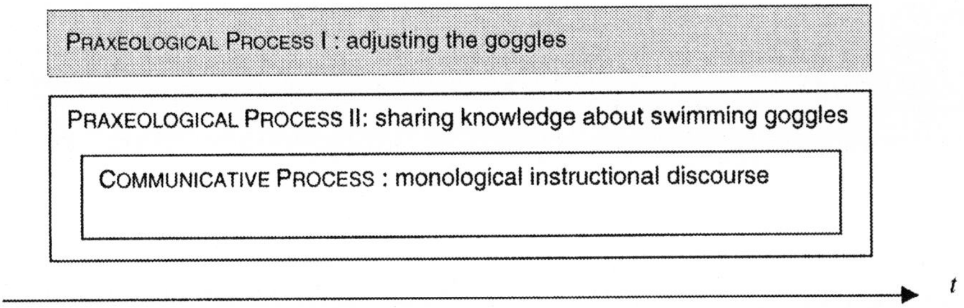

Figure 8.5. Pragmatic Configuration of Segment 4.

assume rather distinct pragmatic properties. The imagistic side of the interaction refers to an individual goal-directed action consisting in adjusting the goggles. As for the linguistic side of the interaction, it consists of an instructional discourse that mediates the joint action of sharing information about how to use swimming goggles. In such a configuration, nonverbal behaviors are not only external to multimodal communicative practices, but they also take the form of distinct praxeological processes. In that sense, they can be seen as autonomous actions.

Concluding Remarks

The sequences described above are but a few instances of the various pragmatic configurations in which nonverbal behaviors may take place in face-to-face interaction. In no way should these examples be understood as an attempt to classify nonvocal components systematically. Rather than circumscribing a finite set of categories, the analysis I proposed aimed at contrasting various empirical expressions of hand movements consisting in handling material or symbolic objects, and to identify the different communicative implications associated with such nonlinguistic entities.

In spite of its preliminary character, my analysis points to interesting phenomena regarding the multimodal negotiation of service encounters. First, it shows that it seems too restrictive to consider gestures and speech as two sides of a single system (McNeill 1992:4). If this may be true with talk-accompanying gesticulations, it is certainly not the case with other nonverbal behaviors like instrumental acts, which co-occur with speech without necessarily contributing to a single semantic unit. Second, my analysis provides evidence for the idea that a clear-cut delimitation between "intracommunicative" (or symbolic) and "extracommunicative" (or instrumental) gestures faces significant difficulties when applied to empirical data.[5] As illustrated by the description of service encounters, instrumental actions such as removing or adjusting objects do not always come down to mere teleological processes performed by isolated individuals: they may be performed in an ostensive way or require verbal contributions as a local support for being accountable. This strongly suggests that in spite of their instrumental nature, nonverbal actions are deeply interwoven with communicative processes, but with various modalities that a multimodal approach to discourse should be able to describe.

NOTES

I am grateful to the Swiss National Science Foundation (project No 12–61516.00) for its financial support. Special thanks are also due to Ingrid de Saint-Georges (Georgetown University) for very helpful comments on an earlier draft of this paper.

1. For such a synopsis, see Brossard and Cosnier (1984), McNeill (2000), or Cavé, Guaïtella, and Santi (2001).
2. I use the following transcription conventions: (.) (..) indicate appropriately timed pauses; (::) indicate that the syllable is lengthened, underlining indicates overlapping talk, and square brackets ([ ]) mark nonverbal behavior. Translations from the original French are my own.
3. In McNeill's terms, one can say that this instance of *iconic gesture* satisfies both the semantic and the pragmatic synchrony rules (McNeill 1992:27–29).
4. "You will have recognized some gestures as re-enactment of the actions that Hussein has recently performed; they are gestures because they are abstracted from the object upon and with which the

original actions are performed. The gesture showing the closing of the choke is a version of gesture that had been made before, but as a 'full gesture' (Flusser), that is, a gesture made with an object in hand and displaying its affordances" (Streeck 1996b:17–18).

5. For further considerations regarding such a *continuum of symbolization,* see Streeck (1996a, 1996b) and Grosjean and Kerbrat-Orecchioni (forthcoming).

REFERENCES

Bronckart, J-P. 1997. *Activité langagière, textes et discours.* Lausanne: Delachaux and Niestlé.

Brossard, A., and J. Cosnier, eds. 1984. *La communication non verbale.* Neuchâtel: Delachaux and Niestlé.

Calbris, G., and L. Porcher. 1989. *Geste et communication.* Paris: Hatier.

Cavé, C., I. Guaïtella, and S. Santi, eds. 2001. *Oralité et gestualité. Interactions et comportements multimodaux dans la communication.* Paris: L'Harmattan.

Clark, H. H. 1996. *Using language.* Cambridge: Cambridge University Press.

Cosnier, J., and J. Vaysse. 1997. Sémiotique des gestes communicatifs. *Nouveaux Actes sémiotiques* 52–54:8–28.

Fillietaz, L. 2001a. Action, cognition and interaction. The expression of motives in bookshop encounters. Paper presented at the 11th Suzanne Hübner Seminar on Bridging the Gap Between Cognition and Interaction in Linguistics, Zaragoza, Spain.

——. 2001b. Discourse, conceptual knowledge and the construction of joint activities. In E. Cho and J. Lim, eds., *The First Seoul International Conference on Discourse and Cognitive Linguistics: Perspectives for the 21st century,* 965–84. Seoul: Yonsei University.

——. 2001c. Coordination and the definition of minimal units of action. In P. Kühnlein, A. Newlands, and H. Rieser, eds., *Proceedings of the Workshop on Coordination and Action at 13th ESSLLI 01,* 49–57. Helsinki: University of Helsinki.

——. 2001d. L'hétérogénéité sémiotique de la gestualité en contexte transactionnel. De la gestualité coverbale à la verbalité cogestuelle. In C. Cavé, I. Guaïtella, and S. Santi, eds., *Oralité et Gestualité. Interactions et comportements multimodaux dans la communication,* 401–4. Paris: L'Harmattan.

——. 2001e. The construction of requests in transactional settings: A discursive approach. Paper presented at the International Conference on Discourse, Communication and the Enterprise, Lisbon.

——. 2002. *La parole en action. Elements de pragmatique psycho-sociale.* Quebec: Editions Nota Bene.

Fillietaz, L., and E. Roulet. 2002. The Geneva model of discourse analysis: An interactionist and modular approach to discourse organization. *Discourse Studies* 4(3): 369–92.

Goffman, E. 1981. *Forms of talk.* Oxford: Blackwell.

Grosjean, M., and C. Kerbrat-Orecchioni. In press. Acte verbal et acte non verbal ou: Comment le sens vient aux actes.

Habermas, J. 1984. *The theory of communicative action.* London: Heinemann.

Laver, J., and J. M. Beck. 2001. Unifying principles in the description of voice, posture and gesture. In C. Cavé, I. Guaïtella, and S. Santi, eds., *Oralité et Gestualité. Interactions et comportements multimodaux dans la communication,* 15–24. Paris: L'Harmattan.

McNeill, D. 1992. *Hand and mind: What gestures reveal about thought.* Chicago: University of Chicago Press.

——, ed. 2000. *Language and gesture.* Cambridge: Cambridge University Press.

Schegloff, E. 1984. On some gestures' relation to talk. In J. M. Atkinson and J. Heritage, eds., *Structures of social action,* 266–96. Cambridge: Cambridge University Press.

Scollon, R. 2001. Action and text: Toward an integrated understanding of the place of text in social (inter)action. In R. Wodak and M. Meyer, eds., *Methods of critical discourse analysis,* 139–83. London: Sage.

Sonneson, G. 2001. De l'iconicité de l'image à l'iconicité des gestes, In C. Cavé, I. Guaïtella, and S. Santi, eds., *Oralité et gestualité. Interactions et comportements multimodaux dans la communication,* 47–55. Paris: L'Harmattan.

Streeck, J. 1996a. How to do things with things. *Human Studies* 19:365–84.

——. 1996b. Vis-à-vis an embodied mind. Paper presented at the annual meeting of the American Anthropological Association, San Francisco.

Streeck, J., and W. Kallmeyer. 2001. Interaction by inscription. *Journal of Pragmatics* 33:465–90.

Van Dijk, T. A., ed. 1997a. *Discourse as structure and process.* London: Sage.

——, ed. 1997b. *Discourse as social interaction.* London: Sage.

Von Cranach, M., et al. 1982. *Goal-directed action.* London: Academic Press.

Wodak, R. 1997. Critical discourse analysis and the study of doctor-patient interaction. In B.-L. Gunnarsson et al., eds., *The construction of professional discourse,* 172–200. London: Longman.

Multimodal Discourse Analysis: A Conceptual Framework

Sigrid Norris
Georgetown University

THIS ESSAY INTRODUCES a multimodal framework for discourse analysis that moves toward an explication of the multiplicity of (inter)actions that a social actor engages in simultaneously, allowing for the analysis of large parts of what has been termed *context* in traditional discourse analysis.[1]

Discourse analysts have long been aware of the dialogicality between naturally occurring language and context. Although context has traditionally been viewed as encompassing everything that surrounds a strip of talk, more recently some concurrent actions have become part of the analyzed aspects.[2] The center of analysis, however, remained spoken language within focused interaction.

This framework for multimodal discourse analysis is practice-based and grew out of my use of the video camera to collect data of naturally occurring interactions within a long-term ethnographic study of two women living in Germany, whom I call Sandra and Anna, and my application of some theoretical notions of Scollon's (1998, 2001a, 2001b) mediated discourse analysis. I collected video data of everyday interactions and found that a primary focus on spoken language severely limited the scope of my analysis. I noted again and again that spoken language was embedded within complex configurations of actions, and the visual data revealed that studying the verbal exchanges without studying the nonverbal actions and the setting actually distorted interpretation of many of the ongoing face-to-face interactions. Mediated discourse analysis, with its focus on action, also encouraged a more holistic investigation.

The conceptual framework for multimodal discourse analysis that I present here permits the incorporation of all identifiable communicative modes, embodied and disembodied, that social actors orchestrate in face-to-face interactions. A communicative mode is loosely defined as a "set of signs with meanings and regularities attached to them" (Kress and Van Leeuwen 2001), giving the analyst a choice to configure the communicative modes as is most constructive to the analysis.[3] A communicative mode in this sense is not a bounded unit. Rather, it is a heuristic unit that is loosely defined without clear or stringent boundaries and that often overlaps (heuristically speaking) with other communicative modes.

The term *heuristic* emphasizes the tension and contradiction between the communicative modes as systems of representation and the dynamic unfolding of real-time social actions. Thus, when speaking of a heuristic unit, the element that indicates the system of representation serves as a means of investigation that we theoretically draw on in order to analyze the dynamic unfolding of real-time social actions.

Through an incorporation of numerous heuristically identifiable communicative modes, the framework demonstrates that social actors are often engaged in various (inter)actions simultaneously at different levels of awareness and/or attention. Awareness and attention are to some degree used interchangeably here, inasmuch as a social actor is aware of the higher-level actions that she or he pays closest attention to. In other words, the analyst can read the level of awareness off of the amount of attention that a social actor pays to a certain higher-level action.

Higher-level actions are those actions which are constructed through the employment of numerous lower-level actions, drawing on a multiplicity of communicative modes. Examples of such higher-level actions are a conversation, reading a magazine, watching TV, or Sandra's action of selecting a CD as described below. Each one of these higher-level actions is made up of many lower-level actions such as utterances, specific manual gestures, maybe a head nod, eye gaze in a certain direction, the social actor's posture, and so on. Whereas a social actor engages in one focused interaction, the social actor usually is also aware of and/or pays attention to other higher-level actions.

Thus, aspects of the traditional notion of context, encompassing much that lies outside of the focused interaction, become analyzable. This framework demonstrates that other (inter)actions and disembodied modes outside of the focused interaction are just as important as the focused (inter)action itself. While the framework allows the analysis of many aspects of what traditionally had been termed context, the notion of context has not disappeared, but rather has been expanded.

Multimodal Discourse Analysis

When viewing modes of communication heuristically, it becomes apparent that they are intricately interwoven, they are not easily separable, and they are interlinked and often interdependent. Figure 9.1 illustrates this point.

In Figure 9.1 Sandra is looking at CDs in a music store. Sandra's gaze is necessarily linked to her head movement and her posture. She would not have to stand facing the CDs in order to look at them. Yet, a different posture would also give this action a different meaning.

The realization that analyzing one mode without the others leaves out much of what is being communicated guided me to establish the multimodal framework for discourse analysis. A focus on one, two, or even three modes always allows us to analyze *some* aspects of an interaction. However, by limiting our focus to one, two, or three modes, we actually lose much important communicative information.

Figure 9.1 emphasizes that Sandra employs many modes of communication in order to perform the higher-level action of selecting a CD. Some of the modes she utilizes are disembodied modes, such as the music that is playing in the store and the layout, both of which determine some of Sandra's actions. Other modes Sandra employs are embodied modes of communication such as gaze, gesture, spoken utterances, head movement, and posture. When a social actor employs complexly interlinked communicative modes, we can speak of modal density. Modal density refers to the intricate interplay of various modes of communication or the intensity of a certain mode that a social actor employs.

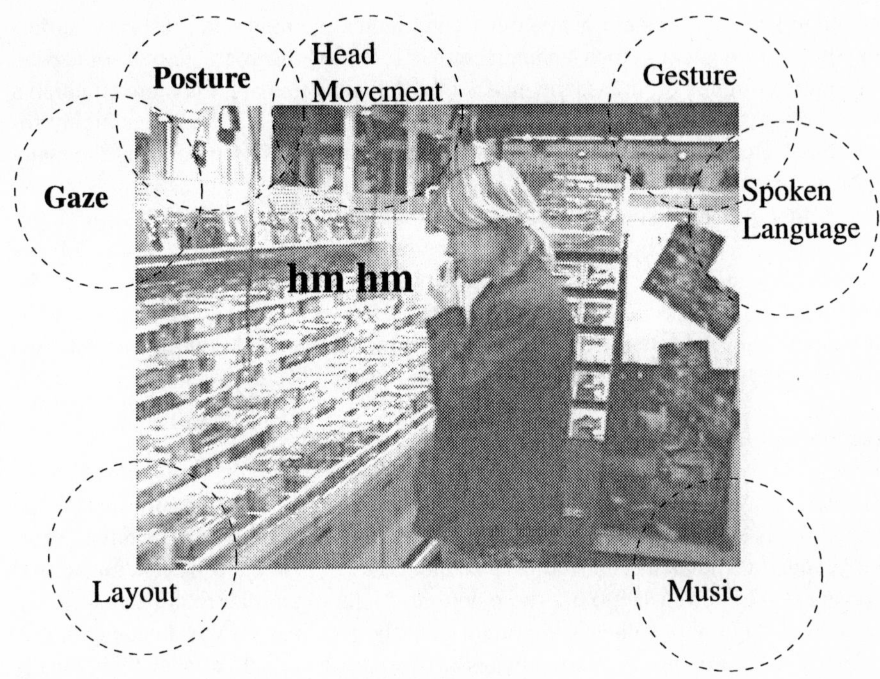

Figure 9.1. Sandra Employs Multiple Modes of Communication.

Modal Density

Any communicative event consists of the interplay among a multiplicity of communicative modes. Social actors draw on certain embodied modes such as spoken language, gaze, gesture, posture, and proxemics. At the same time, the social actors may employ disembodied modes, such as listening to recorded music or reading magazines. Simultaneously, other disembodied modes are present in the environment, giving off messages. Disembodied modes always entail some frozen actions, where the term *frozen action* does not imply one static form but rather a higher level of permanency of a communicative mode. The disembodied mode of the layout of the store in figure 9.1 entails greater permanency than Sandra's utterance (or the mode of spoken language), and yet the layout has been placed in the store by a social actor (or actors) just as the utterance has been uttered by a social actor.

Kress et al. (2001) note that communication is achieved through all modes separately and, at the same time, together. This notion emphasizes the communicative function that is entailed in each one mode, and at the same time highlights the notion that modes are in constant interplay.

Although modes of communication have usually been studied in isolation from one another, this paper focuses on the constant interplay of various communicative modes, embodied and disembodied, that social actors draw on in order to perform mediated actions. Various communicative modes are employed by social actors in order to best perform several higher-level social actions at different degrees of attention and/or awareness, while other communicative modes are just present during the focused and less focused interaction, structuring the interaction in some way. The more complex or intense the modes of communication are, the more attention a social actor pays to a certain higher-level action. In figure 9.1, Sandra is highly focused on selecting a CD, and we can perceive her attention by perceiving the many modes she employs simultaneously.

Although I show specific modes of communication that Sandra utilizes in figure 9.1, I would like to emphasize the *heuristic* notion of communicative modes. Modes of communication utilized by a social actor cannot and should not be counted. The number of modes used is of little importance (even if one could count them); what is important is the complexity of interlinked communicative modes or the intensity of a specific mode or several modes employed by the social actor.

Foreground-Background Continuum

Focused higher-level actions can be theorized as occurring in the foreground of a social actor's awareness or attention. I take the term *foreground* from art, music, and sound. Artists often speak of the foreground or the background of a painting. Similarly, sound technicians and studies in sound (Schafer 1977) and speech, music, and sound (Van Leeuwen 1999) use these notions, including a midground and speaking of a three-stage plan. What is important is in the foreground. Van Leeuwen notes, "*What* is made important . . . will always be treated as a 'signal,' as something the listener must attend to and/or react to and/or act upon" (1999:16). I adopt this notion and add a continuum to it.

The multimodal framework consists of the theoretical notions of modal density, displaying the level of attention/awareness of a social actor through the intricate interplay or intensity of modes employed and a foreground-background continuum, displaying the relative positioning of higher-level actions that the social actor is simultaneously engaged in. When visualizing this in a graph (figure 9.2), modal density builds the y-axis and the foreground-background continuum builds the x-axis.

A social actor's focus of attention in the graph is located at the point where the x-axis meets the y-axis, or more visibly in the foreground of the continuum. In this framework, we can determine what is important to the social actor by viewing what the social actor treats as a signal, what the social actor attends to and/or reacts to and/or acts upon. The higher-level action that the social actor pays most attention to is the higher-level action, which is located in the foreground of the continuum in the graph. Figure 9.2 depicts Sandra's focused higher-level action of selecting a CD in a graph illustrating the modal density foreground-background continuum.

Social actors orchestrate a range of communicative modes in everyday interactions accomplishing various higher-level actions concurrently.

Modal Density Foreground-Background Continuum: An Instance of a Naturally Occurring Interaction

The following example of a brief instance of a naturally occurring exchange illustrates how the conceptual framework for multimodal discourse analysis described

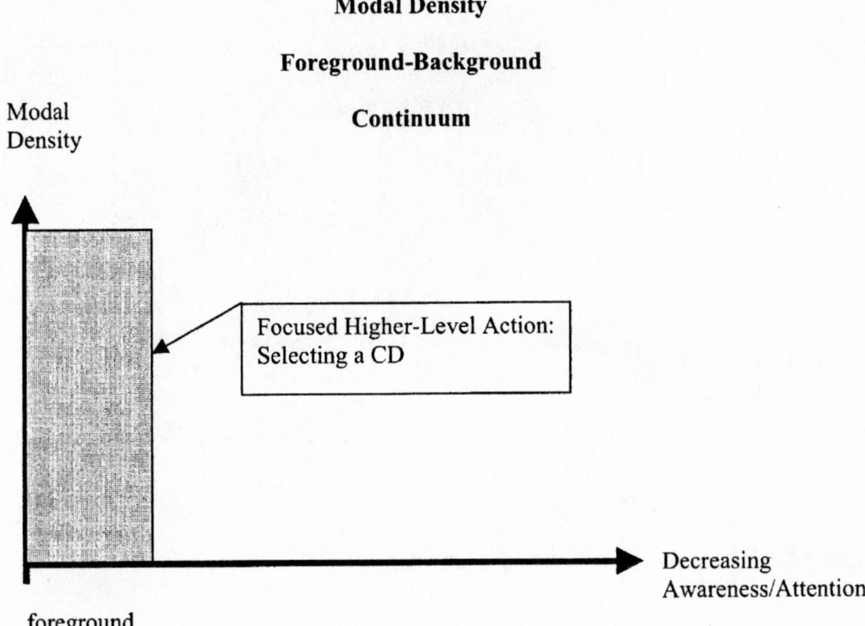

Figure 9.2. Sandra Focuses on Selecting a CD.

above gives new insight into everyday interactions. This excerpt is a representative sample of the many naturally occurring interactions that I collected throughout my year of fieldwork. The participants are Sandra and Anna, my primary informants; Anna's husband, Robert; Anna's three children; Sandra's two boys; and myself.

The interaction took place in the great room of Anna and Robert's apartment. I call it the great room because the kitchen, the dining room, and the living room are all open and easily accessible visibly as well as audibly from any one point in the area.

The camera was placed on a tripod, primarily recording Sandra who is sitting at the dining room table holding Anna and Robert's three-year-old daughter Katie in her lap. While the camera is freezing Sandra's and Katie's actions, verbal and non-verbal, the camera also records all the other ongoing audible activities in the great room. Figure 9.3 shows Sandra sitting at the table holding Katie in her lap, and indicates the relative positions of the others present.

Situation

This excerpt is one small instance from a large sequence of interactions. Just prior to this moment that I will discuss, Sandra had been drawing pictures for Katie, while Anna was reading cook books and writing a shopping list. First Sandra drew a few Santa Clauses. Then Katie requested that Sandra draw her Daddy, who was not present in the room at the time. Shortly after these drawings were complete, Robert

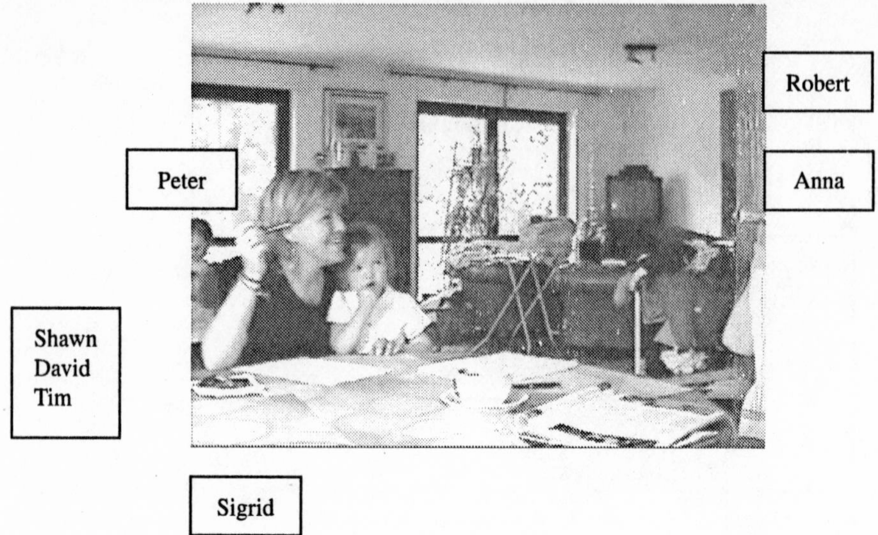

Figure 9.3. Sandra and Katie at the Dining Room Table.

walked into the room, his hair sticking up in the air. Katie looks at her Dad, Sandra makes a funny comment and an exchange between Sandra, Robert, and myself occurs, while Anna is still sitting at the table, writing her shopping list. Then Anna chimes in, gets up from the table, and walks into the kitchen area where Robert is standing. At this point Katie is still watching her Dad, and the following exchange occurs.

Transcription

In this transcript, I make use of some transcription conventions developed in Norris (2002): the utterances are given in regular font, nonverbal actions are *italicized,* and the person or object that is pointed to or looked at is specified in **bold** font. In addition, I underline pronounced nonverbal actions in this transcript. Furthermore, I use some conventions from Tannen (1984), indicating overlap with brackets [and emphatic stress with CAPITALIZATION.

The transcript is given twice. The first time, the utterances are in their original German version, while the second transcript shows the English translation:

Transcript in original German

(1) Sandra: hhh *leans back in her chair; gazing at* ***Robert***
(2) [und dann ne hhh
(3) *gaze shift to* ***Anna***
(4) [wie geht diese eine Werbung hhh
(5) *turns the piece of paper over*

(6) Katie: *gaze shift to* ***piece of paper***
(7) Sandra: Wind [in Ro nee nee nee hhh
(8) | *hand gesture: wiping motion with right hand*
(9) Katie: [hier mal der Papa *hand gesture: pointing at the paper*
(10) Sandra: Sonne [in Rom hhh
(11) | *hand gesture: circling motion with right hand*
(12) Katie: [hier mal der Papa
(13) Sandra: *leans forward in her chair and motions her upper body forward*
(14) *points with pen in her right hand at* ***Anna*** hhh
(15) [*bends her head downward* hhh
(16) Robert: [nein.
(17) Sandra: *her head is bent down and her right elbow is resting on the table*
(18) [*her right hand strokes her hair* hhh
(19) Katie: [hier mal der Papa
(20) Sandra: [*Lifts her head*
(21) Anna: | HAMBURG.
(22) Sandra: [Drei We
(23) [*pointing right hand/pen toward* ***Anna***
(24) [Hamburg, [genau hhh
(25) Katie: | *gaze shift toward* ***Anna***
(26) Anna: [WIND
(27) Sandra: [*pointing right hand/pen toward* ***Anna*** hhh
(28) Anna: [ROM
(29) Sandra: [*pointing right hand/pen toward* ***Anna*** hhh
(30) Anna: [SONNE
(31) Sandra: [*gaze shift toward* ***Robert*** *performing a right-left head beat*
(32) | und dann Drei-WETTER Taft hhh
(33) Anna: [dann New York? Ne
(34) GEnau.

English translation of the utterances

(1) Sandra: hhh *leans back in her chair; gazing at* ***Robert***
(2) [and then you know hhh
(3) [*gaze shift to* ***Anna***
(4) [what do they say in the advertisement hhh
(5) [*turns the piece of paper over*

(6) Katie: *gaze shift to* ***piece of paper***
(7) Sandra: Wind [in Ro no no no hhh
(8) *hand gesture: wiping motion with right hand*
(9) Katie: draw Daddy here *deictic hand gesture: pointing at piece of paper*
(10) Sandra: sun [in Rome hhh
(11) *hand gesture: circling motion with right hand*
(12) Katie: draw Daddy here
(13) Sandra: *leans forward in her chair and motions her upper body forward*
(14) *points with pen in her right hand at* ***Anna*** hhh
(15) [*bends her head downward* hhh
(16) Robert: no.
(17) Sandra: *her head is bent down and her right elbow is resting on the table*
(18) [*her right hand strokes her hair* hhh
(19) Katie: draw Daddy here
(20) Sandra: [*Lifts her head*
(21) Anna: HAMBURG.
(22) Sandra: Three We
(23) [*pointing right hand/pen toward* ***Anna***
(24) Hamburg, [that's it hhh
(25) Katie: *gaze shift towards* ***Anna***
(26) Anna: WIND
(27) Sandra: [*pointing right hand/pen toward* ***Anna*** hhh
(28) Anna: ROME
(29) Sandra: [*pointing right hand/pen toward* ***Anna*** hhh
(30) Anna: SUN
(31) Sandra: [*gaze shift toward* ***Robert***
(32) And then Three-WEATHER hairspray hhh
(33) Anna: then New York? No
(34) THAt's it.

While the transcript of this interaction lends itself to a detailed discourse analysis (extricating the meanings and interactional consequences of Sandra's gaze shifts, her manual gestures, as well as her postural shifts, or her laughing); just as it lends itself to an analysis of the interplay of Sandra's beat gestures (which are the quick back-and-forth movements that Sandra performs when pointing with her hand/pen toward Anna, and Anna's utterances, which follow these short gestures as if timed by Sandra); or Anna's exaggerated utterances like HAMBURG, WIND, or ROME (illustrating the performance of the advertisement); I would like to focus on a different aspect of the interaction in this paper.

Foreground

I would like to focus on Sandra and point out that she utilizes a multiplicity of communicative modes in this brief interaction. She utilizes the modes of spoken language, gaze, gesture, posture, and head movement as described in the transcript. At the same time, Sandra is sitting in a chair at a table, utilizing the disembodied mode of layout of the physical space, as can be seen in figure 9.3. Her proximity to Anna and Robert also plays a role in this interaction, structuring the volume of Sandra's utterances and laughter.

Sandra employs high modal density to perform this higher-level action of joking with Robert and Anna. All of the embodied and disembodied modes which Sandra employs in this exchange are intricately intertwined. The gaze shifts, the gestures, the utterances, as well as the postural shifts during which Sandra is bending backward or forward in her chair and placing her right elbow on the table, employing the disembodied mode of furniture, indicate that Sandra is clearly focused upon the exchange among herself, Robert, and Anna. Figure 9.4 heuristically visualizes the modal density employed by Sandra during this exchange.

This complex of interwoven communicative modes displays Sandra's foregrounding of the higher-level action of joking among the three adults.

Midground

At the same time as Sandra is focused on the exchange with Robert and Anna, she is holding Katie in her lap. The image in figure 9.3 shows Sandra sitting at the table, holding Katie with her left arm, and holding a pen in her right hand.

When looking at the transcript, we see that Katie tried to get Sandra's attention in lines (9), (12), and (19), repeating *draw Daddy here* three times during this brief moment of interaction. Katie's first utterance follows Sandra's action of turning the

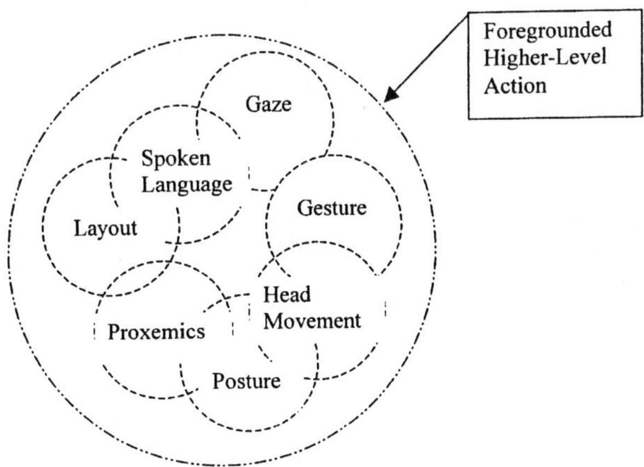

Figure 9.4. High Modal Density: Joking with Anna and Robert.

piece of paper she had been drawing on for Katie just a few moments before Sandra engaged in the joking sequence with Anna and Robert. While it is evident that Sandra does not give Katie her focused attention at this moment, Sandra also does not disattend the interaction with Katie. She is observably aware of the child in her lap and is interacting with Katie by turning over the piece of paper she had been drawing on. Once the paper is turned, there is a blank piece of paper in front of Sandra. At which point, Katie starts requesting to *draw Daddy here.* Thus, Sandra employs the mode of object handling, engaging in interaction with the child in her lap.

Furthermore, Sandra holds on to Katie, employing the communicative mode of touch, which is linked to the mode of posture and proxemics. In addition, Sandra's head movement downward in line (15) and the stroking of her own hair in line (18) are closely monitored by the child, who stops her repetitive request after Sandra's pronounced head movement as indicated in line (20), again looking at Anna. Katie shifts her gaze following Sandra's gaze toward Anna in line (25), shortly after Sandra's performance of the pronounced head movement. It appears that this movement of bending forward and up again was at least in part communicative in the higher-level action between Sandra and Katie.

When employing the notion of modal density, we can determine that Sandra pays much less attention to the interaction with Katie than to the interaction with Anna and Robert. Figure 9.5 heuristically visualizes the modal density that Sandra employs in her interaction with Katie.

Modal density in this interaction is visibly not as high as the modal density that Sandra employs simultaneously, performing the higher-level action of joking with Anna and Robert. Thus, we can say that Sandra foregrounds the interaction with Anna and Robert, while she midgrounds her interaction with Katie. This means Sandra is well aware of Katie and her requests for focused interaction, yet she does not focus upon her at this moment in time. In one of the following interactions in this sequence, Sandra does return her focused attention to Katie, showing that she was aware of the child's request to draw an image of her Daddy on the piece of paper.

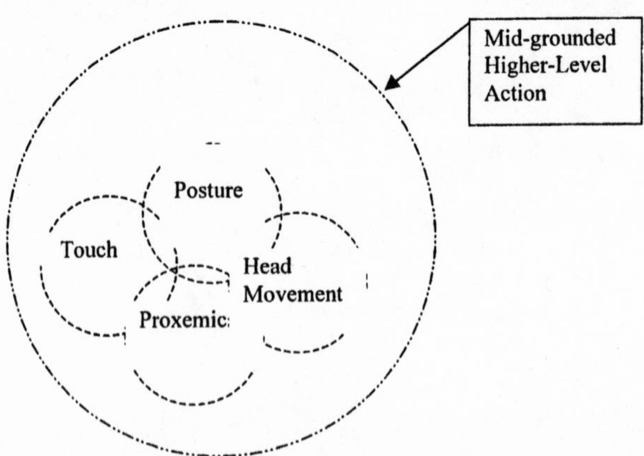

Figure 9.5. Medium Modal Density: Interacting with Katie.

A Relative Position between Midground and Background

At the same time as Sandra is focused on joking with Anna and Robert and is aware of Katie's requests to draw her Daddy, Sandra is also aware of the other children playing in the room.

Due to the close proximity between Sandra and the playing children, Sandra is employing low modal density in interaction with the other children. Figure 9.6 illustrates this low modal density employed.

While Sandra pays little attention to the boys, she is at least vaguely aware of their activities. Such awareness is more evident in the interaction sequence than in this very interaction itself. Within the interaction sequence, Sandra turns to the four boys as soon as they start acting in some undesirable way, for instance, if the children start fighting, open the patio door, run out of the great room, and so on. Such sudden focus of attention shows that Sandra monitors the ongoing activities among the boys at some level of attention/awareness. She does not disregard their presence altogether, but also interacts with a minimum of modal density with the four boys at this time. Van Leeuwen (1999:16) explains that "background sounds are 'heard but not listened to,' disattended, treated as something listeners do not need to react to or act upon." While Sandra disregards much of what the boys are doing, she is ready to avert misbehavior of the children whenever needed, demonstrating that she does not background her interaction with the boys completely.

Background

As mentioned before, Sandra is visiting Anna and Robert in their apartment. The action of visiting is another higher-level action that Sandra performs, backgrounding it at this time, while she is foregrounding the higher-level action of joking with Anna and Robert, midgrounding her interaction with Katie, and monitoring (to some extent) the four boys who are playing in the great room. Sandra does not react to or act upon the higher-level action of visiting Anna and Robert at this time, although she unambiguously is performing it, utilizing many communicative modes including proxemics, posture, layout, spoken language, gesture, and gaze. The modal density

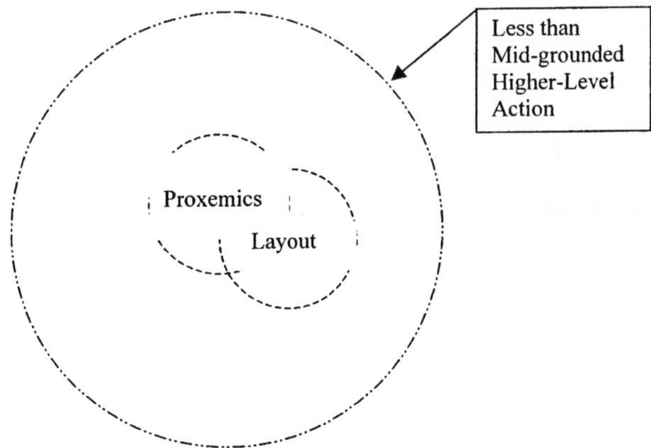

Figure 9.6. Lower Modal Density: Supervising the Four Boys.

that Sandra employs in order to perform the higher-level action of visiting, however, is very low.

While, heuristically speaking, all of these communicative modes make up this higher-level action of visiting, the modes are not complexly interlinked for the purpose of visiting at this time. Rather the modes are loosely present, none of them taking on specific intensity for the purpose of constructing this higher-level action. Figure 9.7 illustrates the heuristic notion of low modal density.

Modal Density Foreground-Background Continuum

When heuristically placing the higher-level actions which Sandra performs simultaneously on the modal density foreground-background continuum, the graph visualizes the relative levels of awareness/attention that Sandra places on the various higher-level actions. Figure 9.8 illustrates the graph.

Sandra performs every higher-level action depicted in this graph simultaneously. The decreasing modal density illustrates Sandra's decreasing level of attention/awareness while performing the higher-level actions.

The higher-level actions that Sandra performs are placed in relation to one another onto the graph. The positions are not fixed, but rather depict the theoretical notion of simultaneously performed higher-level actions by one social actor in real time. The positions of these higher-level actions are by no means static; they are constantly changing and fluctuating with the attention of the social actor. For example, at the beginning of the interaction sequence Sandra foregrounded the higher-level action of visiting. She rang the door bell, exchanged greetings with Anna, Robert, and their children, entered the apartment, and so on. At that moment, the multiple modes that Sandra employed were purposely utilized to engage in the higher-level action of visiting, making this the focused interaction at that point in time. While the action of visiting is ongoing, however, the level of attention that Sandra pays to this higher-level action changes.

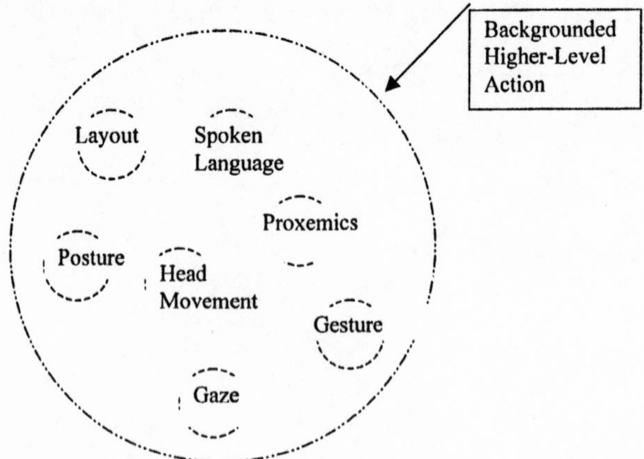

Figure 9.7. Low Modal Density: Higher-Level Action of Visiting.

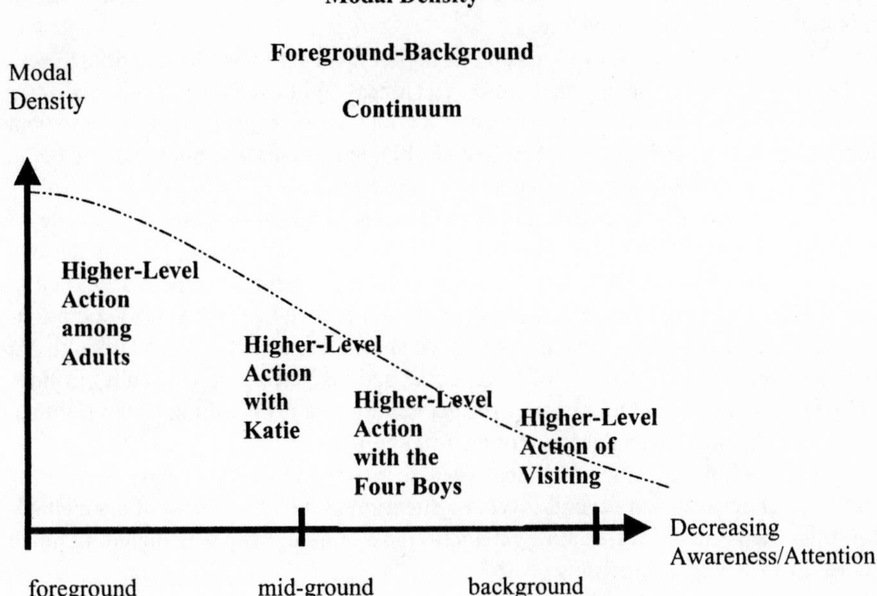

Figure 9.8. Sandra Performs Four Higher-Level Actions Simultaneously.

Conclusion

This conceptual framework for multimodal discourse analysis allows for the integration of all heuristically identifiable communicative modes and the analysis of concurrent higher-level actions that a social actor performs.

Modes of communication are viewed as heuristic and to some extent unbounded units. I tried to visualize this concept by using dotted and unfinished dotted lines. Modal density refers to the complexly interlinked communicative modes that a social actor utilizes to perform a higher-level action (like Sandra's selection of a CD in figure 9.1). The more complexly interlinked and/or intense the modes are, the higher the modal density. The mere multiplicity of modes employed, however, does not indicate high modal density, as illustrated in figure 9.7.

The graph of the modal density foreground-background continuum illustrates that context—be it concurrent actions involving gesture, posture, gaze, for example, or be it the setting in which the interaction occurs—is *not* distinct from the foregrounded or focused higher-level action itself. Often, backgrounded higher-level actions structure the other higher-level actions in some way. Although Sandra disattends the higher-level action of visiting at the moment described above, all of the other higher-level actions she performs simultaneously would not be possible for her to perform in just that way without this backgrounded higher-level action. In other words, the focused interaction of joking with Anna and Robert, the midgrounded interaction of drawing/playing with Katie, and the somewhat further backgrounded interaction of looking after the boys would not come about without this higher-level action of visiting.

Thus, a social actor may focus on one higher level action while attending to several others at differing levels of attention/awareness. While the focus of a social actor certainly communicates the importance of the interaction engaged in at that moment in time, several other interactions are not disattended completely, but rather are being attended to at different levels of attention/awareness.

When a social actor engages in simultaneous higher-level actions, lower-level actions performed through the employment of one or two communicative modes can communicate on several levels. For example, Sandra's head movement described in lines (15), (17), and (20) combined with stroking her own hair in line (18) communicate to Katie that Sandra is not about to give her the requested focused attention. At the same time, the brief string of lower-level actions performed by Sandra in lines (15), (17), and (18) communicates to Anna that Sandra cannot think of the right sequence of the advertisement, prompting Anna to perform.

The multiplicity of communicative actions—higher-level actions as well as lower-level actions—on several levels of attention and/or awareness of a social actor, raise the issue of investigating interaction in a more holistic way including much more than focused interactions. ▒

NOTES

1. For ease of terminology, interactional sociolinguistics is not distinguished from discourse analysis.
2. See Goodwin (1980, 1981, 1986, 1994), and particularly Goodwin (2001), incorporating gaze and images, focusing his analysis on the part played by visual phenomena in the production of meaningful action. Also see, Erickson (1990), Finnegan (2002), Haviland (2000), Kendon (1978, 1980), McNeill (1992), Ochs and Taylor (1992), Ruesch and Kees (1956), and Whalen, Whalen and Henderson (2002). See also Whalen and Whalen chapter, this volume.
3. I would like to kindly thank the participants of the study and their families. Furthermore, I would like to thank Ron Scollon for his supportive discussions, Ruth Wodak and Heidi Hamilton for their insightful comments, and Theo Van Leeuwen for his thoughts. I would also like to thank a group of students at the Research Center for Discourse, Politics, and Identity in Vienna for their constructive questions, and Alan Norris for his attention to wordings.
4. Communicative modes such as layout can be divided into many other communicative modes like furniture, or spatial arrangement of a room/building/area. Depending upon the focus of the study, such division is obligatory or may be insignificant.

REFERENCES

Erickson, F. 1990. The social construction of discourse coherence in a family dinner table conversation. In B. Dorval, ed., *Conversational organization and its development,* 207–38. Norwood, NJ: Ablex.

Finnegan, R. 2002. *Communicating: The multiple modes of human interconnection.* London: Routledge.

Goodwin, C. 1980. Restarts, pauses, and the achievement of mutual gaze at turn-beginning. *Sociological Inquiry* 50(3–4): 272–302.

——. 1981. *Conversational organization: Interaction between speakers and hearers.* New York: Academic Press.

——. 1986. Gestures as a resource for the organization of mutual orientation. *Semiotica* 62:29–49.

——. 1994. Professional vision. *American Anthropologist* 96(3): 606–33.

——. 2001. Practices of seeing visual analysis: An ethnomethodological approach. In T. Van Leeuwen and C. Jewitt, eds., *Handbook of visual analysis,* 157–82. London: Sage.

Haviland, J. 2000. Pointing, gesture spaces, and mental maps. In D. McNeill, ed., *Language and gesture: Window into thought and action,* 13–46. Cambridge: Cambridge University Press.

Kendon, A. 1978. Looking in conversation and the regulation of turns at talk: A comment on the papers of G. Beattie and D. R. Rutter et al. *British Journal of Social and Clinical Psychology* 17:23–24.

——. 1980. Gesticulation and speech: Two aspects of the process of utterance. In M. R. Key, ed., *Nonverbal communication and language,* 207–27. The Hague: Mouton.

Kress, G., and T. Van Leeuwen. 2001 *Multimodal discourse: The modes and media of contemporary communication.* London: Edward Arnold.

Kress, G., C. Jewitt, J. Ogborn, and C. Tsatsarelis. 2001. *Multimodal teaching and learning: The rhetorics of the science classroom.* London: Continuum.

McNeill, D. 1992. *Hand and mind: What gestures reveal about thought.* Chicago: University of Chicago Press.

Norris, S. 2002. The implications of visual research for discourse analysis: Transcription beyond language. *Visual Communication* 1(1): 93–117.

Ochs, E., and C. Taylor. 1992. Family narrative as political activity. *Discourse & Society* 3:301–40.

Ruesch, J., and W. Kees. 1956. *Nonverbal communication: Notes on the visual perception of human relations.* Berkeley: University of California Press.

Schafer, R. M. 1977. *The soundscape: Our sonic environment and the tuning of the world.* Rochester, VT: Destiny Books.

Scollon, R. 1998. *Mediated discourse as social interaction.* London: Longman.

——. 2001a. Action and text: Toward an integrated understanding of the place of text in social (inter)action. In R. Wodak and M. Meyer, eds., *Methods in critical discourse analysis,* 139–83. London: Sage.

——. 2001b. *Mediated discourse: The nexus of practice.* London: Routledge.

Tannen, D. 1984. *Conversational style: Analyzing talk among friends.* Norwood, NJ: Ablex.

Van Leeuwen, T. 1999. *Speech, music, sound.* London: Macmillan Press.

Whalen, J., M. Whalen, and K. Henderson. 2002. Improvisational choreography in teleservice work. *British Journal of Sociology* 53:239–58.

Files, Forms, and Fonts: Mediational Means and Identity Negotiation in Immigration Interviews

ALEXANDRA JOHNSTON
Georgetown University

THE PERMANENT RESIDENCY VISA (or "green card") allows non-U.S. citizens to work and live indefinitely in the United States and to travel abroad as if carrying a U.S. passport. A face-to-face interview with a U.S. Immigration and Naturalization Service (INS) officer is the final requirement and ultimate verdict in the years-long application process. During the interview, an applicant has about twenty minutes to display—through talk, physical appearance, gaze behavior, documentation, and numerous other practices—that they are who they claim they are: an "approvable" applicant. The applicant must claim this identity consistently across multiple modes using verbal, material, and semiotic mediational means. The officer's job is to evaluate the consistency of identity claims across all modes and mediational means. If the use of any mediational means disrupts the identity of "approvable," officers may often employ adversarial tactics to test the strength of applicant claims.

This paper focuses on one such adversarial interview. An immigration officer interviewing an applicant for an employment-based green card developed doubts about the veracity of an applicant based upon the applicant's lack of direct gaze and presentation of a possibly fraudulent document. The use of videotape as a data-collection technique affords the close examination of the (in some ways, quite similar) gaze behavior of both interactants, as well as to pinpoint the source of the officer's evaluation. In the case of the document, the officer did not believe the applicant's employer in Pakistan could have had access to Microsoft Word to produce the document—the same word-processing software used everyday by the officer. Unexpected similarity in practice between officer and applicant resulted in identity imputations of "deniable" to the applicant—which in turn raises questions about when "comembership" may be felicitous or infelicitous for a person in a gatekeeping situation. The analysis of immigration interviews may therefore assist in understanding how gatekeepers make conclusions about similarity and difference and how that affects identity negotiation in gatekeeping encounters.

Research Background and Motivation

The District Adjudications Officers (DAOs) who perform permanent residency interviews wield considerable power over individuals and U.S. society. Incrementally, through thousands of interviews, immigration officers select the future immigrant portion of the U.S. workforce and the pool of potential new U.S. citizens. Their job is also seen to affect U.S. national security; mandatory fingerprint checks and many application questions probe the applicant's past for activity criminalized under U.S. law, including drug possession and dealing, prostitution, and terrorism. For the individual applicant, the DAO's decision to grant or deny an immigrant visa has enormous impact—personally, socially, and economically. In a study of permanent residency interviews I conducted at an INS District Office in the eastern United States, one applicant told me, "This is the most important step in an immigrant's life. The interview determines whether or not you stay in the U.S.—it affects your legality or illegality. If you don't [get] approved, maybe you go back to working [for] underpayment, or work in places you don't want to work. Your life, your family's life, your son, your daughter, your brothers and sisters . . . their life depends on you" (personal communication, April 2001).

An officer's decision to approve or deny a green card rests upon both statutory and discretionary grounds. For example, an applicant applying for an employer-based green card must provide an employer affidavit. The presence of that document in the applicant's file is a statutory requirement. However, the officer's evaluation of that document as legitimate or fraudulent—and of the applicant's discourse about the document as truthful or deceitful—is discretionary. Every officer develops his or her own methods for making discretionary decisions based upon INS regulation and protocol, on-the-job experience, and training.

However, few people other than visa applicants and the immigration officers who screen them realize how negotiable visa decisions may be, or how miscommunications and misjudgments may occur. Immigration lawyer James Nafziger surveyed the review process for visa denials and found that not only did visa applicants have little recourse when they were mistakenly denied a visa, but that officers themselves recognized the potential for discretionary mishaps: "One officer pointed out that she is very much on her own in drawing the proper inferences from the demeanor and other personal clues of applicants. Officers recognized that their decisions were often somewhat subjective and that mistakes were bound to happen" (Nafziger 1991:68).

One area of subjectivity results from the degree of *comembership* between gatekeepers and applicants. As discussed below, comembership has been shown to account for some of the variation in service meted out by gatekeepers.

Comembership in Gatekeeping Encounters

Comembership has been defined as the "active search" for shared attributes of social identity or status that are particularistic rather than universalistic (Erickson and Shultz 1982). Comembership can be signaled by the explicit referential content of the encounter in which interactants realize that they share a facet of social identity, such as supporting the same political party, having the same educational background, or having children the same age. However, the feeling of "we are similar," which the term comembership tries to capture for analytical purposes, may also be less consciously realized. For example, similar use and interpretation of contextualization cues (Gumperz 1982, 1992) such as prosody, kinesics and gaze, listener response behavior (Erickson and Shultz 1982), lexical appropriations, and conversational style

(Tannen 1984), may also produce a feeling of similarity among interactants. I will call this implicitly realized form of comembership "practice-based comembership," as opposed to social-categorical comembership.

What might be the effect of a sense of sameness in an institutional setting? Erickson and Shultz (1982) found that the establishment of comembership positively influenced the outcome of gatekeeping encounters between junior college counselors and their advisees. Specifically, the degree of comembership had a critical bearing on whether junior college counselors acted as a student's *advocate* or *judge*. In situations of high comembership (due to shared educational background or sports activities), the counselor was more likely to provide assistance to the student by offering special help or directly conveying "bad news" of obstacles that might interfere with the student's goals. However, in situations of low comembership, the counselor was more likely to act as a judge who represented the institutional bureaucracy. "Judge" behavior included making the student "work" to express information and expressing "bad news" indirectly.

Erickson and Shultz also showed how different types of listener response behavior—subtle nonverbal cues such as gaze, nodding, and body posture—directly influenced the counselor's interpretation of whether a student was attending to and understanding what the counselor said. In several cases, listener response behavior that differed from the counselor's own style was misinterpreted by the counselor as showing inattention or lack of comprehension—which then correlated with the counselor's stance as "judge" rather than "advocate."

The work of Erickson and Shultz shows how a high degree of practice-based comembership was felicitous for the person seeking access to institutional goods and services. Other research (Cook-Gumperz and Gumperz 1997; Erickson and Shultz 1982; Scollon and Scollon 1981; Tannen 1984, 1989, 1993) supports this finding; similarities in constructing and interpreting conversational "small talk," narratives of personal experience, and body movements all play a role in creating high comembership. This is critical to acknowledge in situations where people have the power to make decisions affecting other people's lives, especially in the face of the false objectivity of bureaucratic "standardization." In what follows, I will show that similarity on a practice level (the use of the same type of word-processing program, document layout, or body behavior such as gaze) sometimes has *infelicitous* results for the person in a position of lower power. A gatekeeper's unexpected sense of similarity to an applicant may be perceived as an incongruous comembership that is refuted rather than ratified. Instead of strengthening the identity claim of "approvable" visa applicant, similarity in practice may result in an immigration officer hardening an identity imputation of "deniable."

Data

The examples that are presented below are drawn from one employment-based permanent residency interview. The interview is part of a corpus of fifty-one videotaped permanent residency interviews between one INS officer and fifty-one applicants of twenty-five different nationalities. When the officer and applicant entered the DAO's office, the officer turned on a mini digital video camcorder and a handheld audiocassette recorder. After the interview concluded, the officer asked if the applicant was willing to step into the neighboring office where I waited to ask permission to use their tapes for research. After obtaining verbal and written permission to use their tapes, I performed a brief exit interview of five to ten minutes with each applicant (and accompanying spouse or lawyer, if present). Following final case action by the INS, applicants were selected for intensive playback interviews of one to two hours.

Although only one officer consented to have his interviews recorded (out of nine DAOs in the field site), his perceptions, assumptions, judgments and interview methods are augmented, corroborated, and challenged by informally structured interviews and conversations I had with many other officers throughout the District Office in several administrative sections. Following Reusch and Bateson (1968) and R. Scollon (1998, 2001b), my goal was to triangulate my analysis by gleaning information from multiple perspectives, including INS institutional members of all levels, applicants and clients, and mediators such as lawyers and immigrant rights advocates.

Theoretical Framework: Mediated Discourse Analysis

The central focus of Mediated Discourse Analysis (R. Scollon 1998, 1999, 2001a, 2001b) is to analyze social issues and theorize social change. This theoretical position draws concepts and tools from several disciplines, including (among others) interactional sociolinguistics (Auer, Couper-Kuhlen, and Mueller 1999; Erickson and Shultz 1982; Gumperz 1982; Tannen 1984, 1989, 1993), ethnomethodology (Goffman 1959, 1974, 1981), linguistic anthropology (Duranti 1997; Gumperz 1982, 1992), intercultural communication (Scollon and Scollon 1981, 2001) and geosemiotics (R. Scollon and S. Scollon 1998, 2000).

Within the larger theoretical agenda of trying to understand social change in sociocultural context, MDA takes human action to be the root of social change. And because, as S. Scollon notes, "if we want to understand social change, we must theorize how social actors orient themselves to the future" (2002), MDA attempts to theorize how actions in the past and the unfolding present allow for or constrain future actions—such as the funnel of commitment (Scollon 2001b) leading an immigration officer to commit to a decision about a visa case. Theoretical and methodological concerns regarding the study of how social actors orient themselves toward the future, termed *anticipatory discourse,* are elaborated by de Saint Georges (2003), Scollon (2002) and S. Scollon and R. Scollon (2000). Anticipatory discourse is a key concept in understanding how the informal practices of immigration officials interweave to transform abstract law into concrete action—a question that is dealt with in detail in the larger study of which this paper is a part.

The unit of analysis in MDA is real-time *mediated action,* a concept developed within the Vygotskian tradition and elaborated by psychologist James Wertsch (1991, 1998). A mediated action is defined as an agent acting with a *mediational means* (Scollon 2001a, 2001b; Wertsch 1991, 1998) within a *social practice* (Bourdieu 1977, 1990). Mediational means include symbolic systems of representation such as a language or specific aspects of language, such as the specialized vocabulary shared by INS officers, or a narrative of personal experience told by an applicant hoping to persuade an officer to approve their visa. Mediational means also encompass any material part of our world that is used by an agent in taking an action, such as an ID card, a binder of documents, or a suit of clothes. The use of mediational means always carries identity implications which may be ratified or disputed by other interactants: for example, after initial denial of a U.S. work visa, one applicant employed bureaucratic language that afforded an identity claim of "savvy client" and "inadvertent sojourner" in order to successfully obtain a U.S. visa after initial denial (Johnston 1999). I will discuss two types of mediational means: gaze and document layout.

Gaze Behavior in Immigration Interviews

Immigration officers often red-flag the lack of direct eye contact by an applicant. Olaniran and Williams spent three weeks in the public waiting room of a U.S. consulate in West Africa observing four consular interviewers and thirty-two visa applicants. Based upon written notes of the interactions, Olaniran and Williams observed that lack of sustained eye contact by applicants seemed to be perceived negatively by all four of the interviewing officers, noting that officers asked "Why are you afraid to look at me when you're talking?" and "Why can't you look at me?" (1995:232). The authors found that 83 percent of applicants (ten of twelve) who maintained direct eye contact or adjusted their behavior upon request by the interviewing officer were successful in obtaining visas. However, 90 percent (eighteen of twenty) of those failing to maintain direct eye contact—even after a direct request to maintain eye contact gaze by the officer—were denied a visa. When applicants were asked why they failed to maintain eye contact when requested, the applicants "pointed overwhelmingly to the discomfort they felt in maintaining eye contact since such behavior suggested impoliteness in their cultural norms" (Olaniran and Williams 1995:233). Some applicants indicated that they tried to maintain eye contact but could not sustain it.

INS officers I interviewed in the U.S. District Office considered the lack of direct eye contact to be polysemous behavior: an applicant who does not meet an officer's eye is seen as deceitful or nervous (or both). However, few officers acknowledged that lack of direct gaze might also be ambiguous. Most officers with whom I spoke were confident that they could tell the difference between an applicant who was "just nervous" and one who was lying. This confidence was exhibited when I entered the office of the DAO after a problematic interview with a Pakistani man applying for an employment-based green card. Referring to the applicant, the officer exclaimed animatedly, "He was ly::ing! Oh, was he lying. He would NOT look me in the eye."

The applicant's eye gaze practices were judged to indicate an applicant who "lied" and was therefore "deniable." Before discussing the applicant's gaze behavior, however, it should be noted that one of the most striking findings of the green-card interview videotapes is that the *officer rarely looks at the applicant.* In fact, the officer rarely *talks* to the applicant. For example, in one successful interview in which an applicant was approved on the spot for his green card, only 5.5 minutes of a 23.5-minute interview were spent in talk. That is, talk comprised only 23 percent of the interview, and fully 77 percent of the interview passed without verbal discourse.

The use of videotape recording affords an even more striking analysis that would have been lost in audiotaped data collection; in the same successful interview, the DAO looked directly at the applicant only 3 percent of the time. Of the period spent in talk (5.5 minutes), when mutual direct gaze might be expected to be most extended, the officer gazed directly at the applicant for a total of thirty-nine seconds. That is, the officer looked directly at the applicant for only 12 percent of their verbal interaction. Meanwhile, the applicant maintained direct gaze orientation toward the officer for nearly 100 percent of the verbal interaction and for the majority of the nonspeaking time as well.

This pattern held for the entire database of interview videotapes. Time spent in verbal interaction between the officer and applicant ranged from 23 to 35 percent of the videotaped interview (taped from the time the officer swore in the applicant until the applicant left the office). Time spent without verbal interaction ranged from 65 to 77 percent of the interview. The amount of time the officer looked directly at the applicant remained under 5 percent of the entire interview. The rest of the time, the officer directed his gaze toward the applicant's file and the documents within, and the databases he pulled up on his computer screen. He was, in effect, interacting with the applicant's file, while the applicant was on conversational hold. The problem was, however, that applicants often did not recognize when a conversational hold occurred and for how long they had to remain on hold—or for how long they should keep their eyes fastened on the officer.

It may or may not seem counterintuitive that the officer expects an applicant to maintain a positively evaluated practice (direct gaze) throughout the duration of the interview that the officer himself practices so rarely (3 percent of the entire interview, 12 percent of verbal interaction). Clearly, the officer does not evaluate himself by the standards he uses for the applicants (that lack of direct eye contact indicates lying), nor does he seem to expect that applicants might draw such a conclusion. And, clearly, an applicant would be unlikely to be approved for a visa if he or she mirrored other officer practices—if an applicant began questioning the officer, fingerprinting the officer, or typing on his computer. However, the officer's use of gaze behavior was evaluated by several applicants as unusual, unsettling, even rude. One applicant wondered if she could have read a newspaper or written lists of errands during the long periods (five minutes and more) of silence and averted gaze. That she would have considered producing behavior she admitted was at odds with her own schema of a formal interview shows how unusual the officer's lack of talk and gaze was to her. She felt frozen; in her words, "like a mouse on a [laboratory] bench, not knowing where to run." It seems that the officer's lack of gaze was salient to several applicants and, therefore, salient to the interaction.

One way in which the lack of direct eye contact by the officer (especially in the beginning of the interview, when DAOs are typically most occupied with file documents and data entry) may affect the interaction is by establishing parameters of behavior that might work against an applicant, especially one whose habitus links direct eye contact with a person in authority with antagonism or disrespect. It may even increase the potential that someone already prone to avoid direct eye contact with an institutional authority will further follow that tendency, resulting in a negative identity attribution. This may serve as a partial explanation of the problematic interview discussed below.

The applicant was a Pakistani man applying for an employer-sponsored green card. The interview video shows that, especially during the beginning of the interview, the officer rarely looked the applicant in the eye. In fact, after the officer swore him in and they were seated, the officer did not once glance at the applicant for the next three minutes. Meanwhile, the applicant kept his gaze anchored on the officer. However, several times when the DAO glanced up at the applicant at the end of a direct question, the applicant often briefly looked away before answering. His gaze then returned when the officer looked back down at the file. The applicant's answers were also marked by long pauses, false starts, clarification questions, and, a few times, "I don't remember."

As the interview progressed, the DAO employed increasingly adversarial tactics: he challenged the truth value of the applicant's testimony, reiterated questions about his place of residence and work history, and read aloud a number of syntactically complex questions about the applicant's legal history ("Have you ever engaged in, conspired to engage in, or do you intend to engage in, or have you ever solicited membership or funds for, or have you, through any other means ever assisted or provided any material support to any person or organization that has ever engaged or conspired to engage in sabotage, kidnapping, political assassination, hijacking, or any other form of terrorist activity?").[1] In a classic example of complementary schismogenesis (Bateson 1972), the applicant began to meet the officer's gaze less and less as the officer gazed at him more and more. Only when the officer looked away did the applicant's dysfluency diminish and his gaze return to the officer's face.

In this interview, a similarity in practice (gazing at an interlocutor who is looking away) resulted in a highly negative evaluation by the interviewing officer ("[The applicant] was lying") and, as we shall see below, an identity attribution of potentially "deniable." Fortunately, in green-card interviews, documentation and oral response trump nonverbal behavior. According to the DAOs I interviewed, it is highly unlikely that someone would be denied a permanent residency visa based solely on interpretations of nonverbal behavior. There must be statutory or other documentary evidence that the application is not approvable. In this case, the officer found it: in the layout of the applicant's employer affidavit.

Document Layout and Font

One of the requirements for an applicant to obtain an employer-sponsored green card is a letter from an employer. In the case of the Pakistani man, the employer affidavit had to attest that he had worked for the employer (a butcher shop in Pakistan) for at least two years (as a meat cutter). In the applicant's file, there was a letter from a butcher shop in a small town in Pakistan that attested to this.

By the interview midpoint, the DAO had taken a heightened adversarial footing. Two turns before this excerpt begins, he told the applicant that he did not believe his testimony. Then, abruptly, the DAO opened the applicant's file to the employer letter and raised it as a topic for the first time in the interview. I include the extended transcript to give a sense of the adversarial tone, which includes repetition, emphatic stress, and tonal variation. (Adjacent periods indicate pauses in seconds.)

Example 1

DAO: This letter.
Where did this letter come from.
The TRUTH.
Where did this letter come from.
..
Who gave you this letter.
Pak Market.
From Pak Meat Shop.
Did you get this letter from the United States or from Pakistan.
..
Have you ever SEEN this letter.
Applicant: Which one,
DAO: This letter here—
you can read English right?
Applicant: Yeah, yeah.
DAO: Okay.
Read that letter.
((20 second pause while applicant reads letter))
Applicant: Yeah, that- that's from Pakistan.
DAO: Okay.
Did you get—
Who-who got this letter,
You or the attorney.
Applicant: No, I got the letter.
DAO: YOU got the letter.
Applicant: Right.

The DAO accomplishes a number of tasks in this excerpt. He obtains verbal confirmation of the applicant's English literacy, he watches the applicant read the letter, he obtains verbal confirmation that the letter originated in Pakistan, and that the applicant (not his counsel) obtained the letter. The DAO follows a protocol analogous to how a lawyer argues a case before trial. He closes every loophole that the applicant or his counsel might raise to later refute an assertion of document fraud ("My client doesn't read English," "My client did not personally obtain this letter"). After further queries about the name of the applicant's employer and the length of time he was employed in the butcher shop, the DAO delivers a preliminary conclusion, narrowing the funnel of commitment to his future case action.

Example 2

DAO:	Here is what I'm going to do.
Applicant:	All right.
DAO:	One thing.
Applicant:	Yes, [sir.]
DAO:	[That] I have a problem with.
Applicant:	Okay,
DAO:	Is this letter.
Applicant:	Which one.
DAO:	Pak Meat Shop.
Applicant:	All right,
DAO:	I am going to . . . contact Pak Meat Shop.
Applicant:	Al—
DAO:	Do they still exist?
	You probably wouldn't know, you haven't been there.
	I'm going to call Pak Meat Shop
	and confirm that you were employed with them.
	If in fact this letter is valid,
	And you were employed with them.
Applicant:	But maybe there's no shop now, I don't know.
DAO:	Okay.
	Then I'll deal with that—
	If that's the case, then that's the case BUT.
	I'm going to find out.
	Even if they—
	I'm going to find out if this shop ever EXISTED.
	Okay?
	If I find out it DID and you worked there, <high tone>fine!>
	I'm approv—I'll approve this,
	No problem.
	If I find out this shop never EXISTED.
	Then . . . of course, I'm not gonna approve it.
	Okay?
Applicant:	All right.

In this segment of anticipatory discourse, the DAO prepares the way for his future actions. His presentation of alternatives narrows the scope of possible future action by outlining two paths the case may take. First, the DAO will call the butcher shop in Pakistan. If the shop exists and the applicant worked there, he will approve the visa. If the shop never existed, he will deny the visa. By explicitly verbalizing the alternatives, the anticipatory discourse warns the applicant that the funnel of future action is narrowing—this is the applicant's last chance to change the course of those actions by providing or withholding further information. In this case, the applicant reiterated that the shop existed and that he had been employed there—and the funnel closed.

After this interview concluded and the applicant had left, the DAO told me that the applicant had lied to him. The two reasons he gave were that the applicant would not look him in the eye, and the employer letter. Were the letter proved fraudulent, the DAO would have the hard evidence required to deny the case. Why did the DAO suspect the letter was fraudulent? According to him: "There's a document [in the file] that looks like it came off Microsoft Word in the U.S. This is PAKISTAN."

The document had a large, curving header that read "PAK MEAT SHOP" in shaded, grayscale bubble letters. The document resembled the format of a type of business letter commonly used in the United States and in international business communication. It contained the addresses of sender and receiver, a salutation, paragraphs separated by spaces, and a signature. The body of the letter showed syntactic, lexical, and discursive features of South Asian English (Kachru 1982, 1983).

The document could indeed have been created using Microsoft Word or similar word processing software. The weight of the paper seemed equivalent to the ream weight commonly used by businesses in the United States for everyday correspondence, and the size was the U.S. standard of 8.5 by 11 inches. However, the point is not which word processing program is used in Pakistan, nor the typical weight of Pakistani letter paper, but that the officer *perceived* a similarity in practice—and then *dismissed* that similarity as highly incongruous. According to his schema of Pakistan, Pakistani businesses, and Pakistani butcher shops, the DAO could not fathom that a letter looking like the one he held had Pakistani provenance. So familiar was the letter in appearance—text layout, font, paper weight, and all other material features—that even dissimilarities in content (South Asian discursive features) did not convey Pakistani geographical origin. In all of his comments, the officer referred to how the letter *looked* rather than how the letter read or what it said. As stated by Van Leeuwen, "typography and handwriting are no longer just vehicles for linguistic meaning, but semiotic modes in their own right" (see the chapter by Van Leeuwen, this volume). In this case, the font, layout, and material feel of the document formed a semiotic mode that signaled access to a means of production refuted by the officer.

Conclusion

This paper shows the importance of two mediational means, one embodied and interactive (gaze behavior) and one external and material (document layout and font style) in the discourse of future action by an immigration officer. In the case of gaze behavior, the officer expected a practice from the applicant in which he rarely engaged himself (direct eye contact) and, in fact, co-constructed initial parameters in which the applicant and DAO engaged in asymmetrical gaze patterns (looking at an interlocutor who was looking elsewhere). In addition, the officer's evaluation of a similarity in material product (a document that looked as if it were produced by word-processing software he uses) refuted the applicant's attempt to claim an identity of "approvable." The examples show that when there are expectations of difference, the use of seemingly homologous mediational means and practices may not result in a felicitous comembership. Multimodal data capture and analysis show the importance of nonverbal mediational means in integrating discourse and action within gatekeeping encounters; in attributing, claiming, or refuting identities of "approvable" or "deniable," as well as understanding how access to institutional resources is distributed.[2]

NOTES

1. All interviews were taped in April, 2001. Long before September 11, 2001, it was INS practice to verbally ask Middle Eastern and/or presumably Muslim men about "terrorist" activities (in addition to the written application questions). In my sample of fifty-one interviews, only two people were asked the "terrorist" question: a Moroccan man and a Pakistani man, both under forty-five years of age.
2. The final outcome for the applicant whose case was examined in this paper was approval. The officer followed through on his promise to verify the existence of the butcher shop in Pakistan by telephoning the embassy of Pakistan to ask for assistance. His telephone contact told him that ascertaining the existence of the shop would take "two years." Under pressure to provide timely final case action for his quota, and unable to prove conclusively that the employer affidavit was fraudulent, the officer approved the application for permanent residency.

REFERENCES

Auer, P., E. Couper-Kuhlen, and F. Mueller. 1999. *Language in time: The rhythm and tempo of spoken interaction.* New York and Oxford: Oxford University Press.

Bateson, G. 1972. *Steps to an ecology of mind.* New York: Ballantine.

Bourdieu, P. 1977. *Outline of a theory of practice.* Trans. R. Nice. Cambridge: Cambridge University Press.

———. 1990. *The logic of practice.* Stanford: Stanford University Press.

Cook-Gumperz, J., and J. J. Gumperz. 1997. Narrative explanations: Accounting for past experience in interviews. *Journal of Narrative and Life History* 7(1–4): 291–98.

de Saint-Georges, I. 2003. Anticipatory discourse: Producing futures of action in a vocational program for long-term unemployed. Ph.D. diss., Georgetown University.

Duranti, A. 1997. *Linguistic anthropology.* New York: Cambridge University Press.

Erickson, F., and J. Shultz. 1982. *The counselor as gatekeeper: Social interaction in interviews.* New York: Academic Press.

Goffman, E. 1959. *The presentation of self in everyday life.* New York: Anchor Books.

———. 1974. *Frame analysis.* New York: Harper & Row.

———. 1981. *Forms of talk.* Philadelphia: University of Pennsylvania Press.

Gumperz, J. 1982 [1977]. *Discourse strategies.* Cambridge: Cambridge University Press.

———. 1992. Contextualization revisited. In P. Auer and A. di Luzio, eds., *The contextualization of language,* 39–54. Amsterdam: John Benjamins.

Johnston, A. 1999. "Aliens" and the I.N.S.: Identity negotiation in bureaucratic events. Unpublished paper.

Kachru, B. B. 1982. South Asian English. In R. W. Bailey and M. Goerlach, eds., *English as a world language,* 353–83. Ann Arbor: University of Michigan Press.

———. 1983. *The indianization of English: The English language in India.* New Delhi: Oxford University Press.

Nafziger, J. A. R. 1991. Review of visa denials by consular officers. *Washington Law Review* 1–105.

Olaniran, B. A., and D. E. Williams. 1995. Communication distortion: An intercultural lesson from the visa application process. *Communication Quarterly* 43(2): 225–40.

Reusch, J., and G. Bateson. 1968 [1951]. *Communication: The social matrix of psychiatry.* New York: Norton.

Scollon, R. 1998. *Mediated discourse as social interaction.* New York: Longman.

——. 1999. Mediated discourse and social interaction. *Research on Language and Social Interaction* 32(1–2): 149–54.

——. 2001a. *Mediated Discourse: The nexus of practice.* London: Routledge.

——. 2001b. Action and text: Toward an integrated understanding of the place of text in social (inter)action. In R. Wodak and M. Meyer, eds., *Methods in critical discourse analysis,* 139–183. London: Sage.

Scollon, R., and S. Scollon. 1981. *Narrative, literacy and face in interethnic communication.* Norwood, NJ: Ablex.

——. 1998. Literate design in the discourses of revolution, reform, and transition: Hong Kong and China. *Written Language and Literacy* 1(1): 1–39.

——. 2000. Physical placement of texts in shop signs: when 'NAN XING WELCOME YOU' becomes 'UOY EMOC LEW GNIX NAN.' Paper presented at the Third Conference for Sociocultural Research, Campinas, Brazil.

——. 2001 [1995]. *Intercultural communication: A discourse approach.* 2d ed. Oxford: Blackwell.

Scollon, S. 2002. Habitus, consciousness, agency and the problem of intention: How we carry and are carried by political discourses. *Folia Linguistica* 35(1–2): 97–129.

Scollon, S., and R. Scollon. 2000. The construction of agency and action in anticipatory discourse: Positioning ourselves against neo-liberalism. Paper presented at the Third Conference for Sociocultural Research, Campinas, Brazil.

Tannen, D. 1984. *Conversational style: Analyzing talk among friends.* New Jersey: Ablex.

——. 1989. *Talking voices: Repetition, dialogue, and imagery in conversational discourse.* Cambridge: Cambridge University Press.

——, ed. 1993. *Framing in discourse.* New York: Oxford University Press.

Wertsch, J. V. 1991. *Voices of the mind: A sociocultural approach to mediated action.* Cambridge: Harvard University Press.

——. 1998. *Mind as action.* New York: Oxford University Press.

Modalities of Turn-Taking in Blind/Sighted Interaction: Better to Be Seen and Not Heard?

ELISA EVERTS
Georgetown University

SINCE ITS INCEPTION, discourse analysis has been used to shed light on ways language use perpetuates oppression, discrimination, and marginalization of various groups of people (e.g., the underclass, women, and minority ethnicities). A realm of society that has yet to reap the full benefit of such linguistically grounded analyses, however, is that of persons with disabilities. Although efforts are constantly being made to change the way we talk about persons with disabilities in both public and private discourse (e.g., we have rejected the terms *crippled* and *handicapped* as demeaning), rehabilitating representations of disability (lexical and otherwise), although important, is in many ways only a superficial attempt to address a problem whose root lies elsewhere: it is at the micro-sociolinguistic level of face-to-face interaction across ability statuses that the marginalization of individuals occurs, with far more fundamental features of interaction at issue than lexicality.[1] The privileging of certain modalities over others in interability discourse is one such aspect of interaction that is critical to the deconstruction of ability-related marginalization.

Blindness as an Object of Linguistic Interest

When the word *language* is juxtaposed with the word *disability,* blindness[2] is not typically the disability evoked in the mind of the linguist. A bias toward the aural/oral modes of communication (essentially speech and its written representations) has generated an extensive literature on the communication of the deaf, and more recently, a growing literature on accommodation in the contexts of cognitive disabilities such as Alzheimer's and aphasia (Coupland et al. 1988; Goodwin 1995; Hamilton 1991, 1994). This is due in part, of course, to the fact that discourse analysis has until recently been largely constrained to the strictly linguistic aspects of communication, a natural artifact of reliance on the audiocassette recorder as the most readily available technology for data management. Both the maturity of the field in the analyses of aural aspects of interaction and the increasing availability of technology for visual data management have brought us to a point where investigation of the roles of various modalities in interability discourse is ripe for the undertaking.

Asymmetrical Modality Constellations

While speech, hearing, and language processing disorders have received liberal attention, what language and communication experts have not treated is how a person with a disability not traditionally recognized as language-related (e.g., a blind person or a person with a prosthetic arm) works within a set or constellation of channels, modes, and modalities for communication that is very particular and significantly alters the receptive and productive playing field of interaction, creating asymmetrical interfaces of these constellations between participants in interability encounters. Paralinguistic and extralinguistic facets of interaction such as volume, pitch, rhythm, gaze, facial expression, gesture, posture, and proxemics, and the degree to which these constraints affect interaction, have often been treated as peripheral or marginal aspects of language, as rapport builders (as if rapport were of secondary importance in interaction), but not as fundamental. Yet it is these subtle, typically off-record modalities that are the locus of social integration or marginalization. Interability discourse can be viewed as a type of intercultural discourse, subject to similar problems: the semiotics conventionalized by one group do not necessarily convey the same meaning to the other. Moreover, as with any subculture, sharing the "same" language (e.g., English) often renders these cultural differences quite opaque. As long as the differences in constellations of modalities available to persons with various physical and cognitive differences remain an informal system (as in Edward T. Hall's [1959] terminology), they will remain inaccessible to the nonspecialist and will continue to be problematic for communication. Only when, as Hall suggests, we come to write a "musical score" for these behaviors, transforming them from an informal system to a technical one that can be recorded, discussed, and analyzed, will we be able to isolate these elements both to exploit them fully and to prevent exploitation.

This paper is a technical analysis of several multimodal features that are fundamental in interaction between a blind woman and several members of her sighted community. It demonstrates how the seeds of the marginalization of blind persons begins with micro-level features of interaction that are typically unconscious, such as those semiotics that constitute the systematics of turn-taking, many of which are visually accessed and are therefore not mutually available across ability statuses (blind and sighted).

The Relevance of Research on Blind/Sighted Interaction

Investigation of blind/sighted interaction, where norms are flouted involuntarily through disability, stands to be of practical use not only to those for whom blindness is a factor in interaction, but also for participants of ordinary sighted interaction as well. To the extent that it constitutes a type of naturally occurring breaching experiment (Garfinkel 1967), it brings into relief much about how these mechanisms operate in unmarked ("normal") conversational contexts. In this study, I apply a multimodal approach to interactional difficulties that result from the lack of access to the visual semiotics of face-to-face interaction that blindness causes, visual cues that are both receptive and productive, and that include both gaze and gesture.

Data and Participants

These data consist of approximately two hours of videotaped interaction between one blind woman and seven of her sighted friends and family members. Dixie, the main subject of this study, is an adventitiously (once-sighted) blind woman in her mid-fifties, whose loss of vision is the result of the gradual progress of retinitis pigmentosa. As I, the researcher, am Dixie's oldest daughter with over thirty years of experience observing and interacting with her, and as the data collected are of interactions with participants with whom both Dixie and I have genuine long-standing relationships, this case study is conducted from an unusually emic perspective.

All of the participants are members or former members of Dixie's church community in Springfield, her small Kansas town. Sister Esther Rose, whose parents founded one of the local churches during her childhood, is in her eighties and has lived in Springfield all her life. Harriet, in her seventies, was raised in another part of Kansas and moved to Springfield when her children were young. Martha, at whose home this gathering takes place, is also in her seventies and moved to Springfield from the deep South with her husband (also present) some thirty years prior. Nana, who moved to Springfield to attend the local university ten years earlier, is a South African woman in her thirties married to an American. Elisa and Anne are Dixie's daughters. Elisa is in her early thirties and is a graduate student in Washington, D.C. Anne is six years younger than Elisa, is married with three young children, and employs Dixie at the daycare she runs out of her home. These women have come together this evening in August 2001 because I have asked them to for the sake of this study, but talk is centered around their interest in the history of their friendships and of the local churches, and the interactional patterns that emerge are those of authentic relationships, decades long. The first hour of conversation takes place in Martha's living room, the second in the kitchen, where Martha serves her guests summer fruit.

An important caveat should be made: Dixie is extraordinarily well integrated into her sighted community (and happens not to have any blind friends), an achievement that is the result of collaborative efforts on both her part and that of her sighted interlocutors. The degree of marginalization that she experiences is minimal relative to what many blind and visually impaired persons experience. What this study demonstrates is that even in very successful blind/sighted interaction where the sighted participants are most invested in integration, blindness limits Dixie's participation and causes various kinds of communicative breakdown.

In this paper I focus on problems of address and reference that emerge in the data in the context of turn-taking, and more specifically, on the complementary aspects of *addressee designation*[3] (turn allocation) and *turn claiming.* Two corresponding compensation strategies emerge in the data: two marked forms of *addressivity* (Werry 1996) for addressee designation by both blind and sighted participants; and the creative exploitation of multiple alternate modalities for getting the floor and claiming a turn on the part of the blind participant.

Related Work on Turn-Taking and Gaze

To be marginalized is to be denied full participation in the mainstream of society. As has already been shown in the existing literature on gaze, the strategies that are used for involvement in conversation are predominantly regulated by gaze—even the perception that one is being involved is largely derived through monitoring others both via receptive gaze and the experience of mutual gaze with other participants. It is this centrality of gaze as a negotiator of various social actions that renders blindness a particularly "social" handicap, as it has been often characterized.

Social psychologist D. R. Rutter (1984) identifies "cuelessness" (Gumperz 1982) as the main stumbling block for the blind interacting with the sighted, though Coupland, Giles, and Benn (1986:54) critique Rutter's work as too generalized because it is does not point to the effects of cuelessness in specific functions of interaction. They observe that "cuelessness can serve as a valuable explanatory concept only when it relates particular cues to particular dimensions of the non-seeing communicator's interactive behavior." An example of such a specific feature of social interaction which they offer is that of turn-taking.

The well-developed literature on turn-taking that has evolved since Sacks, Schegloff, and Jefferson's (1974) seminal article on its systematics demonstrates that it is remarkably complex and requires cooperation between interactants at a very minute level, such that the subtle moves of one party are predicated on the subtle cues of another. It was Sacks, Schegloff, and Jefferson who first argued for an ideal of no gap, no overlap in conversation,[4] and identified Transitional Relevance Places (TRPs) as the crucial points at which floor changes are negotiated. Thus, although cuelessness is a receptive problem, the productive behaviors that constitute participation are also predicated on reception of visual cues. Naturally, this means that the productive behavior of seizing a turn depends on receptive competence, not only in anticipating an imminent turn change slot, but also in identifying potential contenders for that slot.

Assuming that one of the simplest measures of participation in interaction is the number and duration of turns a given participant takes in conversation, it is clear that the problem of turn-taking is fundamental to the problem of involvement. Goodwin (1980, 1981) and Kendon (1967, 1990) show that turn-taking behaviors are primarily regulated through gaze. Kendon shows how TRPs are anticipated through gaze, while Goodwin demonstrates that having listener gaze is so central to the turn claim process that turn claimants will restart their sentences until they have the gaze of the current speaker/addressee as assurance that they have the floor.

Telephone and computer-mediated discourse are subject to some of the same complications that emerge in blind/sighted interaction with regard to turn-taking when gaze is not available as a facilitator. Although overlap occasionally does occur in telephone conversations (especially when the connection is less than perfect), turn-taking in that context is less complex because it is typically dyadic. Moreover, although participants in phone conversations must rely exclusively on aural cues for anticipating TRPs, a crucial difference between this and blind/sighted interaction is that both parties in phone conversations share the assumption that they are working with the same limited set of modalities, so that there is little if any asymmetry.[5]

Participants in Internet chat interaction also share the assumption that they are each working without the benefit of extralinguistic visual cues; however, chat interaction is more often multiparty, a feature which precipitates a need for alternative turn-taking conventions. Particularly germane to blind/sighted interaction is the notion of *addressivity* introduced by Werry (1996) to describe the repeated use of a participant's name to designate the participant as the intended addressee in the absence of visual cues, especially when a dyadic exchange is embedded in a larger, multiparty exchange.

Addressivity strategies rely on participant assumptions and expectations, what Schiffrin (1994) treats in her discourse model as *information state*. In order to realize that she is a potential addressee, for example, a participant needs to know when a current speaker expects her to possess information that she may be able and expected to share. She also needs to know what is expected of other participants. Although there is sometimes linguistic evidence of such expectations, they are often not evidenced at all, so that inaccurate assumptions about information state are among the most common causes of communication breakdown even in sighted/sighted interaction, and will certainly play a role in blind/sighted interaction as well.

Reception and Production of Turn-Taking Cues: Three Forms of Addressivity

An important precondition to claiming a turn is identifying who may be seen as potential addressees or turn contenders at the next transitional relevance place. Participants in a conversation draw on a number of modalities for cues as to who is being addressed at any given point. These may be linguistic (conveyed in speech), paralinguistic (conveyed in the manner of speech), or extralinguistic (conveyed in nonverbal semiotics). While paralinguistic and extralinguistic modalities are often treated as redundant features of interaction, these data show that in some forms of addressivity they are essential to full comprehension of an utterance or a conversational move. Consider the role of gaze in three types of addressivity that occur in face-to-face interaction and the effects that gazelessness will produce in an interability exchange where one or more participants is blind.

Type 1, *You/Gaze Addressivity*, is the unmarked form of address in sighted/sighted interaction (Goodwin 1980; Kendon 1990). In Type 1, addressee is cued through the use of the pronoun *you* without the name of the addressee, (e.g., *Would you like coffee?* <gazing at addressee>). The polysemy of this form is its chief limitation: in multiparty interactions it can refer to an individual, several individuals, or a generalized *you* (meaning *one*). If unaccompanied by a name or unique title, the use of the pronoun *you* to signal an intended addressee requires *modality coupling*, in this case, the linguistic modality of the pronoun *you*, coupled with the extralinguistic modality of mutual gaze. In other words, the pronoun *you* does not accomplish the function of address without gaze, so that the extralinguistic modality of gaze is inextricable from this form. When the intended addressee is a single individual, the

Table 11.1
Three types of addressivity in blind/sighted interaction

Address Strategy	Name	Pronoun	Verb	Gaze	Example
(1) *You/Gaze Addressivity*	0	you	2nd person	gaze	*Would you like coffee?*
(2) *You/Name Addressivity*	Harriet	you	2nd person	[gaze]	*Harriet, would you like coffee?*
(3) *Name/Gaze Addressivity*	Harriet	0	3rd person	gaze	*Would Harriet like coffee?*

speaker normally disambiguates *you* by achieving mutual gaze with that individual. If gaze is not available, other modalities will need to be drawn on for addressee identification or the cue will be missed. Thus gaze is integral to this form of addressee designation, not peripheral or redundant. To compensate for gazelessness when this strategy is employed, nonseeing participants must attend more vigilantly, both in interpreting auditory or other nonvisual cues, and in anticipating speaker expectations about hearer information state.

In Type 2, *You/Name Addressivity,* the addressee is cued linguistically through use of the intended addressee's name coupled with the pronoun *you* (e.g., *Harriet, would you like coffee?*); as Werry shows, this is normative in chat interaction. In this form, gaze is optional but redundant. Moreover, where gaze is available in face-to-face interaction among sighted interlocutors, this device is relatively uncommon. In this data, however, it is used with frequency as a gaze compensation strategy to alert the blind participant that she is being addressed.

The third and most marked type of addressee designation strategy in this data is Type 3 Addressivity, *(Third person) Name/Gaze Addressivity.* This strategy involves naming the addressee and achieving mutual gaze with him or her, but uses third person verb inflection, which precludes the use of the pronoun *you* (e.g., *Would Harriet like coffee?* <gazing at Harriet>). The advantage of this strategy is that a sighted interlocutor can use mutual gaze to indicate to a participant that she or he is being addressed, and through the use of name, can simultaneously convey this information to the blind participant. There are two disadvantages of this strategy, however. The first is that it is highly dispreferred in English to talk about a present party in third person. The second is its linguistic polysemy: third-person reference clarifies who the topic of conversation is, but not who the addressee is. Without the use of gaze to single out a participant, it could be interpreted as an invitation for any participant to answer in an effort to increase involvement.

Knowing Who Is Available as a Potential Addressee: Attending and Resting Gazes

Not only do participants need to know who is being addressed, but speakers also need to know who is available as a potential addressee. If a participant does not appear to be attending to the speaker, the speaker may either address someone else or may use an alternate modality to address the nonattending participant (such as that participant's name or a touch gesture) and wait for mutual gaze before proceeding. The data presented here show that Dixie, as a person socialized in the norms of sighted interaction before losing her sight, can produce convincing gaze behaviors despite the fact that she cannot receive them. She is particularly adept at using gaze to convey the sense that her interlocutor is being attended to when she knows herself to be the primary addressee.

One distinctive aspect that emerges in Dixie's productive gaze behavior, however, is that of a neutral "resting" gaze, which Dixie uses when she is not the primary addressee. This gaze, not focused on the speaker or any other participant, is likely to give sighted interlocutors the impression that she has disengaged from the conversation even when she may still be actively listening. This apparent inattention will affect the turn management behaviors of the sighted participants, particularly in regard to who will be seen as available as a potential addressee or turn contender. It should be noted that although sighted interlocutors may sometimes exhibit behavior similar to the blind resting gaze, the duration and frequency of its production by blind participants are quite marked. On the other hand, the ability to produce a convincing attention gaze may also be a liability when, for example, it miscues to the speaker that information has been successfully transmitted that has not.

Failed Addressee Identification: Type 1, *You/Gaze Addressivity*

Although the failure to claim a turn, a productive aspect of turn-taking, is the most obvious obstacle to active participation in a conversation, receptive participation should be considered first. Although failure to identify the primary addressee of an utterance can be an impediment to a coherent understanding of the emerging discourse, such receptive failures may remain covert without either causing a loss of face to the blind participant or observably affecting the interaction. When a participant fails to identify that she herself is the intended addressee, however, the failure will be observable, preventing her from fulfilling the role of active participant by responding on cue, and inhering a greater risk of face loss.

Type 1, the preferred addressee designation strategy of using the modality coupling of the pronoun *you* with mutual gaze, is not sufficient for a blind participant. A Type 1 failure occurs in the data when Dixie fails to identify herself as the primary addressee of a request for help with the punch line of a joke that Harriet is trying to tell. Harriet is sitting on the left end of the couch and Dixie on the right end, with Esther between them. Because the telling of the joke takes more than seventy intonation units, I have omitted the body of the joke, excerpting primarily the meta-discourse about who knows the joke and might help with the punch line.

Example 1

1	Harriet	Did—Did you hear that one <gazes around Esther to Dixie>
2		About the lady that come home from church . . . (ellipse lines 3–5)
6		And she said—
7		Now help me, <gazes into the air, not at any specific participant>
8		I might get it all wrong—
9		She said—
10		Acts four . . . <puts hand on forehead, thinking>
11		Acts 4 . . . (ellipse lines 12–14)
15		Darnit,
16		I had it and it was real cute,
17		And I liked–
18		YOU gave it to me. <gazes at Dixie and points to her>
19	Dixie	WHO did? <producing convincing receptive gaze to Harriet>

20	Harriet	YOU did.
21	Dixie	I did?
22		No, I didn't.
23		I never heard it before.
24	Harriet	Oh.
25		Anyway, it was, (ellipse lines 26–64) . . .
65	Elisa	That's excellent.
66	Dixie	That's pretty cute.
67	Harriet	Someone gave me that.
68	Dixie	Ahh, it wasn't me.
69		I never heard it before in my life.

Harriet seems to address the first request generally to the whole group as she produces an unfocused upward gaze, trying to remember the joke, "Now help me, I might get it all wrong." This Type 1, *You/Gaze addressivity*, is in the imperative, with an implicit *you.* The polysemy of this form, that it could refer to one or several participants, combined with Harriet's unfocused gaze, suggests that she is addressing the group generally. Her second request, however, is made directly to Dixie, when, after about five seconds of unsuccessful attempts to recall the punch line, Harriet leans around Esther and gazes at Dixie (who appears to be gazing back), and says, "Help me, help me." This is again a Type 1 strategy with the *you* implicit in the imperative, but this time it is disambiguated for the sighted participants by the use of gaze, directed only at Dixie. Having no access to receptive gaze for these nonverbal signs (Harriet's posture, proxemics, and gaze), however, Dixie cannot know that this request is directed to her and does not reply. A few seconds later, Harriet turns to Dixie again and says, "You gave it to me," looking at Dixie and pointing to her. Dixie replies with apparent surprise, "Who did?" Harriet answers, "You did," but Dixie denies this saying, "No, I didn't, I never heard it before."

When the joke is finished, several minutes later, Dixie returns to this point in the conversation, putting on record that she had not initially known who was being addressed. She reports some of her information processing, apparently by way of apology:

Example 2

1	Dixie	When you were saying,
2		Help me
3		I'm thinking,
4		I thought you were talking to Esther or somebody.

The complex of modalities Harriet employs to indicate Dixie as the intended addressee include the linguistic modality of the pronoun *you,* the paralinguistic modality of voice direction, and the extralinguistic modalities of posture, proxemics, and gaze. All of these modalities are available to the sighted participants, but having no receptive gaze, Dixie has no access to posture, proxemics, or gaze, which turn out to be key. Because Dixie does not know the joke ("I never heard that joke before") and doesn't initially realize that Harriet believes her to know it, it takes her longer to put the auditory cues together (linguistic and paralinguistic) to determine that she was the intended addressee.

That she had imagined Esther, seated to her left between Harriet and herself, to be the probable addressee ("I thought you were talking to Esther or somebody"), however, and not someone on the other side of the room, demonstrates that the paralinguistic cue of voice direction made her aware that Harriet's voice was directed toward her end of the couch, though it was not sufficient to specify whether it was to her or to Esther. Had Dixie been privy to Harriet's assumption that she knew the joke, this knowledge would have helped compensate for missing the visual cues and she might have guessed earlier that she was the intended addressee.

Failed Addressee Identification: Type 3 Addressivity, *Third Person Name/Gaze Coupling*

An alternative addressee designation strategy is to use the modality coupling of the addressee's name with gaze, but without the pronoun *you,* in third person. I use this strategy when I raise a new topic of conversation by asking Harriet when she started going to the church they all now attend: "When did Harriet start going to the Assembly?" Linguistically, this third-person reference clarifies who the topic of conversation is, but not who the addressee is:

Example 3

1 Elisa When did Harriet start going to the Assembly? <mutual gaze with Harriet>
2 Harriet W[ell on trai–] <mutual gaze with Elisa on hearing her name>
3 Dixie [ASK her] @ <Harriet turns gaze to Dixie when Dixie speaks>
4 Harriet Tr– ailridge but I–
5 Elisa I AM asking her. @@
6 Anne She IS—<smiles, nods, gazes at Dixie, hits her lightly on the arm>
7 Dixie @@ (XX) <turns to Anne and says something indiscernible>
8 Harriet When it was still on Trailridge, <Anne turns gaze back to Harriet>

The videotape shows, however, that the polysemy of this Type 3 form was disambiguated by the visual cue of my gazing at Harriet to signal that she was the intended designee. Harriet responds to this cue by returning my gaze and beginning to speak immediately upon the completion of my utterance. Moreover, the video shows that the other (sighted) participants also understood Harriet to be the designee, as they all automatically turned their gaze to her upon my finishing the question, "When did Harriet start going to the Assembly?" Dixie, however, draws attention to the markedness of the Type 3 strategy by saying, "Ask her," and giggling. That Dixie gets reproved both verbally and through a touch-gesture by Anne ("She just asked." <hitting her lightly on the arm>), and verbally by Elisa ("I AM asking her.") indicates that Dixie's daughters understand the addressee to be Harriet, and they expect Dixie to understand that too. Because Anne and Elisa are the two participants most familiar with Dixie's limitations and arguably the most attuned to her communication style, their responses to Dixie's utterance suggest that they do not realize that this misunderstanding could be sight-related, and, moreover, suggest a tacit acceptance of Type 3 addressivity as a valid addressee designation strategy.

Addressivity Types 1, 2, and 3 across Ability Statuses: Success, Failure, and Repair

Evidence that both Type 2 (*You/Name Coupling*) and Type 3 (*Name/Gaze Coupling*) addressivity are actually normative in this group of blind and sighted participants is their use by Elisa, Martha, Esther, and Dixie herself at a point earlier in the conversation while they are still in the living room, as shown in Example 4. Esther and Dixie are the current topic of conversation and at least four participants are collaboratively trying to arrive at a consensus on whether Esther and Dixie might have attended the Foursquare Church at the same time.

Example 4

1	Elisa	When did, like—
2		Sister Rose might have met my mom before.
3	Esther	Oh, m—met <touches Dixie's arm, gazes at Elisa>
4		Your mom,
5		Probably over there at Trailridge.
6	Martha	Did you [go to Foursquare?]
7	Elisa	[At the old] [church building]
8	Martha	[Esther, did you go] to Foursquare?
9	Esther	Well, I went to Foursquare but did— <looks & points to Dixie>
10		Dix[ie?]<gazes at Dixie, turns to Martha when Martha speaks>
11	Martha	[Dix—]
12	Martha	Wasn't that where you went, Dixie?
13		Wasn't that where you came from?
14	Elisa	Yeah, we went to Foursquare.
15	Dixie	Ye:::ah, but –
16	Esther	How many years ago? <gazes at Dixie, looks away on completion>
17	Dixie	Well, yeah.
18		Esther has been at Assembly how long? <unfocused gaze>
19	Esther	Well, I'd been at Assembly . . . < unfocused gaze, not at Dixie>

Elisa, who is trying to determine when Dixie met Sister Esther Rose, opens this sequence with Addressivity Type 3 by asking, "When did, like— Sister Rose might have met my mom earlier." This question is asked in third person through the use of Sister Rose's name without the pronoun *you.* In Elisa's subsequent question, "Did you go to Foursquare?" she addresses Esther with Type 1, without using her name, indicating whom she means to address via the pronoun *you,* coupled with the act of gazing at Esther and achieving mutual gaze. However, when Esther answers this question, she uses Type 3, Dixie's name in a third person question: "Well, I went to Foursquare but did Dixie?" As observed above, Type 3 addressivity is ambiguous in that participants cannot tell with certainty whether Esther means to address Elisa, whose question she has just answered, or Dixie, who is most able to answer the question. No reply from Dixie is forthcoming, however, and evidence that other participants view Dixie as the addressee is Martha's stepping in with a Type 2 address, using the pronoun *you* and her first name: "Wasn't that where you went, Dixie?" She then provides a Type 1 address in a second token of the question after the name, "Wasn't that where you came from?" The second token may be in anticipation that Dixie might not be fully attending until after she hears her name. Dixie uses Esther's name in third person, the Type 3 strategy, in reply: "Esther has been at Assembly how long?"

Example 4 illustrates Addressee Designation Strategy Types 1–3. Type 1, the most common strategy in sighted/sighted interaction, often fails in this blind/sighted interaction. Type 2, which sometimes occurs in sighted/sighted interaction, occurs more frequently here and is successful in letting Dixie know that she is being addressed. Type 3, third person reference, a form of addressivity in multiparty interaction which can have the effect of simultaneously addressing the intended party and alerting the unaddressed non-seeing participant as to whom the addressee is, seems to have emerged as an accommodative discursive practice in the habitus of both the blind and the sighted participants in compensation for Dixie's lack of access to the modality of gaze.

Turn Claiming: The Creative Exploitation of Alternate Modalities to Get the Floor

In Example 4, in which Dixie is a topic of conversation, she takes turns that speakers allocate to her in the form of questions with Addressivity Types 2 and 3. There are, however, several noticeable instances in this evening of video-recorded talk where Dixie attempts to initiate turn claims of her own but fails. While she is not the only person who sometimes fails to claim turns in this data, there is evidence that her failures are either caused or complicated by her having no access to the modality of gaze. There is also evidence of frustration on Dixie's part about her inability to get the group's attention. One striking turn-taking struggle of this nature takes place in Example 5. In this instance, however, after her first attempt fails, Dixie assesses the situation, reformulates her approach, and through the employment of no less than nine different modalities, finally manages to get the floor, claim her turn, and obtain the response she desires.

Table 11.2
Instances of three types of addressivity in interability exchanges in Example 4

Speaker	Interability Crossing	Type	Pronoun	Name	Verb	Gaze	Utterance
Elisa	Sighted—Blind/ Sighted	Type 3	X	Sister Rose	did, might have met	mutual gaze, [gaze]	*When did, like— Sister Rose might have met my mom earlier.*
Martha	Sighted—Sighted	Type 1	You	X	did go	mutual gaze	*Did you go to Foursquare?*
		Type 2				mutual gaze	*Esther, did you go to Foursquare?*
Martha	Sighted—Blind	Type 2	You	Dixie	went	[gaze]	*Wasn't that where you went, Dixie?*
		Type 1	You	X	came from	[gaze]	*Wasn't that where you came from?*
Esther	Sighted—Blind	Type 3	X	Dixie	did (go)	[gaze]	*Well, I went to Foursquare, but did Dixie?*
Dixie	Blind—Sighted	Type 3	X	Esther	has been	[gaze]	*Esther has been at Assembly how long?*

Example 5

1	Esther	Fredericksons–
2		They used t–
3		They were musical,
4		And they had a marimba
5		The girl played–
6		XXX
7	Martha	[Fredericksons?]
8	Dixie	[What's a marimba?]
9	Esther	Fredericksons,
10		They were second pastors.
11	Dixie	<looks to Anne, makes face and gesture>
12		<mouths> I know THAT,
13		That's in HERE <pointing to her head>
14	Anne	<laughs>
15		Oh, XX
16	Dixie	<turns to Esther, 'gazes' at her, 'patty-cake' gesture>
17		What's a marimba? <increases volume slightly>
18		What's it look like?
19	Esther	Well, it's <extends hands about 2.5 feet>
20		A kinda keyboard,
21	Dixie	Oh.
22	Esther	That you use some sticks that you–
23		<animated gesture: hitting the marimba w/sticks>
24		Play it with–

Although Martha, the hostess, has indicated that she is ready for everyone to move to the kitchen for fruit, no one moves to act on her suggestion. In the awkward space of nonresponse, she sabotages her own request for action by expressing her interest in Esther's stories about local church history, which initiates another strip of conversation. Dixie becomes very involved in this discussion, but when the topic comes to a close, she stops talking and assumes a posture facing toward the kitchen and away from the rest of the group, apparently in readiness to comply with Martha's wishes. She also assumes an extreme "resting gaze," which gives her the appearance of being disengaged from the conversation. That Dixie is actually still listening, however, becomes evident when Esther raises a new topic by mentioning the marimba that a pastor's daughter used to play, to which Dixie immediately asks, "What's a marimba?"

Because Dixie does not change her posture or the direction of her own gaze, she is not in a position to catch Esther's eye or anyone else's when she asks this question. The volume of her voice is at the same level as the other women's, but unfortunately

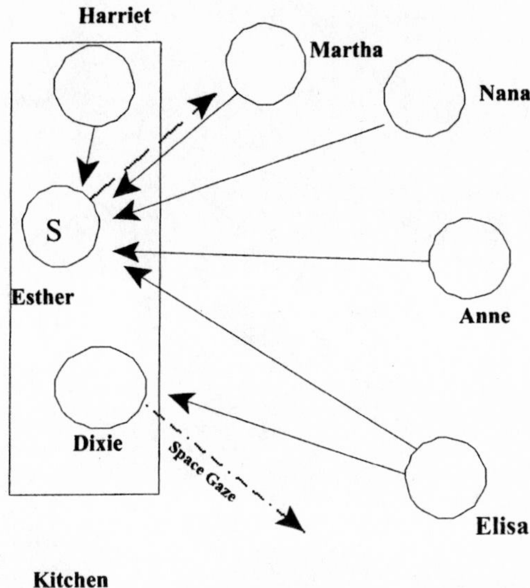

Figure 11.1. Gaze Vectors at Failed Turn Claim Attempt.

for Dixie, Martha repeats the name of the family for confirmation ("Fredericksons?") at exactly the same time that Dixie asks about the marimba, overlapping her utterance completely. Because Esther is looking at Martha, to her left, and not at Dixie, to her far right, she evidently "hears" Martha's question and not Dixie's because she answers, "Fredericksons," with falling intonation. Dixie does not seem to have heard Martha's question over her own voice because she responds as though Esther's answer ("Fredericksons.") were an erroneous reply to her own question ("What's a marimba?"). Because Dixie knows Esther to be hard of hearing, this is a plausible conclusion.

At this point Dixie commences a not-so-subtle display of frustration. She turns her head and her gaze about 20 degrees to the left, in the direction of the speaker and other participants, but specifically locating herself within Anne's line of vision, and makes a comic face. She mouths something like, "I know THAT, That's in HERE," and points to her head, eliciting laughter from Anne. Although Dixie's gesture is directed to Anne, a byproduct is catching Martha's and Harriet's peripheral gaze so that they turn their gaze toward her. Anne's laughter contributed to getting their attention too, but the laugh directs their attention to Dixie, the provoker of Anne's laughter, and not to Anne. Thus Dixie's humor is a discourse strategy that mitigates her complaint, but both contribute to the end of gaining participant attention as a precondition for claiming a turn.

The shift of gaze vectors from Esther to Dixie in figure 11.2 illustrates the net effect of Dixie's animated side complaint to Anne such that now five of six participants are looking at Dixie rather than at Esther (the speaker), who is, for a brief moment, the only participant not gazing at Dixie. Dixie then turns more directly toward Esther (about 15 degrees) and, raising her voice slightly, asks again, "What's a marimba?"

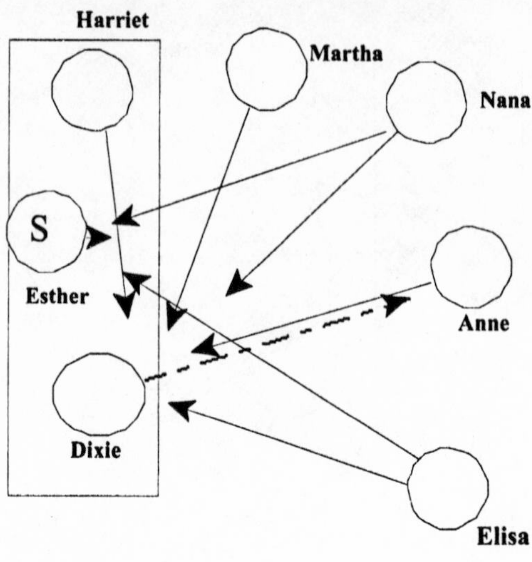

Figure 11.2. Shift of Gaze Vectors as Dixie Gets the Floor.

At this point, Esther raises her face toward Dixie and attends to her. Dixie then makes her second turn-claim attempt, buttressing it with two strategies: repetition and gesture. The repetition, a rephrasing of the first question, appeals to participants' visual imagination: "What's it look like?" She reinforces this question with an animated gesture that is reminiscent of the rolling part of the actions to the popular children's rhyme, "patty-cake-roll-it-in-the-pan." Now that she has everyone's attention, there is no overlap and her question is clearly heard. Naturally enough (if ironically), Esther responds to Dixie's request for a visual description with both a verbal description and a visible gesture, the hand motion of knocking a baton on a marimba.

Dixie's reformulated turn claim strategy was a complex of several modalities. Clearing enough turn space to speak without being overlapped involved linguistic, paralinguistic, and extralinguistic modalities. Linguistic strategies such as humor, complaint, and repetition are discourse strategies that are dependent either on there being no overlap or on the utterance being audible above the overlapping utterance and/or on having the speaker's gaze. Increased volume is a paralinguistic strategy that has the potential to overcome being outside the line of speaker gaze in gaining participant attention so that participants turn their gaze to her.

Some extralinguistic modalities are dependent on others. Notably, gesture, facial expression, and productive gaze are all contingent on the would-be turn claimant being within the line of vision of the person(s) whose attention she would like to procure, so that a necessary precursor to those strategies for Dixie in Example 5 is changing her body alignment (e.g., leaning in, turning, etc.) as a means of locating herself, and particularly her eyes, within the line of vision. Gesture is also a means of capitalizing on participants' peripheral vision and drawing them into a direct focus of the gesticulator, as Dixie's gesture to Anne catches Martha's and Harriet's gaze. By

Table 11.3.
Multimodal strategies for getting the floor without receptive gaze in Example 5

Linguistic		Paralinguistic		Extralinguistic	
Complaint	*I know that, That's in HERE..*	**Volume**	Raises voice slightly	**Gesture**	Pointing to her head, rolling gesture to ask 'what?'
Humor	*I know that, that's in HERE..*	**Intonation**	Falling intonation slightly more commanding	**Posture/ Proxemics**	Turns toward participants, leans in
Question	*What's a marimba? What's it look like?*	**Stress**	KNOW, THAT, MARIMBA	**Facial Expression**	Comical grin with complaint
Repetition	*What's a marimba? (2X), What's it look like?*	**Rhythm, Pace**	Accelerates pace slightly, matches speaker's rhythm	**Productive Gaze**	Directs eyes so that she appears to be gazing at the speaker

getting Anne's attention first, then the other participants', and finally the speaker's through an elaborate web of multimodal discourse strategies, Dixie is able to make herself seen, which is a precursor for making herself heard. Only when all of the participants are looking at Dixie do they stop talking and allow her the turn space to ask her question.

Conclusion

In the absence of mutual access to gaze as a facilitator of turn-management and attention signaling, Dixie and her sighted friends and family have developed a cache of compensation strategies for managing interaction, including several marked forms of addressivity which are used by both blind and sighted participants, as well as the strategic exploitation of multiple alternate modalities for getting the floor on Dixie's part. Though instances of breakdown do occur, these compensation strategies increase Dixie's participation in these interactions and integrate her into her sighted community to a degree that seems exceptional.

The assumption that audibility is the most salient feature of communication in face-to-face interaction has been largely responsible for the neglect of attention to the communication problems of the blind and visually impaired. Microanalysis of blind/sighted interaction is the first step toward technologizing this area of discourse so that strategies for overcoming gazelessness in interaction can be identified and appropriated by both blind and sighted persons in an effort to bridge the ability gaps that inhibit the full integration of blind persons into sighted communities.

Clearly *ableism,* as some scholars in the disability literature have called the marginalization of persons with disabilities, is incompatible with the ideology of a free society, and is an issue that deserves the critical attention of discourse analysts. Because integration cannot be achieved by simply changing the way we talk about members of various groups unilaterally, but must also be made by changing the way we talk to each other, the discrete discursive practices that achieve marginalization must first be identified. When the differences at issue are physical disabilities, one of the most fundamental aspects of interaction to be investigated is the interface of the asymmetrical modality constellations available to each. Privileging certain modalities to the exclusion or neglect of those that may be primary for others, however unconsciously, is the first layer of ableist marginalization that must be treated.

In the case of blind interlocutors, the assumption that speech and hearing are sufficient for ensuring equal access to participation in interaction with sighted interlocutors is misguided. As these data show, visual cues are often the key to gaining full participation in interaction, so that being seen is often a precondition for being heard. In regard to interability discourse in general, moreover, the time has come for discourse analysts to identify the ways that individuals who are ideologically committed to integration are passively or actively complicit in perpetuating both public and private discourses where people with divergent ability statuses are relegated to the margins of our conversations and our society, rendering them too often neither seen nor heard. ▪

NOTES

1. I use *blind* rather than *visually impaired* here both because it is the descriptor that my subject uses in reference to her ability, and to reserve *visually impaired* to refer to individuals who have partial sight.
2. Thus, although there exists a field of study that can be called disability discourse, what I am describing here is more aptly termed *interability discourse*, within which *blind/sighted interaction* is a subfield.
3. Whereas Sacks, Schegloff, and Jefferson (1974) use *turn allocation* when referring to current speaker selecting next, Philips (1983) uses the more specific *addressee designation*.
4. Tannen (1984) and others have clearly shown that the acceptable duration and frequency of gaps and overlap in conversation varies significantly according to culture and individual style differences.
5. Naturally, this is also why it is in the context of phone conversations that blind speakers are most consistently able to "pass" as sighted.

REFERENCES

Coupland, N., J. Coupland, H. Giles, and K. Henwood. 1988. Accommodating the elderly: invoking and extending a theory. *Language in Society* 17:1–41.

Coupland, N., H. Giles, and W. Benn. 1986. Language, communication, and the blind. *Journal of Language and Social Psychology* 5:53–62.

Garfinkel, H. 1967. *Studies in ethnomethodology*. Englewood Cliffs, NJ: Prentice-Hall.

Goodwin, C. 1980. Restarts, pauses, and the achievement of mutual gaze at turn-beginning. *Sociological Inquiry* 50(3–4): 272–302.

——. 1981. *Conversational organization: Interaction between speakers and hearers*. New York: Academic Press.

——. 1995. Co-constructing meaning in conversations with an aphasic man. *Research on Language and Social Interaction* 28:233–60.

Gumperz, J. 1982. *Discourse strategies*. Cambridge: Cambridge University Press.

Hall, E. T. 1959. *The silent language*. New York: Random House.

Hamilton, H. 1991. Accommodation and mental disability. In H. Giles, J. Coupland, and N. Coupland, eds., *Contexts of accommodation: Developments in applied sociolinguistics*, 157–86. New York: Cambridge University Press.

——. 1994. *Conversations with an Alzheimer's patient: An interactional sociolinguistic study*. Cambridge: Cambridge University Press.

Kendon, A. 1967. Some functions of gaze direction in two-person conversation. *Acta Psychologica* 26:22–63.

——. 1990. *Conducting interaction: Patterns of behavior in focused encounters*. Cambridge: Cambridge University Press.

Philips, S. U. 1983. *The invisible culture: Communication in classroom and community on the Warm Springs Indian Reservation*. Prospect Heights, IL: Waveland Press.

Rutter, D. R. 1984. *Looking and seeing: The role of visual communication in social interaction*. New York: John Wiley & Sons.

Sacks, H., E. Schegloff, and G. Jefferson. 1974. A simplest systematics for the organization of turn-taking for conversation. *Language* 50:696–735.

Schiffrin, D. 1994. *Approaches to discourse*. Oxford: Blackwell.

Tannen, D. 1984. *Conversational style: Analyzing talk among friends*. Norwood, NJ: Ablex.

Werry, C. C. 1996. Linguistics and interactional features of internet relay chat. In S. Herring, ed., *Computer-mediated communication: Linguistic, social and cross-cultural perspectives*, 47–60. Amsterdam: John Benjamins.

"Informed Consent" and Other Ethical Conundrums in Videotaping Interactions

ELAINE K. YAKURA
Michigan State University

THE DECLINE IN THE COST and size of equipment has made videotaping much more feasible for researchers studying naturalistic human interaction (Pink 2001). This is an exciting development, for videotaping offers researchers in linguistics and related disciplines such as sociology and anthropology a number of advantages over audiotaping or other forms of data collection. For example, videotaping allows for recording of the nuances of unspoken gesture or other non-audio details. Thus, video has unparalleled power for capturing context and communicative intent (Archer 1997), as well as allowing for "repeated, detailed examination" of interactions that can also be examined by others (Goodwin 1994). At the same time, it is becoming easier to display videotaped data at seminars, conferences, and on the internet (Redmon 2000).

Together with these advantages, videotaping presents a variety of new challenges for parts of the research process. For example, video images clearly identify the research participant, and this lack of anonymity can give rise to sensitive issues in the research process. Due to the widespread deployment of video cameras in our society, nearly everyone has seen images of themselves in home movies, or on store security monitors. Thus, it is likely that research participants have been videotaped and have viewed their videotaped image in the past. In this case, we might assume that informed consent would present no problems. There are, however, more subtle issues at play; research participants might not be fully aware of how videotaping will affect their reactions to being videotaped in a research context. In this case, "informed" consent can be more elusive than a researcher might wish.

In this paper I use concepts from various disciplines to raise questions about how videotaping might affect researcher/research participant relationships in ways that are not explicitly stated in formal guidelines, regulations, or codes of conduct. These issues naturally affect the trust that develops between the researcher and research participants (Kirsch 1999). To explore these issues, I begin with a brief discussion of the unique characteristics of videotaping and the alternative modes of viewing videotaped data ("gazes"). I then present a set of researcher choices in addressing these concerns, and discuss some possibilities for dealing with participants' concerns as they arise. In raising these issues, I am not arguing that existing regulations or codes of conduct require revision. Rather, I am suggesting the need for increased sensitivity and awareness on the part of researchers who choose to videotape naturalistic interactions.

Features of Videotaping

Videotape is a relatively familiar medium; home movies, for example, are commonplace. However, as Chalfen (1998) notes, home movies are typically produced for consumption in the home (although the television program *America's Funniest Home Videos* would appear to belie this). Once the videotape is produced for consumption outside the home, the change in context raises particular issues for research consent. First, because videotaping reveals the image of the subject, there is neither anonymity nor confidentiality. Even subjects who have been repeatedly videotaped in many home movies might react with discomfort knowing their image would be presented in a different context.

Although disguising identity is possible with videotaped images (i.e., one can imagine obscuring the video image of a research participant), doing so is quite awkward (Simoni 1996) and may even compromise the data (Sturken and Cartwright 2001). Thus, unlike surveys, interviews, or even audio recording, subjects who agree to let their images be recorded would typically give up their anonymity as participants in the research. Conventions regarding photographs seem more common; for public figures or public events, permission to take and display photographs freely, without seeking written permission, appears acceptable (Gold 1989; Pink 2001).

Further, because videotaping clearly identifies the research participant, discussion of "touchy" topics is problematic. For example, Simoni (1996), in interviewing medical personnel about HIV, noted that research participants were understandably more sensitive to confidentiality when issues involved possibly stigmatizing patients. Because video has the potential to carry identifying data in a manner that other media do not, it raises potential problems for our research participants.

Gazes: Alternative Modes of Viewing

Videotape is also somewhat different than other media for data collection because it can be viewed in different ways. "Mode of address," like "gaze," is a term that has been used to capture the perspective, or point of view, of a film (Ellsworth 1997). This gaze can take a variety of forms, but two are particularly salient in videotaping research participants.

The first can be characterized as a "surveilling" gaze, made ubiquitous by the presence of video cameras at banks and convenience stores. One well-known example of the surveilling gaze is the repetitive broadcast of "home" movies that have captured momentous events (e.g., the Rodney King beating). This type of gaze, which Renov and Suderburg (1996:xv) characterize as "widespread and pervasive," is ostensibly a neutral and "objective" rendering of events captured by the lens. The surveilling gaze might also be thought of as the academic gaze; it is the typical perspective from which we analyze and present our data. It is also the perspective from which we encourage others to view our data, in that academic norms strongly encourage (if not actually require) us to display our data so that our peers can judge the validity of our analysis for themselves (Goodwin 1994). This type of data might even be published and viewed by a large audience on the Internet (Redmon 2000).

In contrast with this public form of surveilling gaze, there is a more private, or "reflexive," gaze. In viewing videotaped images of ourselves, the video presents us with an "out-of-body" experience, which sometimes contrasts with one's "self" image. This can result in "shock" at viewing oneself on videotape, which Darden (1999) has noted is not unusual. This type of shock can have positive consequences, as well as negative ones. As Henley has noted, viewing video "can generate all manner of new insights as the protagonists' comments bring to light facts or connections that previously they had not thought worthy of comment. . . . [They] make connections that are new even to them" (1998:54).

More than simply recording one's image, video can allow research subjects to create their own identities. Holliday, for example, had her research subjects make video diaries using video cameras; "respondents were asked to demonstrate visually and talk about the ways in which they managed or presented their identities in different settings in their everyday lives" (2000:509). These diaries captured performative aspects of identity. From this perspective, participants are not simply passively videotaped, but create and construct their identities through the video medium.

Researcher Choices

Federal laws and regulations governing the rights of the research subjects do not specifically address the issues raised by new media. These regulations are typically implemented by universities and other research institutions. For example, the Michigan State University (MSU) University Committee on Research Involving Human Subjects offers the following statement as part of its policy:

> Every person has the right to determine what shall be done to him or her, what activities he or she shall engage in and what risks he or she will take. Consequently, research on human subjects cannot be carried out without the subjects' competent, voluntary, and informed consent. (www.msu.edu/user/ucrihs)

Within these guidelines, researchers have discretion along a variety of dimensions, including: (1) the wording of the permission to use the data for various purposes; and (2) degree of access to the raw data and the research products.

Permission

Researchers have a variety of choices in gaining consent from their subjects. At the minimum, researchers ask for permission to videotape the participants in some setting. What is rarely spelled out, however, are all the possible uses of the resulting videotaped images. Permission to record presumes permission to analyze, permission to present (to various academic audiences), permission to publish, and permission to copy and distribute the publication. This may seem obvious to us, but it may be difficult for participants to visualize themselves on display in front of an international audience of strangers. Worse yet, the particular segments we choose to present might not be the most flattering: the data might highlight embarrassing errors.

Participants who have granted permission to record their interactions may be reluctant to grant permission to publish an annotated video clip on the Internet. This raises a question about when informed consent is obtained. The conventional wisdom suggests that participants must consent before the videotaping begins. Even if the potential uses of the data are spelled out, participants have not had the opportunity to see the videotape before consenting. Researchers could potentially allow participants to review the data and then reconfirm their consent for its use.

Access to videotaped materials

Researchers also have choices about the degree of access participants will have to the research materials at each stage of production. Convenient access to these materials would provide participants with a way to monitor the use of their image over time. For example, can participants view the videotaped footage if they choose? Can they retain a copy? Can they get copies of edited research products? Of course, with videotaped data, each of these possibilities involves further expense for the researcher. Offering to provide participants with a particular version of the materials upon request might be a reasonable compromise.

Example: Videotaping in the Classroom

To make these issues more concrete, I consider student reactions to being videotaped. While not an entirely naturalistic setting, classroom interactions provide a relevant example for the purposes of this paper. For the past several years, I have videotaped student interactions in a small (twenty-five students) course on managerial negotiation skills for graduate students in a labor relations/human resources program. I had asked students to sign consent forms (see ten Have 1998 for a sample), for I had intended to include visual images from the videotapes in my teaching portfolio (Seldin 1997; Zubizarreta 1995). These examples would serve to illustrate the classroom videotaping technique as well as to provide evidence of student learning. Although technically not necessary for our UCRHS guidelines, I wanted the students to have an opportunity to "opt out" because the teaching portfolio would be viewed by others. The large majority of the students, who all said they had been previously videotaped in home videos or wedding videos, appeared comfortable with the videotaping and signed consent forms.

However, there were a handful of students who were not comfortable with the process. This discomfort manifested itself at different stages for different people. For example, a few students expressed discomfort at the appearance of the videotape equipment through jokes and body language (such as frowning or averting their gaze). In discussions with these students, one student described how realizing that the video camera would record their interaction made them feel self-conscious (the surveilling gaze). A different student expressed her discomfort after viewing the videotape, which seemed similar to the "shock" described by Darden (1999). She described "seeing" unexpected (and unspecified) things she hadn't previously seen about herself (the reflexive gaze).

These experiences suggest even when students are familiar with videotaping and consent to it, they can have second thoughts later in the process. When they are being videotaped, self-consciousness (the surveilling gaze) may create discomfort. Or, they may not have second thoughts upon being videotaped, but feel uncomfortable viewing the videotape. In a classroom setting, the reflective gaze is encouraged, because the learning objective is to build skills in interpersonal interactions. But the classroom setting is less threatening than a completely naturalistic setting might be.

Conclusion

In summary, videotaped data is (potentially) more personal and (potentially) more public than other forms of data. Anonymity is difficult if not impossible, and the surveilling and reflexive aspects of video create the possibility that the images we record may be loaded with unanticipated significance for the participants. For better or worse, the advent of the Internet has allowed academics to put these images on display in increasingly public forums. Although subjects may grant "informed consent" based on their familiarity with everyday uses of videotape, academic usage may present special concerns. To address these concerns, researchers may choose to augment the basic legal requirement of "informed consent" with increased access and involvement on their part of their subjects. Douglas Harper has argued that the "new ethnography asks for a redefinition of the relationships between the researcher and the subject. The ideal suggests collaboration rather than a one-way flow of information from subject to researcher" (1998:35). Certainly videotaping has the potential to alter the relationship and trust between the researcher and the research participant.

REFERENCES

Archer, D. 1997. Unspoken diversity: Cultural differences in gestures. *Qualitative sociology* 20(1): 79–105.

Chalfen, R. 1998. Interpreting family photography as pictoral communication. In J. Prosser, ed., *Image-based research: A sourcebook for qualitative researchers,* 214–34. Bristol, PA: Falmer Press.

Darden, G. 1999. Videotape feedback for student learning and performance: A learning-stages approach. *Journal of Physical Education, Recreation and Dance* 70(9): 40–45.

Ellsworth, E. 1997. *Teaching positions: Difference, pedagogy, and the power of address.* New York: Teachers College Press.

Gold, S. 1989. Ethical issues in visual field work. In G. Blank, J. L. McCartney, and E. E. Brent, eds., *New technology in sociology: Practical applications in research and work,* 99–109. New Brunswick, NJ: Transaction Publishers.

Goodwin, C. 1994. Professional vision. *American Anthropologist* 96(3): 606–33.

Harper, D. 1998. An argument for visual sociology. In J. Prosser, ed., *Image-based research: A sourcebook for qualitative researchers,* 24–41. Bristol, PA: Falmer Press.

Henley, P. 1998. Film-making and ethnographic research. In J. Prosser, ed., *Image-based research: A sourcebook for qualitative researchers,* 42–59. Bristol, PA: Falmer Press.

Holliday, R. 2000. We've been framed: Visualising methodology. *The sociological review* 48(4): 503–21.

Kirsch, G. 1999. *Ethical dilemmas in feminist research: The politics of location, interpretation, and publication.* Albany: State University of New York Press.

Pink, S. 2001. *Doing visual ethnography: Images, media and representation in research.* London: Sage.

Redmon, D. 2000. Mundane visual technology, digital spectacles, and ludic events. Paper presented at the International Visual Sociology Association annual meeting, Portland, Maine.

Renov, M., and E. Suderburg, eds., 1996. *Resolutions: Contemporary video practices.* Minneapolis: University of Minnesota Press.

Seldin, P. 1997. *The teaching portfolio,* 2d ed. Bolton, MA: Anker Publishing.

Simoni, S. 1996. The visual essay: Redefining data, presentation and scientific truth. *Visual Sociology* 11(2): 75–82.

Sturken, M., and L. Cartwright. 2001. *Practices of looking: An introduction to visual culture.* New York: Oxford University Press.

ten Have, Paul. 1998. *Doing conversational analysis: A practical guide.* Thousand Oaks, CA: Sage.

Zubizarreta, J. 1995. Using teaching portfolio strategies to improve course instruction. In P. Seldin, ed., *Improving college teaching,* 167–79. Bolton, MA: Anker Publishing.

The Moral Spectator: Distant Suffering in Live Footage of September 11, 2001

LILIE CHOULIARAKI
Institute of Film and Media Studies, University of Copenhagen

IN THIS PAPER, I discuss extracts from live television footage of the events of September 11, 2001, from the vantage point of discourse, that is of how the reported event "comes to mean," how it becomes intelligible through television's meaning-making operations (Chouliaraki and Fairclough 1999; Fairclough 1992, 1995; Kress and Van Leeuwen 2001; Lemke 1999; Scollon 1998). My aim is to illustrate how television images and language work to link different locales: both how they create meaning about proximity and how, in so doing, they involve the spectator in certain ethical discourses and practices. To this end, I specifically focus on the question of how television mediates the September 11 excerpts by articulating different space-times—the "here-there" and "before-after" dimensions of events. The epistemic claim that I make is that space-time articulations provide key insights into the ways in which the mediation of the events of September 11 moralizes the spectator; that is, how it shapes the ethical relationship between spectator and spectacle and, so, cultivate specific action-political dispositions.[1]

This epistemic claim derives its force from the major space-time tension in the televised mediation of September 11: the attacks in New York and Washington provisionally, but dramatically, reversed the dominant space-times of the "center," the space-time of safe viewing, and the "periphery," the space-time of dangerous living. On September 11, the "center," and only contemporary superpower, entered the space-time of dangerous living. It became the sufferer. The chronotopic analysis, then, is framed by a specific theoretical concern: how space-time articulations mediate suffering from a distance; how such articulations negotiate the relationship between a spectator, safely situated at home, and a sufferer, whose sudden, violent, and gruesome misfortune the spectator cannot directly act upon.

Suffering, here, is not merely a "phenomenological" description of events. It is primarily a conceptual device for identifying how the semiotic resources of television invest September 11 with certain "normative" discourses, of what is legitimate and fair to feel and do vis-à-vis the event. In this sense, suffering is the discursive principle that constitutes the spectator as a moral subject and, in so doing, organizes the social and political relationships of mediating September 11, of representing it from a distance (Boltanski 1999). Indeed, this shift of the "centre" to the space-time of suffering is interesting because it shows us how television capitalizes on this spectacle to articulate certain moral stances as universal, and, so, link them to hegemonic political projects, such as the "war against terror."

Such substantial links are, obviously, impossible to make under the constraints of this chapter. However, studying the mediation of September 11 for the ways it constitutes the spectator as a moral subject can usefully contribute to theorizing a key moment within a broader sociocultural process, which Mouffe (2002) calls the "moralization of politics"—that is, the contemporary reformulation and reconstitution of political rationalities and practices in discourses of ethics (Rose 1999).

My perspective on September 11 thus concerns the televisual mediation of distant suffering and its "moralizing" effects on the spectator. This focus entails a dual analytical perspective. On one hand, there is the perspective on televisual mediation as multimodal discourse, as visual and verbal meaning-making. What are we to feel when watching the plane crashing onto the twin tower, spectacularly exploding in flames, in front of our eyes? What are we to do when watching fire brigades, medical, police, and municipal forces rushing to help victims just after the Twin Towers' collapse? Or how are we to respond when confronted with President Bush's promise to "hunt down those folks who committed this act"? In the analysis, I identify the distinct role that verbal and visual media play in three television extracts, in order to see how these media represent distant locales, by inserting them in distinct space-time dimensions.

On the other hand, there is the perspective on television as an agent of moral responsibility. How does televisual discourse negotiate the spectator's relationship to the spectacle of suffering? Under which conditions can we expect the spectator to "connect" to far away events with a sense of moral involvement and, even, a will to act upon such events? In the analysis, I identify the semiotic features of the space-times available on screen, with a view to see how these organize the social relationship between the spectator and the images of distant suffering and which distinct emotions and dispositions to action they mobilize in connecting us to the locale of suffering. This perspective makes Boltanski's (1999) work on "media, morality and politics" central to my argument and analysis.

Expanding on this dual perspective, the paper unfolds in the following moves: First, I propose an analytics of televisual mediation, which takes into account the embeddedness of mediation both in multiple media (camera, graphics, telephone) and in social relations. These are what I respectively refer to as the "multimodality" and the "multifunctionality" of mediation. Second, I introduce the problematic of representing distant suffering in terms of what Boltanski calls a "politics of pity." This is a politics that aims to resolve the space-time dimension of mediation in order to establish a sense of "proximity" to the events and, so, engage the spectator emotionally and ethically. Third, I contrast three different modes (or topics) of representing suffering by reference to three live footage extracts from the Danish national channel (DR):

- Street shots of Manhattan, just after the Twin Towers' collapse;
- The summary of the day's events, with shots from the second plane collision and President Bush's first public statement;
- A long shot of the Manhattan skyline burning.

I describe each of these topics in terms of its space-time dimensions, its distinctive semiotic elements, and the affective mode and moral horizon it opens up for the spectator. In concluding, I briefly touch upon implications for the "moralization" of the spectator, involved in the topics of the representation of September 11 as distance suffering.

Toward an Analytics of Mediation

The concept of "difference"

The dual perspective on the September 11 televisual mediation as distant suffering poses a conceptual demand: we need to integrate, on one hand, the problematic of the multiplicity of media and their semiotics and, on the other, the representations of proximity and involvement in the live footage. I propose that we attempt this integration by referring to the concept of "textual difference." This means that we approach the material with a view to tracing down the relationships of "difference" implicated in the Danish television text on September 11. But what does the concept of "difference" refer to, in this context?

In all (post-) Saussurian accounts of meaning-making, including social semiotics and discourse analysis, "difference" is the principle upon which texts are produced (Chouliaraki and Fairclough 1999; Hodge and Kress 1988; Howarth 2001; Kress 1985; Kress and Van Leeuwen 2001). But we need to draw a crucial distinction between two types of difference that traverse the production of texts. On one hand, there is the semiotic medium and its meaning-making "affordances," such as, say, the camera and the privileging of the visual-pictorial vis-à-vis the telephone and the privileging of the verbal—what I term "difference within the semiotic."

On the other hand, there is the semiotic work that these "affordances" perform in concrete television practices; that is, the representations of suffering and the ethical relationships these establish between spectator and sufferer—what I term "difference outside the semiotic." This distinction is analytical, not substantial. In practice, meaning-making and its mediation are not insulated processes. They are embedded into one another. In other words, there is no link to distant locales, which is not, simultaneously, an ethical claim on how to relate to this locale. But the distinction is useful in one important way. It exemplifies and facilitates the logic of an "analytics of mediation." According to this logic, looking upon mediation in terms of both medium and semiotic production draws attention to the "moment" of their articulation. This is the "moment" in which, say, the camera and the telephone are brought together in a single practice to constitute a multimodal complex of representations about the event.

The meaning of September 11 emerges, then, neither through language (the bias in much discourse analytic approaches to the media) nor through the pictorial alone (the bias in much social theory of the media). It emerges as a configuration of meaning-making operations, whereby the shifting salience of such media bears effects upon the intelligibility of the event, the way it "comes to mean," and, thereby, on the "quality" of involvement it establishes for the spectator. I briefly refer to "difference within the semiotic," the specificity of the media that articulate television representations, and "difference outside the semiotic," the specificity of these representations in the empirical material.

Difference within the semiotic: The multimodality of mediation

On one hand, the term *difference* points to difference that is constitutive of semiotic systems themselves. For Derrida, pushing the structuralist legacy to its limit, difference is not a social but a systemic category that resides in the very organization of language (cf. Derrida 1982). The claim is that the sign, rather than being split (à la Saussure) in its sound/image form and its linguistic/conceptual content, is seen as an "instituted trace," a mark that consists of both materialities. Thus, Derrida argues, contra Saussure, that meaning-making does not privilege speech over the graphic but needs both types of sign in order to come to being. Under this dual capacity, as graphic/pictorial and as spoken/conceptual, each mark makes meaning not by presenting itself as a positivity, but by differentiating itself from other marks in altering its meaning as it travels from context to context.

The possibility of repeating, and therefore of identifying, *marks* is implied in every code, making of it a communicable, transmittable, decipherable grid that is iterable for a third party, and thus for any user in general (Derrida 1982:315).

Though Derrida has been criticized for divorcing the workings of meaning production from their social conditions of possibility (Butler 1999), the point here is that the written sign has a distinct "immediate" materiality, a permanence and a capacity for repeatability that differentiate it from speech. Similarly, in social semiotics and discourse analysis, difference within the semiotic is theorized as emanating from difference in the medium of semiosis, as multimodality. Multimodality provides a discourse analytic point of entry into the procedures by which televisual texts articulate language and visuality, orality, and writing; and the procedures by which meaning is inseparably inscribed onto these distinct media: verbal/aural, visual/pictorial, visual/graphic.

What is currently named multimodal discourse analysis marks, therefore, not a radical break from previous analytical frameworks, but an opening. It is an orientation toward the specificity of television's multiple media and toward the ways in which television knowledges and identities are related to the materiality of these media. Telephone and camera, from this point of view, are not innocent vehicles of information. They are constitutive of such information, as each one establishes relationships between spectators and the televisual message specific to the medium's own mode of articulation. For example, the telephone's aural/verbal mode enables the representation of "distant suffering" as a universal condition ("we are now all threatened"), whereas the camera's street shots of Manhattan fix "distant suffering" onto particularized representations of individuals in their local contexts.

Difference outside the semiotic: The multifunctionality of mediation

On the other hand, the term "difference" points to a direction of difference which, albeit always semiotized, lies outside meaning-making systems in power asymmetries that traverse social fields and in the historical and political relations within or between groups and populations. Specifically, the concept of discourse sets up a constitutive relationship between the two. Every move to meaning-making comes about from a position of power—power traversing and structuring the social positions available within a practice. Meaning, then, makes a claim to truth precisely from that power position which enunciates it. This is not the "truth," but always a truth effect, a truth that seeks to reconstitute and reestablish power through meaning.[2]

So, for an "analytics" of mediation, studying discourse, the logic of meaning-making, helps map out the logic of social relations of difference. By the same token, the study of power becomes the study of the social conditions of possibility for meaning-making. Difference outside the semiotic, the meaning-power dialectic, is captured in the multifunctionality of semiotic practice: the claim that social relations are seen to shape and be shaped by the meaning potential of semiotic systems. The multifunctional claim is that each text, simultaneously, represents aspects of the world, enacts social relations between participants in social practices, and cohesively and coherently connects texts with their contexts (ideational, interpersonal, and textual functions of language; Halliday 1995). In other words, studying the semiotics of mediation throws into relief the work of the text to construct reality (the proximity dimensions in the mediation of September 11) and establish interpersonal relations and identities for the participants in the practice, in this case, the moral relationship between spectator (Danish audience) and sufferer (the actors portrayed in the September 11 footage).

Analytics of mediation and discourse analysis

I consider the duality of the concept of difference, as difference outside the semiotic (the multifunctionality of mediation) and difference within the semiotic (the multimodality of mediation), to be a key claim for an analytics of mediation (Chouliaraki 2003). The concept of analytics places the study of mediation within a broader frame of critical interpretation, what Foucault calls an analytics of truth, that is, "the quest to define the conditions under which knowledge is possible, acceptable and legitimate" (Dean 1994:50).

This quest takes as its object specific practices and discourses of the present time in order to analyze how they have been constituted as fields of knowledge and how they have constituted us as moral subjects in specific power relations. In so doing, such an analytics is part of a history of the present, not an objectivist historical project which accurately recovers a teleological route from past to present. It is a project that identifies "the political and ethical issues raised by our insertion in a particular present, and by the problem of action under the limits establishing the present" (Dean 1994:51).

To study a single "moment" of this "insertion" in the present, and a prominent one such as September 11, from the perspective of how it comes to mean, raises the question of the historical and social conditions upon which the possibility for meaning-making rests. It follows that the discourse analytic project is central in an analytics of mediation, inasmuch as it seeks to show that the conditions upon which our involvement in the event, and our dispositions to act on it, rest on "truth effects," not universal and ahistorical potentialities. They are constituted both by contemporary social and political relations and rationalities and by the technologies of representation available in the mass media.

In the analytics of mediation that follows, I operate on both these views of difference. I take the September 11 television texts to be multimodal, focusing on the distinct trace of each specific medium on representations of proximity and involvement. With respect to difference within the semiotic, then, questions include:

- Are the media, brought together in the text, insulated from each other or are they combined in certain ways?
- Which possibilities for the representation of proximity and temporality are enabled (or constrained) through the use of one medium rather than another or through specific multimodal articulations?

I also take the television text to be multifunctional, focusing on the work of the text to propose a certain relationship of involvement to the spectator vis-à-vis the event. So, with respect to difference outside the semiotic, questions include:

- Which social relations are imported onto our text through these articulations of spatio-temporal orders?
- Which specific representations of moral involvement do these spatio-temporalities give rise to?

Such questions guide the analytics of mediation not only in identifying proximity and involvement in language and the visual, but also in identifying the relative salience of specific "technologies of representation" over others, in the selected extract. This is important because it is their relative salience that defines the hierarchy of representations in the multimodal environment of television and privileges certain proximities over others, in certain television texts.

Proximity and Involvement in Televisual Mediation

I have so far outlined an approach to televisual mediation as discourse, as a meaning-making practice, that takes into account the embeddedness of television both in social relations and in multiple media. An analytics so defined addresses the relationship between the spectator and the spectacle of distant suffering, by thematizing the discursive space of mediation—the space in which this relationship is represented semiotically.

For many, this confrontation of the spectator with distant suffering is the very power of television. It is the power to compress distance and bring home disturbing images and experiences that are otherwise unavailable to wide audiences. Its dominant mode of address is "You cannot say you didn't know." It hails the spectator into the subject position of the witness—the most profound moral claim that the medium has made upon contemporary social identities (Ellis 2001). Yet, the function of television as an agent of moral responsibility is a controversial matter. On the one hand, there is optimism. The sheer exposure to the suffering of the world, which television has made possible to an unprecedented degree, brings about a new sensibility to audiences, an awareness and a responsibility towards the "world out there," which had been impossible.

On the other hand, there is pessimism. The very (over-)exposure to human suffering has "anesthetizing," numbing effects upon audiences. Rather than cultivating a sensibility, the spectacle of suffering becomes domesticated by the experience of watching television. As "yet another spectacle," it is met with either indifference or discomfort, and "zapping" is the only possible reaction to it.[3] Ultimately, the debate is polarized between ungrounded optimism, the spectator's involvement to distant suffering is unconditionally possible, and unnecessary pessimism, this involvement is de facto impossible.

However, rather than attempt direct responses, we should instead set in motion the key dialectic implicit in the controversy: proximity-distance. The proposal for an analytics of mediation focuses precisely upon this dialectic as an accomplishment of discourse. Space-times, here, operate to suspend the spectator's geopolitical center, the home in its national context, and reconfigure new senses of proximity and sensibility toward suffering, which are inscribed onto the geopolitical shifts on the television screen. The assumption is that the multimodality of this text (television's camera, talk, and graphics) and their semiotic modes (verbal, visual, aural) bear a constitutive effect upon these articulations and, so, upon the production of the moral universe of the spectator. We are, then, interested in how the medium mediates suffering, by producing certain forms of ethical relating, by inserting suffering in a "politics of pity." How are we to understand this politics of pity?

Pity is not to be understood as the natural sentiment of human empathy. Rather, pity is a historically specific and politically constituted principle for relating social subjects under the capacities of a spectator and a sufferer. The former are safely removed from the unfortunate condition of the latter. As the principle for establishing a generalized concern for the distant "Other," pity intends to resolve the inherent tension in this spectator-sufferer relationship. This tension arises from the dimension of distance: "distance is a fundamental dimension of a politics [of pity] which has the specific task of *unification* which overcomes dispersion by setting up the 'durable institutions' needed to establish equivalence between spatially and temporally *local* situations" (Boltanski 1999:7; emphasis in original).

It is precisely the capacity of such a politics to rearticulate different spatio-temporal orders and establish proximity at a distance, which renders pity instrumental in contemporary conceptions of (Western) sociality and indispensable in the constitution of modern democratic collectivities. Importantly, in order for pity to act as a principle of relating, it has to act discursively, to produce meaning about suffering. The idea of a politics of pity, then, points precisely to that mobilization of semiotic resources that constitute suffering, and the spectator's involvement in suffering, in strategically distinct ways: "in order to generalise, pity becomes eloquent, recognising and discovering itself as emotion and feeling" (Boltanski 1999:6).

Let us now turn to the chronotopic analysis of the empirical material, in order to see the various ways in which pity "becomes eloquent" in the "direct link" with New York, in the summary of September 11 events and in the long shot of the Manhattan skyline.

The Moralization of the Spectator

Distant suffering in the direct link with New York

This eight-minute long sequence is a telephone link between the DR studio in Copenhagen and the Danish Embassy in New York. The anchorperson interviews the embassy consul, who describes the situation as a firsthand witness, expresses his personal feelings and evaluates the event's longer-term consequences. The visual frame is the DR studio interior. Almost halfway through, this frame is interrupted twice to move to street shots from Manhattan, before the interview ends with a frame back to the studio. The main features of the Manhattan visuals are random shots, erratic camera movements, imperfect focus and framing, and the camera lens covered in white dust.

This is clearly a projection of unstaged reality. Through these visuals, we enter the concrete, almost tangible, reality of Manhattan: the omnipresence of dust and ashes; scattered bits and pieces of brick, stone, concrete; people, covered in dust, walking or running away; professionals with helmets on, suggesting that relief work is already under way. Indeed, other shots show ambulances, fire brigades, and municipal workers setting up street barriers in the scene of suffering. These visuals are framed by the consul's vivid verbal description of vehicles howling, hospitals on emergency, and bridges closing down, as well as of authorities trying to get an overview of the situation to maximize their assistance to victims and collect information for the wider public.

Which space-time are we entering here? This involved camera moves us "right there" in the scene of suffering, "right now" as events are unfolding from moment to moment. This is a space-time of instantaneous proximity, the space-time par excellence of the witness function of the spectator and of the direct link genre. Simultaneously, however, this same projection of unstaged reality in "real time" gives us a sense of distance from the scene. This is evident, for example, in the ways in which the very technology of mediation makes itself visible to the spectator: the camera is covered in dust; the satellite transmission fails for a brief moment; there are no sound effects, which cleanses the sense of presence in the scene of action. We are called to witness suffering, yet we are aware of our own situatedness: we are watching it from home, with plenty of time to comment and analyze. We inhabit the space-time of safety, of the "center." No matter how close we get, it is not we who have to breathe the ashes or shake dust off our clothes. All we can do is keep on watching.

Obvious as this point may be, it throws into relief another fundamental tension in televisual mediation, a tension that undercuts the spectator as a moral subject, as a witness who feels compelled to act upon suffering. This is the tension between the sense of "being there" and the powerlessness to act, given the distance that separates the spectator from the "there." And it is at this point of tension that the politics of mediating distant suffering comes into focus. It is at this point that pity becomes eloquent. The logic of such eloquence is a logic of displacement. Precisely because the spectator cannot act in the scene of suffering, the politics of pity displaces the feelings the spectator may have toward the sufferer upon other actors, who are already represented in the scene of suffering. Different possibilities of displacement give rise to distinct topics of suffering, depending on the figure that organizes the spectator's feeling potential. Sentiment, if feelings are organized around the benefactor, the figure that attempts to alleviate suffering; denunciation, if feelings are organized around the persecutor, the figure that provoked suffering in the first place; the sublime, if feelings are organized around the spectacle of suffering itself, generating aesthetic appreciation of its scenic setup. Which topic of suffering is the direct link enacting?

The direct link and the topic of sentiment

There are three semiotic elements in the "direct link" that suggest that September 11 is constituted via the topic of sentiment: the figure of the benefactor, the emotionality of language, and the move toward common humanity.

The figure of the benefactor emerges primarily through the visual texts but also through the general consul's vivid description of the scene of suffering, Manhattan. The ambulances, the fire engines, the closing of the bridges and the hospital emergencies constitute a semantic field in which the "protagonist," though not explicitly named, is present as the collective agent of all such "first-aid" operations. The benefactor is thus visualized and linguistified as the resource for the relief and comfort of suffering in a context of frantic activity, at a time that takes no waiting. Emotionality seeps through the general consul's description and evaluation of the event, via constant references to his own feelings ("dramatic," "impossible to overview," "shocking," "undescribable"). Notice also the anchorperson's question, "General Consul, you are not only a political person, you are also a human being. How does it feel to witness such a terrible catastrophe?" Unlike denunciation, which is premised upon a metaphysics of justice, mobilizing indignation toward the unfairness of the event, the topic of sentiment rests precisely upon such an explication of emotion vis-à-vis the tragedy, upon a "metaphysics of interiority." As Boltanski puts it, it is not enough for the spectator to report the suffering, but "at the same time he [*sic*] must also return to himself, go inwards and allow himself to hear what his heart tells him" (1999:81).

The consul functions, in this topic, as the witness of a suffering that fills his heart with empathy. Finally, the move towards common humanity comes about when the consul is called to evaluate the consequences of the event. Here, spectator and sufferer are joined in a common fate, exemplified in the consul's shift from a descriptive "they" (the sufferers) and through a personal "I" to an all-inclusive "we," referring to the globe as a whole. The future of the globe is here scripted onto a gloomy scenario ("we are entering a new phase," "we don't know how it will escalate," "worry, deep anxiety, a terrible, terrible, terrible event with deep political consequences for all of us"). What we have here is a crucial leap for the topic of sentiment from the spectator's particularity toward a contemplation of universal values. This leap, Boltanski's "imagination of the heart," also installs the moral horizon of this topic: to empathize with the tragedy of the other as a human being, and to reflect upon this suffering as, ultimately, part of our common fate as human beings. Indeed, the topic of sentiment "consists in 'feeling oneself in one's fellow man,' in recognising, in a 'gesture of humanity,' the common interest which links the one it touches to others" (Boltanski 1999:92).

The summary of events and the topic of denunciation

This two-minute text was put together to provide Danish spectators with a chronology of events up to the present moment and was inserted in the flow of the live footage in regular intervals. It is primarily a visual text capitalizing upon the enormous news value of some of the September 11 shots. It begins with shots from the first burning tower, then the second plane crash, cutting to Bush's first public statement from Georgia, before showing the two towers' collapse; it then moves to Washington and the Pentagon burning. The verbal text includes no commentary, no evaluation. There are only time and space details of the events, information on the number and route of flights as well as the passenger numbers on board. Bush's statement is not quoted or reproduced but, predictably, directly shown. In terms of space-time, we are at a space of omnipresence, everywhere where the camera takes us (Manhattan, Atlanta, Washington), at the time of immediate past (that same morning of September 11).

Which feeling potential is activated here? I point to three elements that semiotically constitute September 11 in terms of the topic of "denunciation": the figure of the persecutor, the aura of strict objectivity, and the claim to justice.

The persecutor is faceless and will remain largely invisible even though, eventually, he will be given a face. Nonetheless, the persecutor as the causal agent of suffering is already evoked in this text. The semiotic procedure is visual editing. The second plane crash, a shot with filmic spectacularity that the camera fixed upon for several seconds after the plane's explosion on the tower and without verbal text, cuts directly onto Bush's first public statement from Georgia. The presidential address begins by condensing the national sentiment, "today we've had a national tragedy" and locating the source of evil "in an apparently terrorist attack against our country." The crash visuals and the verbal text are woven together in an intertextual link, which evokes the figure of a persecutor and organizes the spectator's feeling potential around the cruelty and unfairness of the persecutor's act (terrorist attack).

Indeed, the evocation of the persecutor is here closely related to another one of "denunciation's" properties, the appeal to justice. This is formulated in the concluding part of the address, in the promise 'to hunt down those folks who committed this act.' Here, the president is articulating the collective expectation to identify and confront the persecutor. This claim to justice entails an "eye for an eye" logic of reiteration, which plays upon feelings of anger, indignation, and revenge. Unlike the topic of sentiment, denunciation is not grounded on emotions based on empathy or subjective involvement. The emotional potential of denunciation is grounded upon the rational assessment of facts: "two planes crashed on the WTC in an, apparently, terrorist attack against our country." It is regulated by coordinated and calculated actions: "I have talked to the vice president, the governor of New York, the director of the FBI." In this manner, the aura of strict objectivity, which marks the voiceover of the summary of events, also traverses the presidential statement. Both texts manage the shift from indignation (the national sentiment) to denunciation (the appeal to justice) via a careful backgrounding of the personal emotionality of the speaker, the effacement of the speaker. "The discourse of denunciation, thus, appears at the same time indignant and meticulous, emotional and factual" (Boltanski 1999:68).

To sum up, the extract as a whole inserts the spectator in a space-time where the witnessing of suffering is not from a "real space-real time" perspective, activating empathy with the sufferer. Rather, the witnessing of suffering takes place from successively alternating positions of witnessing the escalation of the attack. It is from the standpoint of "aperspectival objectivity," as Boltanski puts it (1999:24). The moral horizon of this space-time is undercut by a metaphysics of justice, the promise to restore justice by hunting down the persecutors and, so, it contains the promise of practical action in terms of the logic of reiteration. It is this disposition to act practically upon the suffering, which is, perhaps, most transparently related to the massive military and political alliance that a month later culminated in the "war against terror" in Afghanistan.

The Manhattan skyline long shot and the sublime

This is an eight-minute shot of the Manhattan skyline burning. It is unusually long in duration for television's tempo and shot from a distance. We are given plenty of time to study visually this overview of the scene of suffering. The verbal voiceover is the talk of the Danish expert panel speculating on possible causes, commenting on international reactions, and evaluating political consequences. This talk, like the visual, distances us from the specificities of the lived environment and functions as a "macro" perspective on the history and politics of the event. Indeed, both visual and verbal texts take us away from the "here and now" of the direct link, as well as from the everywhere in immediate past of the summary. We are now situated in the space-time of what we may call a "tableau vivant"—a painting depicting "still action." Like in perspectival painting, proximity is total here; you can see everything there is to see, and the temporality is an eternal present time without contingency or evolution. Let us look at three semiotic elements that constitute the suffering from this space-time: the long shot and iconic meaning, the contrast between the beautiful and the sublime, and the rhetorical tropes of "anachronism" and "anatopism."

Long shots universalize. They abstract from indexical, context-specific meaning and foreground the iconic. Indeed, this image works generically, though obviously there are particularizing elements (such as, for some, the New York City skyline). In its generic form, as an icon, the long shot represents one space, the contemporary metropolis of high buildings, modern architecture, and dense mass volume. The frame centers on the fumes covering the city, and, simultaneously, it couples two image themes onto one another: the gray sky and the clear turquoise seawater. In aesthetic terms, the camera couples the horror and awe of the sublime with the domesticity and friendliness of the beautiful. These two elements visually cohere on the basis of a set of equivalential contrasts: landscape (land in smoke but the water peaceful), color (gray-turquoise), and activity (obscure, suggestive on land but explicit and readily available to vision in the water). Indeed, it appears as if the boat activity is oblivious to, rather than interacting with, the city mayhem. In this tableau vivant, the September 11 spectacle lends itself to aesthetic appreciation. It is the visual medium that brings the city close to the spectator, by establishing a relationship of contemplation to it. The feeling potential of this contemplative proximity is displaced neither onto the benefactor nor onto a persecutor. It stays with us as an experience of aesthetic indulgence. This is what Boltanski discusses as the sublimation effect of representing distant suffering, an effect which constitutes aesthetic pleasure in a double moment: "an initial movement of horror, which would be confused with fear of the spectator was not . . . personally sheltered from danger . . . is transformed by a second movement which appropriates and thereby appreciates and enhances what an ordinary perception would have rejected" (Boltanski 1999:121).

Even though the aesthetic register of this topic entails the possibility of a "radical rejection of pity" (Boltanski 1999:132), in fact, the sublime does moralize the spectator, but in a different way from the previous two topics. This happens through the use of other media that frame the visual. Indeed, if the camera abstracts from the particular to project an aestheticized view of the city as an icon, the television graphics and the voiceover particularize this abstraction.[4] The graphic message on screen, the recurrent "New York" bar, anchors the image of the burning metropolis onto the temporality of the present an open sense of present time as unfolding actuality. This semiotic combination brings into focus the crucial inversion of the "center-periphery" relationship that September 11 performed. New York, the invincible center, is in mayhem. The visual thematization of the "center" as a sufferer, a novel and "paradoxical" representation, further allows for a couple of interesting inversions in this topic: an inversion in time, "anachronism," and an inversion in space, "anatopism" (Bakhtin 1986).

On the axis of time, the "unfolding actuality" of the bars combined with the "eternal presence" of the camera's "tableau vivant" evoke a new temporal context for the representation of suffering in the centre, that of Pearl Harbor in World War II. The effect of anachronism is precisely to produce, for events present, a past reference, thus linking the two, as repetitions or mutations, in the eternal flow of history: is this a 1941 déjà vu? The "depth" thus attributed to the present event contextualizes it in a discourse of the national past as a recurrent motive that, yet again, requires a response—though the nature of the response, retaliation as then, or diplomacy, is an open matter.

On the axis of space, the graphic specification of the scene of suffering as "New York" combined with the long shot on the burning skyline evokes a new spatial context for the representation of suffering in the "center," that of any Western metropolis. The effect of "anatopism" is to establish equivalence among disparate locales, thus producing a new configuration of possible connections among them. Here, "New York" as the sufferer becomes a crucial signifier, connecting the space of dangerous living with the space of safety, inhabited by other cities of the "center": if this is possible there, which place comes next? The spectator engages with this space as a potential sufferer herself. Anatopism, then, introduces into this "sublimated" representation of distant suffering a new dimension of proximity, "proximity as vulnerability."

In sum, the complex space-time of the sublime, with its anachronic and anatopic effects, construes a moral horizon radically different from either of the previous topics. At the absence of a benefactor or a persecutor, and, so, free of the urgent obligation with which these figures engage the spectator in emotion and commitment, the sublime seems to rest upon the spectator's reflexive contemplation on the scene of suffering. Reflexive contemplation can be understood as an arrangement that turns this scene into a passive object of the spectator's gaze, and the spectator into a gazing subject aware of her own act of seeing, a "meta-describer" (Boltanski 1999:19). Crucial, now, for the moralization of the spectator is the fact that this arrangement does not entail redemptive sympathy, empathetic or indignant, but sympathy distantiated from its object: "The beauty extracted from the horrific through this process of sublimation of the gaze, which is 'able to transform any object whatever into a work of art,' *owes nothing therefore to the object*" (Boltanski 1999:127; emphasis added).

The implication of the nonobligation to the suffering object is this: the spectator is given the option to make links between September 11 and other temporal and spatial contexts, and so to evoke points of contact with the past and with the rest of the world. Though both the links performed here belong to predictable discourses of Western history and politics, it is crucial to notice that the space for a reflective and analytical exercise is opened up. It is perhaps not by chance that, in the expert-panel voiceover, what was subjected to the most critical scrutiny, during those eight minutes of the long shot, was the concept of sympathy ("sympati") itself. September 11 was discussed as an opportunity for the United States to gain a long-lost sympathy all over the world. The superpower, far from invincible, has its own vulnerabilities; this sympathy, however, is conditioned upon the superpower's mode of response to the event. Retaliation, it was said, would put such sympathy under strain. It is in the topic of the sublime, then, that the certainties of common humanity (sentiment) and of world alliance (denunciation) become explicitly formulated and critically evaluated.

Conclusion

In this paper, I have attempted to show how a politics of pity constitutes the spectator of September 11 as a moral subject; how pity becomes eloquent in modalities of emotion and dispositions to action, through the multimodal and multifunctional semiotics of television. Crucial, in this process, is the articulation of space-times—the management of the distance that separates the spectator from the scene of suffering. We saw that the discursive logic of mediating suffering, a logic of displacement, inserts suffering into a broader universe of space-times, and, in doing so, contextualizes it in different topics: sentiment, denunciation, the sublime. Each topic is articulated through a combination of different media, the salience of which varies by topic. The topic of sentiment, in the direct link, relies on the telephone and the visual shots from Manhattan, construing a space-time of instantaneous proximity for the representation of suffering. Denunciation, the topic in the summary of events combines high value visuals with brief voiceover, construing a space-time of omnipresence in the immediate past. Finally, the sublime, in the long shot of Manhattan, prioritizes camera work and establishes a relationship of visual contemplation with the Manhattan skyline—a "tableau vivant" of the scene of suffering. It is via the insertion of suffering in distinct space-times, and the social relationships these space-times evoke, that certain moral horizons and orientations to the "Other" became possible, acceptable, and legitimate in the televised spectacle of September 11.

And it is in this sense that space-times work as what Bakhtin calls "conditions of representability" of suffering, as chronotopes of suffering that carry specific ethical values.

But which specific representations of suffering do these space-times, both within the scene of suffering and between the scene and the spectator, make possible? Whereas the topic of sentiment moralizes the spectator by inscribing her onto a relationship of empathy with the sufferer, the topic of denunciation moralizes the spectator by inscribing her onto a relationship of indignation against the perpetrator of evil. Each topic constitutes these relationships on the basis of a specific metaphysics, a universal discourse that stabilizes the representation of suffering upon a specific truth claim. In sentiment, a metaphysics of interiority grounds the moral horizon of the spectator upon a claim to universal humanity that is evoked through a sense of being there "right now." In denunciation, a metaphysics of justice grounds this moral horizon upon a claim to the objective access to truth that is attained through an omnipresence in the immediate past, or a perspective "from nowhere."

Finally, what is the effect that each "topic" has upon the representation of suffering in September 11? Their effect is, predictably, that of significant exclusions. Each topic attempts to close off the possibility of representing suffering in alternative ways. Instantaneous proximity articulates a discourse of universal humanity, by excluding the possibility of historicizing the position of the sufferer in the field of contemporary political relations. In emphasizing the human dimension of suffering, it suppresses the political specificity of, and hence a cause-effect reasoning upon, this suffering as suffering from the center. Aperspectival objectivity articulates a discourse of impartial truth, by excluding the possibility of attributing justice outside a logic of reiteration. In tightly binding the immediate truth of terror with the promise for hunting down (and, ultimately, counterattack), it suppresses other possibilities of alternative political, diplomatic or military action.

The third topic of suffering, sublimation, installs a relationship of reflexive contemplation with the spectacle of suffering itself. It dispenses with the figures of benefactor and persecutor and, in so doing, it considers the suffering to be neither heartbreaking nor unfair. Rather, it invites the spectator to indulge in the aesthetic pleasure of a "tableau vivant," the visual image of the Manhattan skyline. Thus, the moralization of the spectator takes on a different twist. The rhetorical tropes of anachronism and anatopism open up a continuity-discontinuity tension, either in time (World War II) or in space (any Western metropolis): how related is the past event to the current one? Which is the connection between this city and others? The voiceover capitalizes on this "openness" to contextualize the event in terms of the conditions of possibility upon which sympathy toward the United States can be sustained or not. Though none of these elements fixes the event within an explicitly historical and political discourse, the "sublime" entails the seeds of a representation of September 11 that foregrounds its historicity. Historicity is here used in the Bakhtinian sense, where the present is not a derivative of what went on before, but a profoundly unfinalizable process, that contains multiple potentials: no retrodiction or prediction can definitely determine the nature, causality, or consequentiality of the event. The invitation to contemplate the spectacle is, then, not only an aestheticizing move that divorces the spectacle from history and politics. It is, perhaps, a potentially rehistorizing and repoliticizing move that offers the spectator a distance and a temporality of reflection.

Of course, my description of the three topics does not aspire to capture the full dynamic of the September 11 live footage, as it unfolds in time—the "eventness" of this event, in Bakhtin's words. In reality, none of the topics is able to bear the weight of representing September 11 alone. All three alternate, fuse and complement each other, constantly recontextualizing the event in a universe of "heterochronies" and "heterotopias." This is important. In the face of events like this one, with a complex and massive impact upon all, we, as spectators, need to engage multiply with its multiple "truths." Indeed, to humanize, to denounce, and to reflect. The point is rather to explicate and theorize the conditions of possibility upon which our different engagements with the September 11 spectacle rest. Looking upon such a spectacle from the perspective of how it comes to mean thematizes the claim that our knowledge of the event, our emotions about it, and our dispositions to act upon it are "truth effects," not universal and ahistorical potentialities. Though by no means any less real for that, their status as effects foregrounds, rather, their historical specificities and their political complicities. I regard this critical project, what I earlier referred to as an analytics of truth, crucial for our own practices as ethical subjects, for reflecting upon the possibilities we have to think, feel, and act politically in contemporary times—especially in these post–September 11 times.

NOTES

1. In this paper, I draw on Bakhtin's approach to space-time analysis, what he terms "chronotopic analysis." The term *chronotope* captures the historical, context-specific constructedness of space and time dimensions and points to their analysis, "*chronotopic analysis,*" as a way of examining the basic frames in which our everyday experience is contextualized—and conceptualized: "In chronotopic analysis, time and space are regarded 'not as "transcendental" but as forms of *the most immediate reality*' (1981:85; emphasis added). As such, space-times are not explicitly thematized in our consciousness; they are not visibly present in the representation of events. Rather, they act as "conditions of representability" of events; they structure and organize such events "from within," and, so, their analysis gives us insight into the social and cultural implications of forms of representation (see Morson and Emerson 1990 for a theoretical discussion on the "chronotope"; see also Chouliaraki 1999 and Ekecrantz 1997 for analytical applications of the term on media texts).
2. This has been one of Foucault's basic claims and a major premise for the poststructuralist anchoring of discourse analysis in critical research, e.g., Morrow and Brown (1994), Fraser (1997), Torfing (1999). For a discussion, see Chouliaraki (2002).
3. In media studies, see particularly Tomlinson (1999) for the question of how the reconfiguration of space-times can effect a closing of moral distance: "How are people to think of themselves as belonging to a global neighbourhood? What does it mean to have a global identity, to think and act as a 'citizen of the world'—literally as a cosmopolitan?" (1999:184). See also Thompson (1995) and Mafessoli (1996) for a similar understanding of the relationship between "deterritorialization" and the spectator as a moral figure; and see Robins (1994) for the opposite view that the media "anesthetize" or numb the spectator's ethical sensibilities.
4. By graphics, I here refer to CNN-type information bars that alternate messages in the lower end of the screen. These include "New York," "Pentagon in flames," and "One more plane crash reported in Pennsylvania."

REFERENCES

Bakhtin, M. 1981. *The dialogic imagination.* Ed. M. Holquist. Austin: University of Texas Press.

——. 1986. *Speech genres and other late essays.* Ed. C. Emerson and M. Holquist. Austin: University of Texas Press.

Boltanski, L. 1999. *Distant suffering: Morality, media and politics.* Cambridge: Cambridge University Press.

Butler, J. 1997. *Excitable speech: A politics of the performative.* London: Routledge.

Chouliaraki, L. 1999. Media discourse and national identity: Death and myth in a news broadcast. In R. Wodak and C. Ludwig, eds., *Challenges in a changing world: Issues in critical discourse analysis,* 37–62. Vienna: Passagen Verlag.

——. 2002. The contingency of universality: Thoughts on discourse and realism. *Social Semiotics* 10(2): 83–114.

——. 2003. *Discourse and culture.* London: Sage.

Chouliaraki, L., and N. Fairclough. 1999. *Discourse in late modernity: Rethinking critical discourse analysis.* Edinburgh: Edinburgh University Press.

Dean, M. 1994. *Critical and effective histories: Foucault's methods and historical sociology.* London: Routledge.

Derrida, J. 1982. *Writing and difference.* Chicago: Chicago University Press.

Ekecrantz, J. 1997. Journalism's 'discursive events' and sociopolitical change in Sweden 1925–87. *Media, Culture & Society* 19:3.

Ellis, J. 2001. *Seeing things: Television in the age of uncertainty.* London: I. B. Tauris.

Fairclough, N. 1992. *Discourse and social change.* Cambridge: Polity Press.

——. 1995. *Media discourse.* London: Edward Arnold.

Fraser, N. 1997. *Justice interruptus: Critical reflections on the post-socialist condition.* London: Routledge.

Halliday, M. 1985. *Introduction to functional grammar.* London: Edward Arnold.

Hodge, R., and G. Kress. 1988. *Social semiotics.* Cambridge: Polity Press.

Howarth, D. 2001. *Discourse.* Philadelphia: Open University Press.

Kress, G. 1985. *Linguistic processes in sociocultural practice.* Oxford: Oxford University Press.

Kress, G., and T. Van Leeuwen. 2001. *Multimodal discourse: The modes and media of contemporary communication.* London: Edward Arnold.

Lemke, J. 1999. Multiplying meaning: Visual and verbal semiotics in scientific text. In J. R. Martin and R. Veel, eds., *Reading science,* 87–113. London: Routledge.

Mafessoli, M. 1996. *The contemplation of the world: Figures of community style.* Minneapolis: University of Minnesota Press.

Morrow, R., and D. Brown. 1994. *Critical theory and methodology.* London: Sage.

Morson, G., and C. Emerson. 1990. *Mikhail Bakhtin: Creation of a prosaics.* Stanford, CA: Stanford University Press.

Mouffe, C. 2002. For an agonistic public sphere. Public lecture, Centre of Public Administration, University of Copenhagen.

Robins, K. 1994. Forces of consumption: From the symbolic to the psychotic. *Media, Culture and Society* 16:449–68.

Rose, N. 1999. *Powers of freedom: Reframing political thought.* Cambridge: Cambridge University Press.

Scollon, R. 1998. *Mediated discourse as social interaction.* London: Longman.

Thompson, J. B. 1995. *The media and modernity.* Cambridge: Polity Press.

Tomlinson, J. 1999. *Globalisation and culture.* London: Sage.

Torfing, J. 1999. *New theories of discourse: Laclau, Mouffe, and Zizek.* London: Blackwell.

Ethnography of Language in the Age of Video: "Voices" as Multimodal Constructions in Some Contexts of Religious and Clinical Authority

JOEL C. KUIPERS
George Washington University

HOW DO PEOPLE PROCESS, manage, and control information while speaking? When engaged in communicative interaction, people can and do rely on a wide variety of acoustic (Feld 1984), visual (Goodwin 1999; Keating 1998, 1999; Kendon 1990), and even gustatory (Kuipers 1993) information sources, not just linguistic ones. Video data can be especially helpful in demonstrating that actors are responding to a rich variety of stimuli in any given communicative event. Faced with the growing availability of video data, some scholars have argued that gestural, proxemic, and other forms of nonverbal communication are reflections of the communicative intents produced in language; others argue, in contrast, that visually based, nonverbal forms of communication play a primary role, with some even arguing that gesture is primary, while spoken language is derivative in an evolutionary sense (McNeill 2000).

Rather than debating the primacy of one form of data over another, I explore in this essay a form of ethnographic holism by placing spoken discourse in a multimodal context (Howes 1991; Kress and Van Leeuwen 2001). The importance of the visual modality is becoming increasingly apparent because of the near universal availability and increasing use of video-based methods of recording ethnographic and linguistic data. Although the title of this paper may sound a bit apocalyptic—the phrase "age of video" perhaps implying a radical break from earlier "ages"—in fact I want to suggest that an ethnography of language in our current "era" is not so different from the ethnography of earlier generations, but it is, and must become, more multimodal. At the same time, I also want to point out that for the ethnographer, video does not necessarily provide more data; instead, it forces us to confront ethnographic subjects as actors who are managing information in a multimodal environment. These subjects may actually be attending to *fewer* things than we might have suspected if we were relying on acoustic information alone. By proposing an ethnographic perspective to discourse as a form of information management, I hope to develop a way of examining and appreciating not only the formal conventions by which people communicate, but also the diverse ways in which actors function in multimodal environments as they construct, organize, manipulate identities, statuses, roles, power, and authority (Kuipers 1990, 1993). Specifically, I want to give some examples of the management of *voices* not only in a contemporary medical setting close to home but also a more exotic setting in eastern Indonesia, and discuss briefly how video contributes to these analysis.

Let me underscore the phrase *information management.* By using the term *information,* I want to move beyond a preoccupation with meaning in a narrow linguistic sense, and focus on the communication of knowledge by any modality; by *management,* I want to suggest a focus on actor-oriented control over time, sequential patterning, unfolding scenarios, and temporal developments. This widening of perspective, I would argue, is partly required by the new media to which we are exposed and now also have available to us. Video, for ethnographers, is a particularly important one. It is a medium in which, as cultural critic Fredric Jameson (1991:76) has put it, the "ultimate seam between time and space is the very locus of the form." That is: video provides not only a rich audio visual snapshot (and all the various simultaneous sensory inputs), it also places that snapshot in the context of the various meanings attached to the sequential flow of those snapshots over time. Thus we can use a phrase like *information management* to understand this seam between space and time in video.

How is the agency of this "management system" distributed? Cognitive approaches focus on the role of the brain in information management over time. Wallace Chafe's book *Discourse, Consciousness, and Time* (1994) is a good example of this. Though I believe the cognitive approach tells us part of the story, there is another part, a part that comes from an ethnographic perspective. This approach examines the management of the relations between discursive forms and their social functions in culturally defined situations. One of the things we learn from this perspective is an appreciation of the diversity of styles, in relation to management of identities, which in turn are interpreted in various ways in diverse value systems.

From within this ethnographic perspective, perhaps the most well known is that of the ethnography of speaking: it arose in the 1960s and focused on the analysis of relatively stable communities and genres according to a rigorous model. According to this model, "an adequate ethnographic description of the culture of a particular society presupposes a detailed analysis of the communicative system and of the culturally defined situations in which all relevant distinctions in that system occur" (Conklin 1962). Following our multimodal perspective, one may extend the analysis of *communicative* systems to *information* systems.

This ethnography-of-speaking perspective resulted in many detailed analyses of particular genres of communicative expression, descriptions of stylistic variation, and also resulted in some new genres of academic publication that sought to describe the way of life of a culture from the standpoint of language (Bauman and Sherzer 1989; Kuipers 1990; Urban 1991). That is, particular moments of discourse were shown to fit together into larger cultural patterns. Such integral systems are increasingly difficult to find. More recently this model has been extended to develop a theory of change, mostly in the framework of work on language ideologies, and how this affects the transformation of local communities, as evidenced in form function relations (Kuipers 1998; Schieffelin, Woolard, and Kroskrity 1998; Silverstein 1998).

Another promising line of inquiry is based on a model of artifact-mediated and object-oriented action, so-called activity theory associated with Vygotsky (Vygotsky and Cole 1978), Luria (Luria and Wertsch 1981), and Leont'ev (1978), who in turn were influenced by Bakhtin (1981), Voloshinov (Voloshinov, Matejka, and Titunik 1973) and others. More recently scholars such as James Wertsch (1985), Jean Lave (Lave and Wenger 1991), and Michael Cole (1996) have developed very interesting activity-based models of ethnography of language and learning that examine how individuals integrate stimuli not only from language but also other sorts of symbols in the context of action. It offers a nonreductionist and holistic approach to ethnographers interested in the dynamic pluralism of communicative activities.

One of the problems I would like to discuss using this ethnographic approach is the concept of voice. Examined with video, it is a multimodal, sight-and-sound phenomenon, not just an acoustic one. By voice, I do not mean it in the traditional grammatical sense (active voice, passive voice) or voice in the purely auditory or acoustic sense, but voice in the broader textual sense of an answer to the question: Who is speaking? As such, voice can be considered a linguistic construction of a social persona (Keane 1999). This is perhaps similar in some ways to the uses of voice in the work of Voloshinov (Voloshinov, Matejka, and Titunik 1973) and Bakhtin (1981), although I will be applying it to interactional data, and examining its functions in concrete social activities, much as in Goffman's concept of "footing" (1974).

As I use it here, the term *voice* includes, but is analytically distinct from, reported speech, because the way in which voices are marked off linguistically is not always with reports of speech; in fact quite often they are loose paraphrases or even, as Deborah Tannen points out, "constructed dialogue" (Tannen 1989). Some voices are not really quotes, as in the case of one patient who said "I'm like, 'whoa.'" The patient in that case is creating a voice of her inner self, a self who says "Whoa." It is not an actual utterance, but rather something that might have been said. Nor can the linguistic construction of social personae be always called "constructed dialogue," because one of the ways of creating a voice is using a "reading voice." The "reading voice"—although it answers the question of "who is speaking?"—is not part of a dialogue in any ordinary sense of the word. Voice in this sense resembles Goffman's concept of "footing" insofar as it signals a participation framework (1974).

The overall analytical strategy is to link details of linguistic form with shifts in speaking positions, identities, and alignments with social structure. I want to demonstrate some examples of how the management of voices is a richly collaborative (although not necessarily harmonious) multimodal activity, engaging both sound and sight in an integrated and often skillful way, particularly in contexts in which issues of identity, power, and authority are at stake. The import and export of voices—their flow in and out of a stretch of discourse—is a complex and social activity. I begin with some background on my own work in Indonesia, and then suggest—perhaps somewhat presumptuously—that the general problem of how voices are managed might have some relevance to the issues facing people engaged in a rather different kind of ritual activity—the verbal exchanges between patients and clinicians in psychiatric interviews in suburban Washington, D.C.

Voices from the Weyewa Highlands of Sumba, Eastern Indonesia

When I arrived on the island of Sumba in the summer of 1978, I soon realized that the tradition of couplets that I had come to study was much more than simply poetry (Kuipers 1990). On this island located about 250 miles east of Bali, this distinctive style of speaking was used not for aesthetic contemplation but for all sorts of ritual performances, from prayers to politics and healing. Although highly accomplished individual speakers spontaneously drew from a stock of about three thousand fixed and conventional couplets and assembled them according to the rules of sacred genres—which often required that a performance be fluent, eloquent, and last all night, in fact this ritual speech was not regarded as a virtuoso demonstration of individual competence but the "voice of the ancestors" *(li'i marapu)*. As such, it was regarded as the centerpiece of their indigenous religious and political system. The rituals, feasts, and performances associated with ritual speech were the very enactment of that tradition: that is, the "voice of the ancestors." This is important, because as the Indonesian government pressed them to abandon their traditional ways, they sought recognition for the voice of the ancestors. Their efforts have so far failed, and the indigenous form of religious practice is rapidly declining (Kuipers 1998).

Voice *(li'i)* has been an integral concept for the indigenous Sumbanese cultures (Kapita 1976; Kuipers 1990). Long ago, in the Weyewa highlands in the western part of the island, where most of my data were gathered, the ancestors gave their living descendants their "word, voice" *(li'i)*. The lexeme *li'i* exhibits a lively tension between two related senses, one emphasizing collective moral obligation and the other focused on short term and individualized performance. In the first sense, *li'i* refers to a message, mandate, a promise, and a duty; it is a temporally structured network of (deferred) obligations. For example, a common way of describing a promise to exchange something in the future is *katukku li'i,* "to plant the word"—a reference to the customary act of erecting a pole to signify the declaration of a promise. More generally, *li'i inna, li'i ama* "words of the Mother, words of the Father" refers to a set of (verbal) instructions handed down from generation to generation, and which descendants should fulfill. In the broadest sense, *li'i* refers to "Weyewa culture": all the customary, changeless and ancient obligations and responsibilities that those words engender.

Li'i also refers to the "voice" as a more individualizing feature of oral performance. As I have pointed out elsewhere,

> this sense of "voice" often assumes an audience, and the highlighting of aspects of delivery: it may be described with adjectives such as "hoarse," "thin," "powerful," "broken," "flowing," "soft," and "deep." In this sense, the "voice" is individualizing, particularizing, and reflects a distinct speaking personality. For instance, when a ritual spokesmen presents his point of view in a ceremony, it is called "to put forth the voice" *(tauna li'i)*. "Voice" also has to do with the features of performance organization, such as rhythm, melody and harmony. The verses of a song, for instance, are called "steps of the voice." If ritual actors fail to coordinate their performances properly, in

either rhythm or meaning, the offense is represented as a vocal problem: "their voices were out of step;" or "their voices were like untuned gongs." (Kuipers 1990)

The tension between individuating and collective senses of *li'i*—as promise and performance—comes together in the Weyewa "ritual speech" *(panewe tenda)* (Fox 1988). When descendants—inevitably—neglect the promises they made to their ancestors, misfortune is believed to ensue. Sumbanese then hire specialist performers of ritual speech, who (1) identify the angry spirit through divination, (2) reenact the promise through a placation rite *(zaizo)*, and (3) fulfill the promise through one of a number of "rites of fulfillment."

In this system, the initial, individuating senses of "voice" involve more visual interpretation. When misfortune takes place, diviners assume that something marginal, wayward, and deviant has occurred. As they try to answer the questions "What are the spirits saying to us?" and "Who is saying it?" they are thus looking for individualized voices. They do not assume that relatively unpredictable misfortune is the collective will of the ancestors; rather it is the voice of an individual, angry spirit.

Thus it is interesting that it is at the initial phases of the ritual process of atonement that visual interpretation is most crucial. Diviners use visual means to assist them in their verbal process of questioning the spirits to identify the angry ones who are responsible for the misfortune. In figure 14.1, the diviner is dramatically reaching along the length of a spear to determine if the spirits agree with his statements, depending on whether he is able to reach the tip of the spear or not.

These visual cues are closely watched by the onlookers as evidence of the truth or falsehood of utterances. At this stage in the ritual the answer to the question "Who is speaking?" is answered visually as much as acoustically. The diviner also

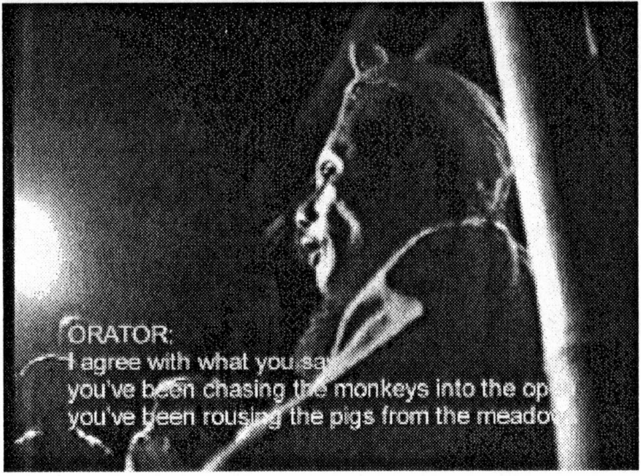

Figure 14.1. In this still frame taken from a videotape, the orator speaks without focusing his gaze in any single direction. Ultimately, his audience consists of an unseen group of "ancestral spirits" *(marapu)*. Orator: I agree with what you say/You've been chasing the monkeys into the open/You've been rousing the pigs from the meadow.

constructs the voices of other participants using quotation expressions in the Weyewa language called locutives (Kuipers 1992).

In the placation rite, or *zaizo,* there is less of a visual focus, and indeed the acoustic focus is somewhat diffuse as well. In these all-night-long ritual speech performances, a singer *(a zaizo)* is accompanied by a four-piece gong orchestra and two drums. The drums *(bendu)* and gongs *(talla)* are given ritual names and are said to convey the singer's voice of reaffirmation up to the ancestral spirits living unseen in the attic reliquary of the house. The singer in turn conveys the voices of the orators *(a tauna lii)* and the support of the ululators *(a pakallaka)*. In addition, the orators often convey the voices of other parties—both present and absent—through reported speech.

In the final stage of the ritual process of atonement—rites of fulfillment—the goal of the event is to express unity among the descendants through a common "voice." The focus is on the verbal expression of unity through unison singing of a song that conveys their commitment to the ancestors. There is little or no reported speech and little visual evidence suggesting an ancestral voice (such as the evidence of divination or omen). Even gongs are absent in the final stage of these rites, because the gongs and drums represent their own "voices," thus detracting from the sense of unity.

Among the voices one can distinguish in a *zaizo* performance are:

1. the "ancestors" *(marapu)*—the gongs and drums are heirlooms from ancestors and they are the voices of intermediaries conveying the word to the ones higher up.
2. the singer *(a zaizo)*
3. the orator *(a tauna lii)*
4. the "ululators" *(a pakallaka)*. It is interesting to note that the ululators only participate through overlap, and use of simultaneity. This is not viewed as an interruption, but as a form of complementarity.

Formal Ways of Differentiating Voices

There are several formal ways in which social personae are differentiated in ritual speech performances:

1. reported speech markers
   a. the root *lu-* inflected for person in various ways
   b. other formal reported speech markers
2. the distinctive pitch and rhythms of ululation, zaizo singing, and ritual oratory
3. channels: drums and gongs themselves convey the voices of the ancestors in this context

In these rituals, by identifying, enumerating, and distinguishing the names of various individuals within the clan, and by expressing, through ululation, the voices of the women, a sort of census of the totality of the community of voices is symbolically constructed. The drum, the gong, the different ritual speakers, and the ululators all

Table 14.1.
Voices and modalities in the Weyewa ritual process of atonement

Ritual Stage	Goal	Acoustic Voices	Visual Voices	Event Focus	Reported Speech
Divination	Identify broken promise, offended spirit	Diviner's voice	The Spear, omens	The spear activity (visual)	Very frequent
Placation	Reaffirm promise	Singer, Orator, Ululators, Gongs, Drums	Omens (pig, chicken)		Present
Fulfillment	Fulfill Promise	Singer and audience in unison	Omens	Singing activity (acoustic)	Nearly absent

build up a sense of the totality of the community, and eventually an acoustic image of unity is constructed. Thus gradually over the course of the ritual, signaled by a reduction in the indications of distinct voices, a consensus is reached. Symbolized by the performance of an a cappella song or chant, there are no reported speech markers, no discordant channels of communication, no distinctive pitches or rhythms other than joint song performed by the chorus of the whole group.

Thus, as the ritual process moves toward its climactic moment of fulfillment, individual voices and quotations are increasingly rare. They seek to minimize any individual identity in a performance, and instead to emphasize the collective nature of the voice being transmitted.

Changing Concepts of "Voice" in Ceremonial Settings

The function of voices in ritual speech is changing. As the Indonesian government puts pressure on the Sumbanese to abandon their devotion to the ancestors and embrace modernity, officials have encouraged elementary schools to develop hybrid versions of ritual speech performances for displays in regional competitions of local customs and dance. These elementary school performances exhibit a remarkably different construction of social personae, constructed through different sensory media. Visual media are more significant in the school performances than in the climactic ritual speech performances (see figure 14.2).

Ritual speech as displayed in these elementary school events has a number of features worth noting:

1. Ululation becomes a separate turn, a distinct voice and social personae rather than an overlapping or complementary feature. The woman performing ululation (marked by an arrow) waits her turn.
2. It has a distinctive visual focus—face front—rather than the more diffuse verbal and acoustic focus of the indigenous ritual events.
3. The ritual speech is choral and written out prior to the event. Note the couple reading from the text.
4. Ritual speech is an adjunct to the dancing. Note that the dancers face front.

Had I focused only on the transcript, I would not have been aware of the fact that this is in many ways really "about" the dance, which is quite literally foregrounded. Also, compared to the clip of the ritual performance, where the performers have multiple body orientations (they are surrounded by the ancestors), this performance is focused in a single direction, pointed toward a unified gaze of an audience. The music has a regular rhythm, designed for the dancers, and the ritual speakers coordinate to it. As a reorientation of the role of visual and auditory modalities, the voice of the ululators is now a support for the dancers, not the singers, but the referential content of their song becomes privileged and supported with written text, which is completely void of reported speech. The ululation is now its own turn at talk. These performances are designed for audiences with relatively little connection to the meaning of the event, including tourists, visiting dignitaries, and even television audiences.

Figure 14.2. Still frame from a video of a ritual performance of elementary school children, prepared for the provincial governor's wife. Note the face-front orientation of the participants. The man and woman on the right perform ritual speech by reading together from a text. The woman on the left waits her turn to ululate. The costumed boys in the foreground dance to a gong and drum orchestra.

The shape of ritual discourse has undergone a multimodal reorientation, guided by social, cultural, economic, architectural, and technological constraints.

Toward a Video Ethnography of Language

Struck by this reorientation of visual and auditory modalities, I began to learn more about digital video as an ethnographic tool. A laboratory for all the technology to digitize, store, retrieve, and analyze this digital data seemed crucial, and with the support of NSF and George Washington University, I was able to set one up that met our needs.[1]

Video ethnography of some clinical encounters

Can lessons learned about the management of information through voices in a faraway island provide insight into cases closer to home? I have analyzed videos of some low-income African American women who have been diagnosed with depression and enrolled in an NIH-funded study for medication treatment. This might seem rather presumptuous of me, but I think some of the same issues apply in both the cases of the ritual of misfortune and in the clinical encounter closer to home. Why? Partly because the nature of the activity in both cases requires the synthesis of a lifeworld and a specialized "professional" world. In both cases, the clients must struggle to integrate information from outside the setting and bring it to bear on the unfortunate situation. In both cases, the actual speakers providing other voices are not usually there in the room; they are voices from outside.

In collaboration with a clinical research psychiatrist at Georgetown University, I have examined these videotapes to identify the ways in which language and other communicative channels are used by both clinicians and patients in the course of the interview. Using the concept of voice, we can begin to see how the patients and clinician together manage the flow of information and relations to each other. Thus voice is not merely a grammatical device used to create meaning, but also a resource used by actors to organize and control information.

The reason the psychiatrist, Dr. Joyce Chung, approached me to work on this study was that she was already part of a much larger study funded by NIH and designed to find the most practical and effective ways of disseminating antidepressant pharmaceuticals in underserved, low-income communities, and she wanted to know more about what actually happens in the interview process. As part of that larger study, researchers obtained signed consent to videotape the interviews, but there was very little in the way of a plan to study the tapes. She hoped that we could learn more about the nature of the patients' experience in the clinics and perhaps gain insight into their ideas about depression. She was also particularly interested because she was aware that in psychiatry, verbal communication is the primary data; there are no x-rays or blood tests for depression.

To investigate the tapes more carefully, we transcribed them using Capmedia software to link the transcriptions with the digital videos; we made use of a transcription system developed by DuBois et al. (1993) with some modifications. Then we imported the transcriptions into Atlas.ti, a database program that handles video. Atlas.ti allowed us to code the video tapes and the texts for things like gaze, reported speech, gesture, interrogatives, and laughter. In addition, the transcriptions were analyzed using Wordsmith—a text analysis program that creates concordances, cluster diagrams, keyword analyses, and other analyses.

At this point, we do not have enough information to generalize on whether these findings are representative of psychiatric interviews, of African Americans, women, or of depressed patients, so I will focus my remarks on the issue of voice.

Voice in psychiatric interviews

Voices abound in the data we collected. Indeed, there were more voices than one might have expected, given the private and intensely personal nature of a psychiatric encounter. To identify ethnographically the voices in these interviews, it is not enough to simply identify the speaker (see Mishler 1984). Speakers cannot be regarded as unified entities, from the standpoint of the actors in the event. The patients speak for themselves, but also for their husbands, their mothers, fathers, children, neighbors, friends, other clinicians, and sometimes the clinicians in the room. They also speak for themselves in a variety of ways, depending on the degree of responsibility that they wish to claim for their speech, or their particular feelings about the veracity of what they are saying. The clinicians in this study also adopt other voices, but the variety of these adoptions is fewer and the functions are different.

The main way in which voices are constructed by both patients and clinicians is through reported speech. This device allows the patient to bring her lifeworld into the clinic—that is, the social, emotional, and private concerns of her personal, nonclinical life. Using reported speech she is able to bring the personae that most affect her into the room and create a dialogue with them for the clinician to witness and participate in. This invocation of the lifeworld allows her to position it in various ways vis-à-vis the world of the clinic: in order to challenge it, validate her own position, or to create solidarity with the clinician. The clinician, on the other hand, tends to create voices in different ways and with different effects. One of the most common ways is that she constructs the voice of the patient and "plays it back to her." Another common voice is the reading voice or the "voice of medical authority" in which the clinician invokes medical knowledge in order to provoke a dialogue with the patient. In the one case, the function of the voice is to create "fact." In the second case, the function is to contrast her own voice with that of medical authority in order to create rapport and solidarity between patient and clinician.

Forms by which voices are constructed

In order of prevalence, the most common ways of differentiating voices are through use of the verbs *say, like,* and *go;* another significant, but less frequent way of constructing a social persona is through intonation, gaze, and gesture, as when signaling that one is reading. As part of a reported speech construction, the verb *say* can be either direct or indirect, as in, "I said, 'OK,'" [direct] or "She said she takes it at night," [indirect]. The direct version implies a more or less faithful recounting of what actually got said, while an indirect construction of someone's voice suggests interpretative *involvement* on the part of the recounter. Patients used *like,* particularly *I'm like,* much more often than did the clinicians, usually to signal a subjective state, but not to report (or to take responsibility for reporting) what they actually said (Romaine and Lange 1991). A patient says, for instance, when her husband is yelling at her, "I'm like, 'Oh my goodness'"—this is not a report of what she actually said at that time. Use of *like* is always direct, and it never occurs as an indirect paraphrase or with the use of the pronoun *that. Go* is a somewhat less common but also important verbal form by which reported speech voices are constructed—as in, "So he goes, 'I'm coming to get her'"—and it also only occurs in the direct mode. The clinicians create voices exclusively with the say verb and through intonation and gesture in the reading voice. Overall, patients' use reported speech increases over the course of the therapy sessions, possibly linked to increasing familiarity among the participants, which gives wider scope to expressions of individuality and the lifeworld experience. This is in marked contrast to the ritual speech example, where the number and variety of voices decreases as the process heads toward consensus and its conclusion.

Some Functions of Voices in Clinical Encounters

In what follows, I present some examples that illustrate these different modes of constructing voices and how they function in their clinical context.

▒ Function 1: Alliances between the clinician and patient against an absent third party

Describing her husband's negative attitude towards her depression diagnosis[2]:

P: "aw your mother's depressed" he's . . . going around the house ***telling*** *my daughter this]*

C: [(:)]

P: ***I was like . . .*** *"oh my goodness"*

C: ***so*** *he was giving you a hard time about it?*

In this excerpt from a transcript, there are three main voices: the clinician, the patient, the patient's husband's voice. The patient performs her husband's voice directly, signaling it through intonation, and then juxtaposes it to her own voice, which she marks off as her own subjective experience using the *I'm like* construction. When she says, "I'm like," she is calling attention to her own subjective inner speech. It creates the vividness without the responsibility for exact quotation. Its function in a sequential sense is that it produces an affiliative statement from the clinician as against her husband. The clinician implicitly evaluates the husband's behavior negatively in her question, "So he's giving you a hard time about it?" What is interesting here is the playing off of one voice against another for social functions. The function is evidenced in its sequelae (Silverstein 1999)—what comes after. The use of this form of self-report is indeed almost immediately followed by an affiliative response. The *I'm like* phrase is much more likely to be followed by an affiliative head nod or other affiliative response than is ordinary speech without an embedded reported speech frame. This reminds me in some ways of similar processes of creating affiliation, alliance, and opposition described Marjorie Goodwin (1990) in her book *He-Said-She-Said,* and by Amy Shuman in her work on adolescent fight stories (1993).

An example with very similar functions occurs in the following excerpt, in which the patient is ventriloquating her husband's voice as he reprimands her for asking him to do things he is physically incapable of:

P: "you know I can't do it . . . you know . . . you know I have these problems . . . you know I can't <HI I said ok (TSK) HI>

C: so he's yelling at you and stuff?

She constructs her own quiet voice in response to his rant: "*I said 'OK,'*" and this produces a sympathetic response from the clinician.

▪ Function 2: uses voice of quoted person to deliver implicit challenge

Another function of reported speech is not to create solidarity but to create an implicit challenge. In this excerpt, the patient describes her friend's reaction to anti-depressants:

P: she said [her the <wa > I don't know the ww medicine] she's on she said she takes it at night [too because it makes her sleepy]

The clinician's response indicates that it functions to some extent as a challenge, because the next three turns are devoted to a lengthy discussion about side effects.

In another instance, a patient reports on her grandmother's skepticism about her cousin going to a psychiatrist:

P: she was like "what do you need to go for?"

As in the previous example, the clinician takes up the implicit challenge, devoting the next several turns to an explanation of the possible benefits of psychiatric treatment.

Function 3: External validation

A third function of reported speech for patients in the clinical encounter is bringing in external validation for subjective experience. In the following example, the patient explains she does not refer to her illness as postpartum depression anymore:

P: no because they told me it would go away

C: *um hmm..It never has. . .*

P: uh uh

The quotation marks off her contention that the source of this comment is not herself; that is, she is not making this up. She immediately gets a validating response from the clinician, who repeats and affirms the patient's statement, "It never has. . . ."

Function 4: Rapport

A fourth function of the construction of voices is used by the clinician to create rapport. In this excerpt, the clinician alternates between reading voice and her own voice. She signals the distinction through intonation, gaze (looking up), and through using gestures when she's speaking for herself. One of its functions is that it differentiates her from the text, and creates a sort of solidarity between the clinician and the patient over against the text. Part of the video confirmation of this comes from the patient's immediate use of nods and other affirmative gestures whenever the clinician departs from the text and reading voice and begins to speak in her own voice.

CI1:um . . . <R there is some indication however that major depression and dysthymia R> which is that chronic kind of depression <R may be diagnosed less frequently in African American women and slightly more frequently in Hispanic women than Caucasian women R>

P: (::)

CI1: um . . . and they're just saying that . . . maybe cultural issues affect the way that

Function 5: highlight evidence

A fifth function for the clinician is to foreground the source of evidence for a particular clinical judgment. The function is not on creating alliances or rapport so much as a kind of assent in yes or no in format. In this excerpt, the clinician is attempting to clarify with the patient the symptoms of her depression:

C: (:) (H) you said that . . . your depression makes you <: not want to . . . answer your phone and see people.

C: and it makes you . . . want to sleep a lot? [is that what you said?] . . . you sleep more?

Conclusions

In both Sumbanese ritual and U.S. clinical settings, videotaped ethnographic data provide a permanent and shareable record of both the visual and acoustic aspects of an activity system in which actors are engaged. By focusing specifically on the "voices" in the data, and specifically trying to answer the question Who is speaking?

we can see in the Sumbanese data a reorientation has occurred between visual and acoustic modalities in the answer to that question: visual media become more important in the more recently developed ritual speech performances for elementary school children. In both the traditional and the more modern performances, voices of absent third parties—the ancestral voices—are imported into the present setting. In the traditional ritual context, the ancestral voices are progressively foregrounded verbally over the course of the ceremonial process, while visual cues of ancestral voices diminish in importance. In the modern context, the individual voices are visually and sequentially differentiated. Each voice has a single visual focus, oriented towards a central gaze of the spectator; ritual speech is performed from a written text.

In the clinical setting, the patients and clinicians both import the voices of absent third parties into the therapeutic encounter. Patients draw on their "lifeworld" of friends, children, husbands, relatives, and employers in order to construct a dialogue that the clinician can understand and participate in. The clinicians draw from a narrower range, importing only the voices of medical authorities (in the form of a reading voice) and the past voices of the patients themselves in order to construct rapport and authority. Unlike the Sumbanese ritual process, where the presence of multiple, distinct voices in a discourse is a sign of disorder, in the U.S. data on the therapeutic process, the appearance of multiple voices in a patient's discourse is a sign of lively rapport with the therapist.

The role of video in the ethnography of language

The head nods and the use of gestures and gaze are crucial to the construction of voice in these texts, and to our understanding of how they function. Without video, these crucial aspects of the encounter would be lost.

But video ethnography has its drawbacks. To name a few:

- Analyzing video is labor-intensive and time-consuming work;
- Video analysis tends to privilege a brief segment of a life (usually one in which a visually rich activity is occurring);
- Video analysis can be technically demanding, requiring laboratory facilities;
- Video analysis poses particularly complex confidentiality and human subjects issues.

On the positive side, in addition to some of the benefits mentioned previously, however, I think it should be said that often we tend to assume video data necessarily results in *more* data for the ethnographer. This is not always the case. In the Sumbanese traditional ritual performance, for example, it is clear that the actors are not really attending to many of the visual aspects of their performance, because most of the event is conveyed by the acoustic channel. In the modern school performance of ritual speech, however, this has changed: the visual aspects of the performance carry a significant amount of information. A transcript containing only verbal aspects of the event would miss important information conveyed through other modalities, especially visual.

I would like to end this discussion with a plea for more attention to the role of video in ethnographic research. Like many of my colleagues, I did not enter the field of linguistics expecting to spend my time preoccupied with electronic equipment, and learning technical jargon. I was attracted to the field because I wished to study and learn more about the role of discourse in social life. Increasingly, however, our information about the role of discourse in social life is mediated by video.

The good news is that technically things are getting simpler over the past as new standards emerge and new technologies develop. Interpretively, though, things are not so positive. There are lots of pseudo-interpretations of video available. Charles Goodwin (1994) has documented the Simi Valley interpretation of the Rodney King video, an interpretation that resulted in devastating consequences. Following the events of September 11, 2001, the videotapes of Osama bin Laden have stimulated many different analyses in television and newspapers (many focusing on the possibility of hidden messages), but none of these analyses so far has adopted an ethnographic perspective.

Video as a medium does not appear to be going away any time soon. Video media arrive now on CDs in cereal boxes, in your mail, email, and now even to your Palm Pilot. The role of video as a form of evidence, data, and teaching support in fields of law, medicine, and education continues to grow. While distribution possibilities for the medium have increased, the interpretive frameworks for such video data do not appear to be keeping pace. Many of the pioneers in the ethnography of nonverbal communication have retired or gone into other fields, and their university positions have not been renewed. Very few appointments are being made in linguistics and anthropology that are devoted to this field, leaving other fields to define the terms of the analysis. We need more ethnographically oriented studies that use video to overturn conventional wisdoms based on single modalities. Let's get to work. ▒

NOTES

I would like to thank Enos Boeloe, Petrus Malo Umbu Pati, and Mbora Paila for their assistance carrying out field research in Indonesia. LIPI, the Indonesian Institute of Sciences, helped facilitate the visa application process. Financial support came from the National Endowment Indonesian for the Humanities, Fulbright CIES, Social Science Research Council, Wenner-Gren Foundation, Woodrow Wilson International Center for Scholars, George Washington University Facilitating Fund, and the Southeast Asia Council of the Association for Asian Studies. This support I gratefully acknowledge.The psychiatric discourse project was funded with support from the National Institutes of Mental Health, the National Science Foundation (instrumentation grant), the Bayer Foundation, and the Banneker Foundation. I also gratefully acknowledge the assistance of Matthew Wolfgram, Lauren Lastrapes, Michael Sieberg, and Andrew Johnson. I am especially grateful for the advice, comments, criticisms, and encouragement of Dr. Joyce Chung. She is not responsible for any errors contained in this paper.

1. Video files are digitized and stored in MPEG-1 or MPEG-4 (divx) format; they are retrieved, coded, and analyzed using Atlas.ti, as well as other programs for parsing, concordancing, and acoustic analysis.
2. A note on the transcription conventions: (:) refers to a single, affirmative head nod; (::) refers to a double affirmative head nod, and so forth; (;) refers to a negative head shake; (;;) refers to a double head shake, and so forth.

REFERENCES

Bakhtin, M. M. 1981. *The dialogic imagination.* Ed. M. Holquist. Austin: University of Texas Press.

Bauman, R., and J. Sherzer, eds. 1989. *Explorations in the ethnography of speaking.* New York: Cambridge University Press.

Chafe, W. L. 1994. *Discourse, consciousness, and time: The flow and displacement of conscious experience in speaking and writing.* Chicago: University of Chicago Press.

Cole, M. 1996. *Cultural psychology: A once and future discipline.* Cambridge: Harvard University Press.

Conklin, H. C. 1962. Lexicographic treatment of folk taxonomies. *International Journal of American Linguistics* 28(2): 119–41.

DuBois, J. W., S. Schuetz-Coburn, S. Cumming, and D. Paulino. 1993. Outline of discourse transcription. In J. A. Edwards and M. D. Lampert, eds., *Talking data: Transcription and coding in discourse research,* 45–89. Hillsdale, NJ: Erlbaum.

Feld, S. 1984. Sound structure as social structure. *Ethnomusicology* 28:383–409.

Fox, J. J. 1988. *To speak in pairs: Essays on the ritual languages of eastern Indonesia.* New York: Cambridge University Press.

Goffman, E. 1974. *Frame analysis.* New York: Free Press.

Goodwin, C. 1994. Professional vision. *American Anthropologist* 96:606–33.

——. 1999. Vision. *Journal of Linguistic Anthropology* 9: 267–70.

Goodwin, M. H. 1990. *He-said-she-said: Talk as social organization among black children.* Bloomington: Indiana University Press.

Howes, D., ed. 1991. *The varieties of sensory experience: A sourcebook in the anthropology of the senses.* Toronto: University of Toronto Press.

Jameson, F. 1991. *Postmodernism, or, The cultural logic of late capitalism: Post-contemporary interventions.* Durham: Duke University Press.

Kapita, U. H. 1976. *Masyarakat Sumba dan adat istiadatnya.* Waingapu: Panitia Penerbit Naskah-Naskah Kebudayaan Daerah Sumba Dewan Penata Layanan Gereja Kristen Sumba.

Keane, W. 1999. Voice. *Journal of Linguistic Anthropology* 9:271–73.

Keating, E. 1998. Honor and stratification in Pohnpei, Micronesia. *American Ethnologist* 25:399–411.

——. 1999. Space. *Journal of Linguistic Anthropology* 9: 234–37.

Kendon, A. 1990. *Conducting interaction: Patterns of behavior in focused encounters.* New York: Cambridge University Press.

Kress, G. R., and T. Van Leeuwen. 2001. *Multimodal discourse: The modes and media of contemporary communication.* New York: Oxford University Press.

Kuipers, J. C. 1990. *Power in performance: The creation of textual authority in Weyewa ritual speech.* Philadelphia: University of Pennsylvania Press.

——. 1992. Obligations to the word: ritual speech, performance, and responsibility among the Weyewa. In J. Hill and J. Ervine, eds., *Responsibility and evidence in oral discourse,* 88–104. Cambridge: Cambridge University Press.

——. 1993. Matters of taste in Weyéwa. *Anthropological Linguistics* 35:538–55.

——. 1998. *Language, identity, and marginality in Indonesia: The changing nature of ritual speech on the island of Sumba.* Cambridge: Cambridge University Press.

Lave, J., and E. Wenger. 1991. *Situated learning: Legitimate peripheral participation—learning in doing.* New York: Cambridge University Press.

Leont'ev, A. N. 1978. *Activity, consciousness, and personality.* Englewood Cliffs, NJ: Prentice-Hall.

Luria, A. R., and J. V. Wertsch. 1981. *Language and cognition.* New York: J. Wiley.

McNeill, D., ed. 2000. *Language and gesture: Language, culture, and cognition.* New York: Cambridge University Press.

Mishler, E. G. 1984. *The discourse of medicine: Dialectics of medical interviews—language and learning for human service professions.* Norwood, NJ: Ablex.

Romaine, S., and D. Lange. 1991. The use of like as a marker of reported speech and thought: A case of grammaticalization in progress. *American Speech* 66(3): 227–79.

Schieffelin, B. B., K. A. Woolard, and P. V. Kroskrity. 1998. *Language ideologies: Practice and theory.* New York: Oxford University Press.

Shuman, A. 1993. "Get outa my face": Entitlement and authoritative discourse. In J. Hill and J. Ervine, eds., *Responsibility and evidence in oral discourse,* 135–60. New York: Cambridge University Press.

Silverstein, M. 1998. Contemporary transformations of local linguistic communities. *Annual Review of Anthropology* 27:401–26.

——. 1999. Functions. *Journal of Linguistic Anthropology* 9:76–79.

Tannen, D. 1989. *Talking voices: Repetition, dialogue, and imagery in conversational discourse.* New York: Cambridge University Press.

Urban, G. 1991. *A discourse-centered approach to culture: Native South American myths and rituals.* Austin: University of Texas Press.

Voloshinov, V. N., L. Matejka, and I. R. Titunik. 1973. *Marxism and the philosophy of language.* New York: Seminar Press.

Vygotsky, L. S., and M. Cole. 1978. *Mind in society: The development of higher psychological processes.* Cambridge, MA: Harvard University Press.

Wertsch, J. V. 1985. *Vygotsky and the social formation of mind.* Cambridge, MA: Harvard University Press.

Multimodality and New Communication Technologies

CAREY JEWITT
Institute of Education, University of London

THE DISCUSSION OF THE IMPACT of new communication technologies on social interaction and discourse is increasingly accompanied by the discussion of multimodality (and vice versa). Through these discussions medium and mode have become woven together like two threads in a cloth. In order to understand the impact on social interactions and discourses themselves that these technologies have this chapter argues that the complex relationship between new communication technologies and multimodality needs to be explored. One way to do this is to understand their relationship as one between technologies of representation (the modes of "multimodality") and technologies of dissemination (the media of multimediality).

This paper attempts to untangle some of the complex connections between technologies of dissemination or medium (new technologies as much as old, like the classroom) and modes. Medium refers to how texts are disseminated, such as printed book, CD-ROM, or computer application. Mode refers any organized, regular means of representation and communication, such as, still image, gesture, posture, speech, music, writing, or new configurations of the elements of these (Kress et al. 2001). Through two illustrative examples, this paper examines this relationship to explore the affordances of technologies of dissemination (media) and the affordances of the technologies of representation (modes). The first example focuses on the transformation of the John Steinbeck novel *Of Mice and Men* (1937) from print technology to digital technology, that is, from the medium of the book to the medium of the CD-ROM (1996). This move from one medium to another enables the designer of a CD-ROM (and the reader of it) to engage with the affordances of a range of representational modes in ways that can both reshape entities ("things to think about and things to think with"), such as character, and the practices of reading. The second example analyzes the modal affordances of three computer programming applications that rely on the *same* medium, but that make available different representational modes for programming.

The contention of this paper is that research on new communication technologies tends to foreground the affordances of medium at the cost of neglecting the affordances of representational modes. The point I want to make is this: the meaning of a text is realized by people's engagement with both the medium of dissemination *and* the representational affordances (whether social or material) of the modes that are used.

Mode as Technology of Representation: The Move from Page to Screen

The CD-ROM as a medium of dissemination has the potential to bring together the mode-aspects of gesture, movement, sound-effect, speech, writing, and image into one multimodal ensemble. Writing remains within the space of new technology in all its forms, but with specialized tasks. The question of what affordances this new space has, and what are the representational modes which are most apt in relation to it, remains (Lanham 2001).

Reading the CD-ROM version of the novel *Of Mice and Men,* the reader is required to select their preferred version of the text: the "written" version of the book or the "visual" version of the book, which includes video clips and drawings alongside the writing. The novel as CD-ROM includes hyperlinks to definitions of colloquial words used in the novel and to a map of the area the story is set in, and it, in its turn includes hyperlinks to information on the population and industry of the towns.

The potential of the medium to link texts via visual hyperlinks enables the reader to move between the entity character in the "fictional domain" of the novel and the entity character in a "factual domain" beyond the novel—the historical-social context of the novel. The two domains of fact and fiction provide the potential for a complex notion of character and text to be realized. Text and character are represented as the multimodal outcome of interaction with many voices and modes over time—as dynamic and emerging from a social rather than an individual reading, which reflects the implicit mechanisms of studying text and character in school English.

The two versions of the novel as CD-ROM offer the designer and the reader of the CD-ROM different resources for meaning-making. The move from page to screen realizes a changed compositional relationship between image and writing. Image dominates the space in the majority of the screens. The relationship between image and writing is newly configured and is itself a visual meaning-making resource. In the context of the screen the writing has become a visual element, a block of "space," which makes textual meaning beyond its written content. The blocks of writing are positioned in different places on the screen (the left or right side, along the bottom or top length of the screen). Depending both on the size and position of the block of writing different parts of the image layered "beneath it" are revealed or concealed. In this way a block of writing (and its movement across screens) can change the screen image fundamentally, as is the case in these three screens shown in figure 15.1. These three screens are taken from chapter 1 of the novel as CD-ROM. They depict the two main characters in the story, George and Lennie, having an argument as they are traveling to start a new job together at a ranch.

In the first screen, the block of writing is positioned above George's head as he talks to Lennie about what he could do if he left him. In the second, Lennie is visually obliterated and George visually foregrounded by the block of text that "contains" George's angry talk of leaving. In the third, the block of writing is placed on the screen in a way that makes both George and Lennie visible as George's anger subsides. The interaction of the blocks of writing and the still image on the screens serve

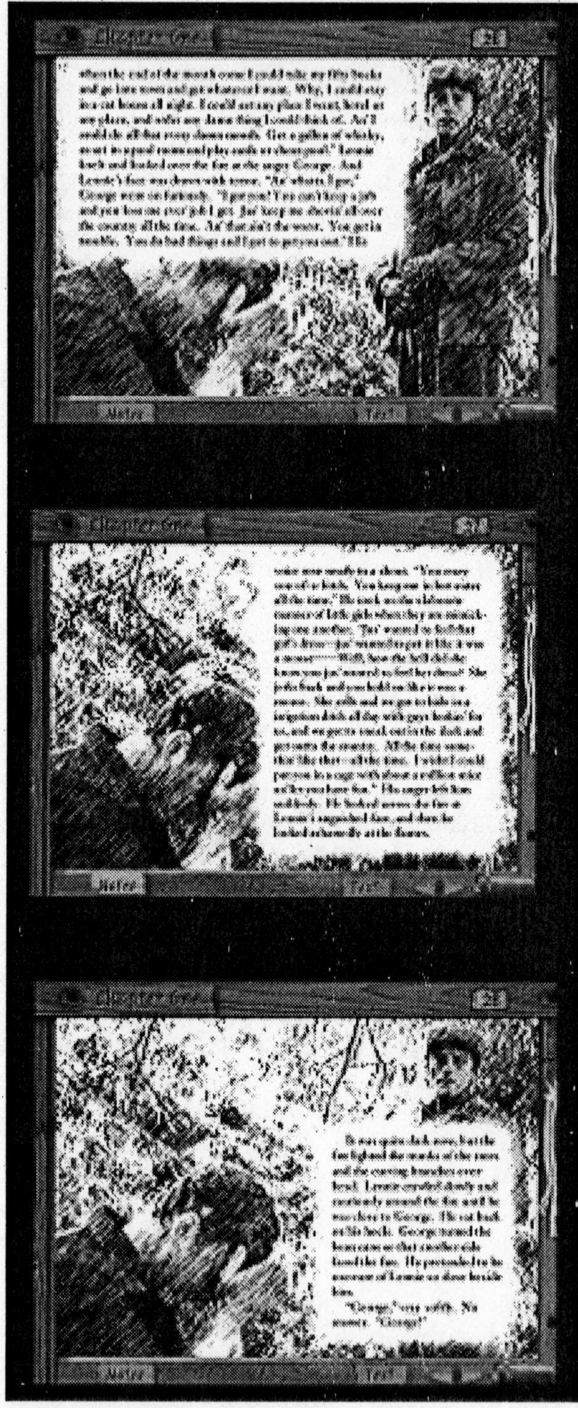

Figure 15.1. Chapter 1 of the *Of Mice and Men* CD-ROM.

to foreground or background the two characters, and to visually mark the intensity of a moment through the persistence of an image on screen.

The modes of writing and image are also used differently in realizing the characters. For example, writing focuses on the thoughts, worries, and dreams of George, while Lennie is more frequently visually represented as expressing himself actionally. Writing is used to indicate reflection, and image is used to indicate action, and through this specialized use of mode these different qualities are associated with the characters George and Lennie.

Throughout the visual version of the novel as CD-ROM, the modal resources of the video clips, drawings, and layout (image, gesture, writing, and speech) are used differently to realize the characters George and Lennie and to emphasize particular characters and moments from the novel. George and Lennie are literally given a voice and appearance through the configuration of movement, gesture, posture, and speech in the video clips at the start of each chapter. Lennie appears in all these clips, while George appears in about half of them. In these clips Lennie is made visually salient (through framing, size, and so forth), and he speaks very little—it is George or the other characters who speak. Some characters are represented only in the still images and writing on screen—they have no voice or movement, while others are represented only in the writing; they are not visualized by the designer of the CD-ROM.

Technologies of Dissemination: The Move from Page to Screen

The transformation from book to CD-ROM brings with it the affordances of a different technology of dissemination. A central point is the potentials for interaction that the medium (the book or the CD-ROM) makes available to the "reader." In reading a book, the reader is given a clear reading path—from the top left corner of the page, to the bottom right and so on, from page one to the end. She or he might move to a footnote, to the index, return to the contents page, or abandon the book altogether: but the reading path is nonetheless there. By contrast, when using a CD-ROM in a lesson a teacher may impose an order on the students' reading of it, but there is no internal grammar to be broken—there is no essential "wrong order," because there is no prior reading path. The CD-ROM makes possible, brings forth, a different kind of activity from that of the book or the film. This enables the reader to some significant extent, to determine their own route through materials (Andrews 2000).

One of the affordances of the technology of dissemination is that it is also a technology of production, and as such it enables students to produce their interaction through different genres, through different forms of engagement. The openness of the "novel as CD-ROM" not only extends but also alters the traditional notion of reading from a matter of interpretation to design (Kress and Van Leeuwen 2001). Students (aged 14–15) were observed using the Steinbeck CD-ROM over a series of five school English lessons in an Inner London secondary school (for a fuller discussion see Jewitt 2002). Two of these students used the Chapter Menu Bar as a navigational tool to move almost seamlessly through the "novel as CD-ROM" as a series of video clips. Another pair of students "flicked" through the still images of the chapter in a way that "animated" the text like a cartoon. While two other students selected characters with audio clips of songs, they learned some of the words, sang, and tapped along—they momentarily transformed the novel into "music." The students' genre of interaction with the text reshaped the entity character through a shift from the literary genre of "novel" to the popular textual genre of comic, film, and song. That is, their engagement introduced a shift from the literary aesthetic to the popular, and from the world of fiction to the students' everyday lifeworlds.

The CD-ROM brings forth a different kind of reading that requires a different kind of imaginative work. The reader of the novel as CD-ROM has to choose from the elements available on screen, to decide what elements and modes to take and make meaningful, and then to order them into a text.

This example illustrates the relationship between mode and medium and the potential for the reshaping of meaning and of practices in the move from the medium of book to the medium of CD-ROM. The second example focuses on the relationship between mode and medium by comparing in some detail the modal choices made by designers working within the same medium.

Modal Representation in Three Computer Programming Applications

This part of the paper focuses on three computer programming applications—Logo, Pathways, and Playground, which aim to make give children access to a conceptual understanding of mathematics through the process of building computer games. This analysis shows that although the affordances of medium and mode often seem to run in parallel, they are independently variable and need to be considered separately. The representational modes that are potentially available in a medium are one matter. How a designer makes use of these is another. A designer need not avail herself or himself of the modes that are potentially available in a medium. The modal resources are the result of a designer's choice from a range of available potentials—not an automatic consequence of the choice of medium in and of itself. A CD-ROM *can* rely primarily on the mode of writing. A book *can* rely nearly entirely on image and in the case of children's books include sound effects.

It is perhaps important to be clear here that it is not technology that determines people's meaning making: the medium of book, or the CD-ROM, like all media, is shaped by the people who use it, and what it is that they do with it. Although the focus of this paper is on the potentials of the medium and modal resources of these programs, how students engage with these potentials in the process of game-making differs. (Student game construction is discussed elsewhere; see Jewitt 2003). It is this complex interaction between people and technologies, often in ways that have not been intended or previously imagined, that shapes and transforms technologies (both old and new) (Castells 2001). Nonetheless, the resources of any technology *do* provide different kinds of constraints and possibilities for their use. With this in mind this section compares the use of mode in the three computer programming applications.

The three computer programming applications share the same technology of dissemination, and the same potentials for modal representation. However, the designers of each of the programs have made different modal selections and combinations that the user cannot alter.

The modal selections made by the designer of a medium (e.g., image and writing) are central to the engagement of a user with it. The modal choices which the designer of an application makes serve to constrain the user of it in what they can do and provides them with different features for realizing and thinking about aspects of programming, rule, game, and so forth.

In order to draw this out this section focuses on one entity, that of "rule," in the three computer programs. The different modal resources of the three applications realize the entity "rule" in quite different ways as shown in analysis of a small piece of programming, in this instance "move the object (t1) 15 units to the right when the control button is pressed."

Logo

In Logo the program mode consists of lexically represented instructions and quantities represented by mathematical symbols. This mode represents particular aspects of the entities condition and action. In Logo the program for the action "move the object (t1) 15 units to the right when the control button is pressed" is represented in figure 15.2.

The "condition" is represented in the form "to move/if key? [case key [ctrl." The agent involved in realizing the condition, the person who presses the key, is not represented in the program mode. (This is not the case in both Pathways and Playground, where the agent is represented.)

The action "move" is represented as a recursive combination of three elements "unit of position," "object," and "the horizontal coordinates of the object," represented as: [t1' xcor = xcor +15]]]. Movement is represented as the addition of a number of units (in this case 15) to the horizontal coordinates of the position of the object. The programming mode does not require the object to be lexicalized, "named," or visually depicted, beyond its horizontal coordinates and t1—in everyday terms the object is not specified. The direction of the object's movement is represented by the sign "+."

Through the arrangement of the elements in the program code sequentially from left to right, and top to bottom, condition and action are represented as two distinct elements. This arrangement signals that condition is prior to action and it foregrounds condition within the entity rule.

```
to move
if key?
        [case key[ctrl
                [t1'xcor = xcor + 15]]]
move
end
```

Figure 15.2. The Logo Expression of the Rule "Move an object 15 units to the right when the control key is pressed."

The mode of Logo is realized in the scientific/technological coding orientation. Logo offers the user of it a way of thinking about movement that is different from an "everyday" understanding or concept of movement. The entity movement is constructed in Logo as through the conceptual resources of science/physics. The representation of movement enables an experienced programmer, through their knowledge of the Logo modal representation of movement, to imagine the movement of the object (t1). Logo represents phenomena as reliant on the "natural laws" of physics, and the user can recreate the entities of the world by engaging with these laws via the Logo programming mode. The specialized programming mode is realized within technical/scientific realism to produce a version of the world as a generalized and analytic system. In Logo, the things that have significance in the everyday world, such as the nature and context of an object, are not represented as being significant.

Pathways

Pathways is a visual object orientated programming system. Programming in pathways is realized through still images in the form of stones that represent a range of specific conditions and actions. Color and shape are used to classify "action" and "condition" stones. The function of a stone is represented by still images with runelike characters; these symbols are graphic within a written genre of mark-making.

The organizational rules of Logo, and the written page in the west more broadly, govern the arrangement of elements in Pathways (Kress and Van Leeuwen 1996). A rule is made by placing a condition stone and an action stone in a linear sequence from left to right on a "scroll." The shapes and textures of the condition and action stones visually "fit" together into "clauselike" structures. As in Logo, the condition comes first in the sequence it is foreground semantically—it is the theme of the rule. The program "move the object to the right by 15 units when the control button is pressed" is represented in figure 15.3.

In Pathways, the condition "when the space bar is pressed" is represented by a still image of a thumb pressing a key. Condition is therefore treated as something a generalized human user creates via interaction with the tools of the system (in this case the control key). This visual representation of "move to the right by 15 units" movement is broken into three parts: a symbolic visual representation of movement—a person jumping; an arrow to indicate the direction of the movement; and a slide bar to represent the "amount" (or rate) of movement. This visual classification of movement breaks the connection with the object and its spatial position. Whereas in Logo movement is fused with the spatial position of the object, in Pathways movement is transformed into a quality independent of the object.

The cartoon genre of still images (e.g., the generic human figure jumping) in Pathways stands in stark contrast to the "equation" genre in Logo. The genre and sensory images of Pathways are located within the everyday world of the user. The representation of "move" as a person jumping is a visual metaphor in which the "behavior" of the object—in this case the movement of a turtle—is represented by an abstracted image of "human action."

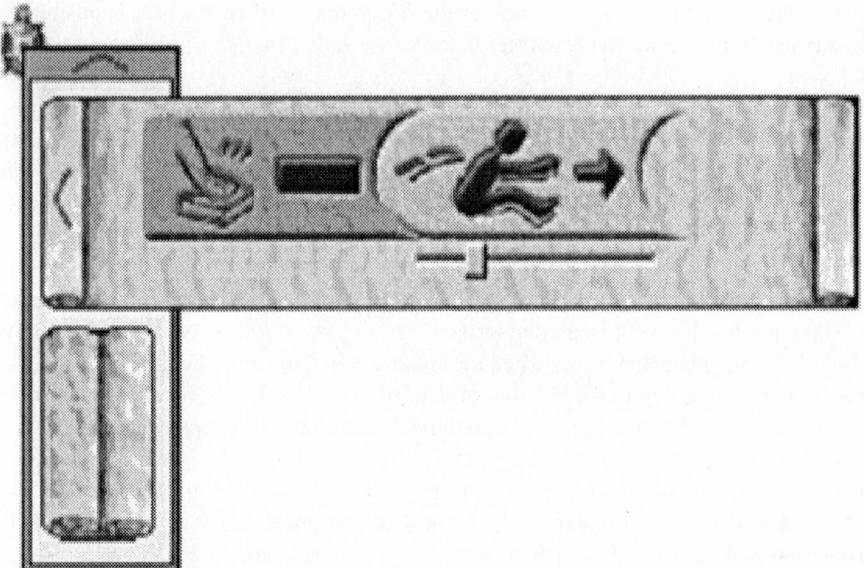

Figure 15.3. The Pathways Expression of the Rule "Move an object 15 units to the right when the control key is pressed."

In Logo, direction and units of movement are represented as mathematical concepts: right is represented as the conjunction of the horizontal coordinates of an object plus units of position, and left as the horizontal coordinate of an object minus units of position). In Pathways direction and rate of movement are represented as fused everyday concepts. The direction of movement is represented visually by arrows with direction—right, left, up, and down. "Units of movement" are represented by the position of a marker on a visual slide. This transforms the entity "rate of movement" from the addition of a discrete numerical unit (in this case "15") to a visual continuum of "amount."

The mode of Pathways and Logo offer two different coding orientations, each of which are appropriate to the different versions of the "world" that these programs provide. What each mode represents as "real" differs. In Pathways, we see a representation of the "real" world, and so the entities have to have a "real world" appearance, they are lexicalized, named, and visually depicted. The object (in this case a turtle), the condition (the image of key being pressed), and the action (the image of movement) are represented as discrete visual entities. In this way an action is realized as a quality that can be "attached to" an object.

In Logo, as mentioned earlier, the user deals with the rule system and its process. In Logo the user is required to engage with movement as a mathematical concept in order to "write" a piece of program. In Pathways the user is required to engage with movement as an inherent characteristic embedded in the action stone. The principles that the user of Pathways and Logo is provided with to interrogate or deconstruct the concept of movement differ, and through these principles the entity movement is itself constructed differently in each of the programs. Further, the user is positioned as a consumer of ready-made entities in Pathways rather than as a producer of them.

Playground

Playground is a multimodal object oriented programming system and the mode combines animation, still images, some written Lexis, and numerical symbols. The rule "move the object to the right by 15 units when the control button is pressed" is represented in Playground code in an animated sequence represented by the stills in figure 15.4.

The condition of the rule (i.e., "when the control key is pressed") is represented in three modes. It is represented in *written mode* by the "yes" in the first box held by the robot. The condition is met when the condition in the box in the thought bubble of the robot matches that in the box the robot is holding. In other words, a met condition is represented as "sameness"—the matching of the boxes. It is represented in *still image* by an image of the control key and an arrow. And it is represented in *animated movement* by the robot placing the number 15 onto the horizontal coordinates of the object, and the moving image of the control button on screen. The animated representation realizes the rule in which condition and action are "fused."

Robots are available from the Playground toolbox. When a robot is selected from the toolbox it is animated, it "waves" at the user and it "hovers"—it "comes to life." The visual representation of the robots, with a "mind" (visually represented as a thought bubble), hands, and eyes, is a signifier of the robots' "trace of humanness." The movement of the robot represents it as a generalized potential for action, and for interaction with the user. When the user trains a robot to carry out a rule, she or he "enters" the "thought bubble" of a robot. In this domain the user's movement of the mouse controls the movement of the arm of the robot. Through animated movement the robot is represented as an extension of the user, and the user is represented (positioned) within the programming mode itself.

The "addition" part of the rule is represented by the interaction of the robot and the tool "Bammer." Bammer is an animated character tool within Playground—a mouse with a large red mallet. Once the robot has dropped the number 15 onto the horizontal coordinates of the object (the box containing the 517 figure), Bammer runs out of the toolbox and bangs the 15 onto the 517. This joins the two numbers. The number in the middle box changes to 532 and the visual representation of the control key moves to the right. Bammer is an everyday cartoon representation of "add," banging things together, squashing them into one form. In this way, the robots and Bammer (and the other animated tools in Playground) mediate the mathematical world that is represented in numbers and sensor positions and the everyday world of the child user. Just as Logo and Pathways draw on particular genres (the equation genre and cartoon genre of still image, respectively) Playground is realized within a highly sensory animated cartoon genre.

In Logo and Pathways the user has to switch from programming mode to game mode in order to see the program actionalized. In Playground programming mode and game mode are simultaneously available—they exist at the same level. The player can see the mechanism of the rule and the result of it at the same time. They

Figure 15.4. The Playground Expression of the Rule "Move an object 15 units to the right when the control key is pressed."

can see the repeated animation of the robot picking up a number and placing it on top of the numerical representation of the horizontal coordinates of the object, the animation of the tool Bammer banging the number in place, and the object moving to the right. This serves to make the programming process continuous with processes in the everyday world. The animated action of the robot holds the tension between the mathematical concept of rule and the everyday experience of movement. Both of these versions of movement are simultaneously available to the user. The user is able to attend to the mathematical code via its actional realization. This iterative move provides a potential for the user to make links, to come to understand rule as both a mathematical and an everyday entity.

As the spatial resource of the page is superseded by the spatial resource of the screen, the logic of the compositional meaning space is also altered. The seemingly fixed directionality of the written text that is present in both Logo and Pathways, is not apparent in Playground. In Playground the arrangement of the different elements of programming mode have multiple directionality, which disturbs the logic of the "line" as a "textual/written unit" in which elements move from left to right. The user's task (as with the CD-ROM discussed earlier) is to select and order the elements made available to them.

Playground locates the mathematical laws of natural phenomena within the social forces of people/community (realized by the Playground representation of the user on screen, the robots, the personified tools, and the overarching metaphor of a city). The modal resources of Logo, Pathways, and Playground offer different modal resources for ways of thinking about rule, condition, and action. They provide the user with different kinds of principles for organizing and understanding the world, and they position the user in different ways to the system itself.

Conclusion

These two illustrative examples demonstrate that the semiotic potentials made available via a multimodal text, whatever its technology of dissemination, contribute to the shaping of what can be "done with it"—how meaning can be designed. This chapter concludes that in order to understand the practices of people engaged with new (and old) technologies we need to understand *what it is* that they are working with. Understanding the semiotic affordances of medium and mode is one way of seeing how technologies shape the learner, and the learning environment, and what it is that is to be learned.

The relative newness of new communication technologies still shines, making digital and computer technologies appear to stand apart from older technologies, such as pen and paper—naturalized everyday technologies that no longer glitter. Nonetheless, the question of how technologies of dissemination shape meaning is always present.

The representational shifts that are so often associated with new communication technologies go well beyond it. The increased intensity of the use of image, the increased visualization of writing is present on screen, page, and elsewhere. The assertion that "we are entering a historical epoch in which the image will take over from the written word" (Gombrich 1996:41) appears to have some value. History shows that modes of representation and technologies of dissemination are and always have been inextricably linked. Understanding new communicational technologies as the differently configured combinations of the affordances of representational modal resources and technologies of dissemination offers one way to understand how multimodal representations between or across technologies reshape knowledge. ▩

NOTE

This chapter draws on my work with Ross Adamson from The Playground Project, directed by Richard Noss and Celia Hoyles at the Institute of Education, University of London, and funded by the European Commission Directorate-General XIII under the ESPRIT Programme (Project 29329: Playground).

REFERENCES

Andrews, R. 2000. Framing and design in ICT in English. In A. Goodwyn, ed., *English in the digital age,* 22–33. London: Cassell.

Castells, M. 2001. *The Internet galaxy.* Oxford: Oxford University Press.

Gombrich, E. H. 1996. The visual image: Its place in communication. In Richard Woodfield, ed., *The essential Gombrich: Selected writings on art and culture,* 138–40. London: Phaidon.

Jewitt, C. 2002. The move from page to screen: The multimodal reshaping of school English. *Visual Communication* 1(2): 171–96.

——. 2003. Computer mediated learning: The multimodal construction of mathematical entities on screen. In G. Kress and C. Jewitt, eds., *Multimodal learning: Moving beyond language.* New York: Peter Lang.

Kress, G., and T. Van Leeuwen. 1996. *Reading images: The grammar of visual design.* London: Routledge.

——. 2001. *Multimodal discourse.* London: Arnold.

Kress, G., C. Jewitt, J. Ogborn, and C. Tsatsarelis. 2001. *Multimodal teaching and learning: The rhetorics of the science classroom.* London: Continuum.

Lanham, R. 2001. What's next for text? *Education, Communication, and Information,* 1(1): 15–36.

Steinbeck, J. 1937. *Of mice and men.* London: Penguin.

——. 1996. *Of mice and men.* CD-ROM version. New York: Penguin Electronic.

Origins: A Brief Intellectual and Technological History of the Emergence of Multimodal Discourse Analysis

FREDERICK ERICKSON
University of California, Los Angeles

THE THEME OF THIS YEAR'S Georgetown Round Table was the use of new technologies in the study of talk, and the development of new conceptual and empirical approaches to multimodal discourse analysis (see Scollon and LeVine chapter, this volume; Kress and Van Leeuwen 2001; Van Leeuwen and Jewitt 2001). As we look forward it is also useful to look back, for as the aphorism has it, "Those who cannot remember the past are condemned to repeat it."

Accordingly I want to recount a selective history of the study of talk in social interaction, and to do this in the form of reminiscence. My account emphasizes the role of information technology in that history, and it also emphasizes that history's brevity, its recency. The systematic study of oral discourse has arisen within the lifetimes and academic careers of those of us who assembled at the conference, and within the lifetimes of a few of our immediate forebears.

One of those forebears is Edward T. Hall. The organizers of this Round Table had invited him to present a plenary address, but illness prevented him from doing so. As a former student of his, I was asked to discuss his work in relation to our current situation. I have therefore given his ideas and his pioneering uses of information technology some prominence in my account—an emphasis that is justified by the influence he has had on many of us, directly and indirectly. My remarks are intended as a tribute to him on behalf of this year's Georgetown Round Table.

Reminiscence: Conceptions and Tools Evolving Together in the Study of Talk

The close study of naturally occurring talk is a little more than fifty years old. That is in part an intellectual matter—the scientific study of language began with a concern for phonetics, moved to phonemics, and then moved to sentence-level grammar. Fifty years ago, "discourse," in Zelig Harris's sense as the study of connections and patterning beyond the level of the sentence, lay just beyond the horizon (Harris 1952).

It is also in part a technological matter, this turn to studying human social interaction in its detailed complexity. Because the behavioral phenomena of the real-time conduct of talk and listening were so complex and fleeting, it was necessary to capture them for purposes of analysis by means of machine recording. Analysis proceeded by exhaustive, repeated relistening and relooking as the machine recording was replayed and transcripts of speech and nonverbal behavior were constructed, using the machine recording as a primary information source.

There had been precursors—the first visual recording of locomotion in humans had been done in the 1880s by Eadweard Muybridge, who attached threads to the shutters of a set of cameras aligned in a row along a walkway and then had research subjects walk forward at right angles to the strings, in parallel with the row of cameras. As each successive thread was broken by the walking man or woman, the shutter of each successive camera in the row was tripped, thus producing a series of still pictures that were the functional equivalent of the succession of individual frames on a strip of cinema film—cinema not yet having been invented (see the collection of photographs on the human figure in motion in Muybridge 1955).

Edison had invented the phonograph in 1877, and in the mid-1890s he and, in parallel invention, the Lumière brothers in France, developed cinema cameras and projectors. Cinema film does not seem to have been used early on for the study of human social interaction, but wax-cylinder sound recording was immediately adapted by folklorists and the early ethnomusicologists, as well as by linguists—G. B. Shaw's Henry Higgins in *Pygmalion* being a fictional example. (As a graduate student in the mid-1960s, I prepared shipping manifests of copies of the recently deceased anthropologist Melville Herskovits's field recordings onto audiotape reels—then the state of the art in sound recording. Herskovits's collection included wax-cylinder recordings of music from Dahomey, West Africa, and from the Caribbean. The collection also included recordings (not on wax cylinders) of radio broadcasts from African American churches on the South Side of Chicago in the 1930s—Herskovits had recorded the preaching as well as the singing in those worship services.

In the late 1930s Gregory Bateson and Margaret Mead used silent cinema film and still photography to record Balinese dancers teaching their apprentices (Bateson and Mead 1942). By the early 1950s Bateson was involved in making research cinema film with audio tracks in collaboration with Jürgen Ruesch and Weldon Kees. They made a set of sound cinema films of psychotherapy interviews that were being conducted in the San Francisco Bay Area (Ruesch and Kees 1956). Then in 1955–56, during the inaugural year of the Center for Advanced Study in the Behavioral Sciences (CASBS), which had just begun its operation on the Stanford University campus, Frieda Fromm-Reichmann formed a seminar at the Center. Members of the seminar group included the linguist Norman McQuown and the anthropologist Bateson, who at that time was working in a psychiatric research unit at the Veterans' Hospital in Palo Alto.

The CASBS group used sound cinema film of therapy sessions and of interviews with various family members that had been made in a project that was one of the early manifestations of what was later to be called "family therapy." The group members, coming from differing disciplines, decided to do parallel analyses of the differing kinds of information available on the film. The result, across the separate transcriptions, was a loosely unified study of verbal and nonverbal behavior in face-to-face communication.

The group continued its work sporadically after the year at the Center had ended, and Margaret Mead, Ray Birdwhistell, George Trager, and others also participated.

They produced an unpublished report, titled "The natural history of an interview," consisting of chapters authored by the various participants (Bateson 1971). There was a detailed phonetic transcription of speech prepared by linguists and various analyses of nonverbal behavior were done by the anthropologists Birdwhistell and Bateson.

The parallel multimodal analyses were made possible technically by the use of sound cinema film. The work of the group was supported theoretically by a particular set of heuristic assumptions: that in the real-time conduct of social interaction all the verbal and nonverbal behaviors that occurred had potential communicative significance and that at any given moment in the course of interaction, whatever each and every member was doing was contributing to an overall social ecology of mutual influence among interactional participants.

The semiotic means remained to be discovered by which verbal and nonverbal behavior came to have significance, as also remained to be discovered the workings of participation in an ecosystem of mutual influence in speaking and listening activity. But the assumption was that all these phenomena were of potential research interest. Thus, in the "Natural History" group, the study of speech was not privileged over the study of nonverbal communicative means and the two modes of communicative action were studied together, in order to determine relationships of related function among them and relationships of mutual influence between the actions of differing individuals during the conduct of face-to-face interaction.

Such an approach to the analysis of human communication is tremendously labor-intensive. Thus it is no surprise that the "Natural History" group spent years in the intensive, multimodal analysis of a few strips of cinema film, and that the manuscript collection of separately authored chapters that they produced was never finally published. The primary copy of it resides now in the Harper Library of the University of Chicago. (We can conjecture that the other reasons this collaborative work did not reach publication are that the principals in the work were senior scholars with very full schedules and very large egos.)

At any rate, it is important to note that the "Natural History" group presumed theoretically that meaningful social interaction proceeds by means of a locally enacted social ecology in real time—an ecology that resides in the multimodal communication behaviors of all the members of an interacting group. The technology of sound cinema film made it possible to study human communication in immediate social interaction from such a theoretical perspective.

Just a few years before 1955, another interdisciplinary collaboration had taken place. This was a collaboration between the anthropologist Edward T. Hall and the linguist George Trager, who were faculty colleagues with Ray Birdwhistell at the postwar Foreign Service Institute in Washington, D.C. Trager was developing an approach for the study of what he called "paralanguage," the sound qualities of speech such as pitch, volume, open or closed throat sound production, and head or chest resonance. Trager published a programmatic essay on the study of paralanguage (1958) that followed the then current principles of American structural linguistics.

Hall had become engaged in the study of patterns of spatial relationship and of timing in human communication, including the close study of the organization of interpersonal distance in face to face interaction, which he called "proxemics." Hall and Trager wrote together a training manual that considered verbal and nonverbal communicative behavior together as a unity, and this formed the basis for a coauthored article (Trager and Hall 1954). Hall further developed this model as "a map of culture" in his paperback *The Silent Language* (1959), which addressed a popular audience and also was read by some scholars. He was interested not only in nonverbal behavior and its visual perception but in humans' use of the entire sensorium in communication. Hall's paper "A system for the notation of proxemic behavior" was published in a special issue of the *American Anthropologist* (Hall 1963), and a subsequent monograph, *Handbook of Proxemic Research* (1974) was published by the Society for the Anthropology of Visual Communication, and he also published a book on proxemics, *The Hidden Dimension* (1966). His overall research program is reviewed in an autobiography (Hall 1992).

In the study of proxemics, Hall made extensive use of still photography, capitalizing on the flexibility of the 35mm single lens reflex camera, which had become generally available after World War II. (He had had training as an artist, and his earliest anthropological work involved the study of decorative patterns in Native American pottery from the Southwest.) Later, in the 1960s, he made use of the then new Super-8 cinema cameras, which used silent film cassettes containing three minutes' worth of film. I remember watching with him films he had made of small groups of shoppers going from stand to stand at the open air craft market in Santa Fe, New Mexico. (Hall taught us as students to walk around our homes looking through the lens of the still camera or cinema camera. Our equipment, he said, should be so familiar to us that we would treat it as an extension of our bodies. Then, in our use of the camera, we would not make our research subjects nervous.)

The capacity to make an audio recording in social circumstances where nothing special was going on involved technology that was not generally available until after World War II. The first such research recording, to my knowledge, was made by William Soskin and Vera John in 1953 at a summer camp for faculty and graduate students operated by the University of Chicago. Their study was published ten years later in a book edited by Roger Barker titled *The Stream of Behavior: Explorations of Its Structure and Content* (1963). In that volume Barker and the other authors considered social interaction multidimensionally, in the spirit of the work of the "Natural History" group.

Soskin and John recorded two newlyweds conversing casually. To keep the interlocutors from being interrupted by others, they put them in a rowboat. The battery that powered the audio recorder in the boat was about the size of a modern automobile battery—not a very portable recording apparatus!

By this means Soskin and John (1963) were able to record interesting examples of naturally occurring speech—an interest due in part to serendipity. As the rowboat was being sculled forward by the wife, it was almost hit by a ferryboat, a circumstance that occasioned considerable vehemence in the utterances that were exchanged between the recently married pair (Vera John-Steiner, personal communication 2002). (This would have provided a good opportunity for the researchers to develop transcription conventions for indicating pitch and volume stress and vocal tone quality in speaking.) The wife, who had been rowing while facing backward, had been depending on the husband's guidance from his position facing forward while seated at the rowboat's stern. Thus the location and orientation of the interlocutors in space and the differing visual information available to them in their distinct spatial situations were quite consequential for the content (and social process) of their discourse, in this earliest instance of a study of naturally occurring talk. Recall that at this time, neither the term *discourse* nor the term *deixis* had begun to have currency.

It was not until the late 1960s, when the small, battery-operated, quarter-inch audiocassette and recorder became commercially available, that it would be easy to record speech as it occurred in its most mundane circumstances—at the post office, on the telephone, at the family dinner table. The research possibilities of the cassette audio recorder were exploited early on by Harvey Sacks, Emanuel Schegloff, and others in what became the approach of "conversation analysis" and by John Gumperz and others in what became the approach of "interactional" sociolinguistics.

One of my own students, Jeffrey Shultz, was the first to record the naturally occurring speech of bilingual preschool children. He did this in 1970 (a year before I met him) using a cassette audio recorder placed in a small backpack which was worn by a child, with a microphone pinned on the front side of the backpack's shoulder strap. As the child moved in space and time, her talk with other children could be recorded continuously by this simple means. But before the advent of the cassette recorder such recording would have been much more difficult and expensive.

Another instrument that had a major influence on our work was the IBM Selectric typewriter, which appeared on the office supply market in the mid-1960s as the "state of the art" electric typing machine. Using the Selectric in the early 1970s, Gail Jefferson, while still a secretary for the researchers Harvey Sacks and Emmanuel Schegloff, helped them develop the set of transcription conventions that became the standard for the emerging field of conversation analysis and that has influenced as well many of those who do other kinds of discourse analysis. Jefferson and her colleagues used a play script approach to the transcription of speech, presenting speech in lines that are limited in length by the width of a sheet of typing paper and by the left and right margin settings and tab stops on the typewriter. The combination of quarter-inch cassette audiotape recorder and the electric typewriter with a moveable ball of type (now replaced by the desktop computer) made a powerful combination that has been used in the close analysis of speech that has developed since the early 1970s as conversation analysis, interactional sociolinguistics, and oral discourse analysis.

It was also in the early 1970s that portable video-recording equipment became available. This is where I came in on the story I am recounting. I had begun doctoral study at Northwestern University in the mid-1960s. There I encountered Ethel Albert and Edward T. Hall. Albert had been a colleague of John Gumperz, Dell Hymes, and Erving Goffman at the University of California at Berkeley. She had recently come to Northwestern as the first woman professor to hold tenure there. With her I learned to read the then brand new work in ethnography of communication. I remember that in an advanced seminar on language and culture Albert said, "the next frontier will be the analysis of discourse." By that she meant exactly what Zelig Harris had meant in his 1952 paper—"discourse" as connections across utterances beyond the level of the single sentence.

From Hall I had learned about proxemics and about what he called "situational frames" (1976). He also introduced me to the approach taken by the "Natural History" group and by Ray Birdwhistell (1970) and William Condon (Condon and Ogston 1967). Accordingly, I was ready to try audiovisual recording of occasions of talk.

In my doctoral thesis research I had been making audio recordings and transcriptions of talk in small discussion groups of young people in their early teens. Usually these groups met in late afternoons after school. The young people talked about the lyrics of popular songs, which were played on a record player and then discussed.

At the very end of data collection in that study I arranged for one of the groups, from the South Side of Chicago, to come up by car to Northwestern after the rush hour and hold one extra discussion session, which would be videotaped. The young people arrived at a room in the School of Education, where there was a studio video camera on a large wheeled tripod. The camera was connected to a stationary Ampex video recorder, which used videotape reels that were one inch thick and about twelve inches in diameter. We made the video recording and, after a small party with pizza and sodas in the recording studio, the young people were driven home.

The next morning I watched the videotape, which had a profound effect on me. By that time I had reviewed about sixty audiotaped group discussions, each lasting about three quarters of an hour, and I had pored over transcripts made from the audiotapes. Part of what I was studying were rhetorical processes in the young people's discourse—how they argued with one another and attempted to persuade one another. With the videotape I could look at a speaker and see who that speaker was addressing at any particular moment—a single interlocutor or a set of interlocutors. I could identify the verbal and nonverbal listening reactions of those primary addressees. The interactional processes of arguing could be much more richly understood when the conjoint verbal and nonverbal speaking and listening actions of the participants were available to me as an analyst. Bateson and the rest of the "Natural History" group were right—it seemed that multimodal analysis of social interaction was the direction to take.

Leaving the videotape in the recording studio—I couldn't afford to buy it, nor did I have a way to replay it—I resolved to make more videotapes when the next research opportunity came. I was able to do that, and also to make use of slow motion analysis of sound cinema film, in a study of interaction in job interviews and academic advising interviews that began in 1970 and eventually resulted in the book *The Counselor as Gatekeeper* (Erickson and Shultz 1982).

Thirty-five years after I made my first videotape, we now have available digital video cameras, fairly inexpensive high-quality wireless microphones, and digital multimedia data storage and retrieval capacity in our desktop computers. For data collection the equipment is so small that for videotaping in a school classroom with two cameras, two wireless microphones, a small shotgun microphone, and a day's supply of videotapes I can carry all the necessary equipment in a briefcase. When, in

1974, I first began long-term videotaping in classrooms, the equivalent items of equipment filled the back of a small station wagon. Before that video wasn't portable at all, as the anecdote of my own very first video recording illustrates.

Moreover, contemporary digital video playback systems include functionality that certain cinema film viewing equipment had, but which had gotten lost during the era of videocassette use. Once digital video is copied on the hard disk of a computer it can be reviewed moving instantly back and forth across long strips of recorded material. One can view faster and slower than life, with or without sound. With 16mm cinema film we also had that capacity, using a special Bell and Howell projector with a hand crank, or a "Moviola" editing machine, or the Steenbeck editing table. For a whole academic generation that capacity in reviewing had been lost. Instead, on the videocassette machine, the fast forward and reverse were imprecise, and one couldn't easily see images on the screen "faster than life." At normal playback speed there were always slight pauses between playing forward and playing reverse. With the cinema viewing equipment one could rock the moving visual image and sound backward and forward in instant alternation.

These differences between video and cinema film review may seem trivial, but I believe they had substantive sequelae—that is, differences in scholars' routine looking and listening practices which resulted from the differing affordances of different kinds of audiovisual reviewing equipment did, in my judgment, account for some of the differences in approach from that used by the "Natural History" group. It was those differences that characterized the development of what we now call discourse analysis. Scholars who never saw what analytic review of sound cinema film could do, by way of flexibility and precision in reviewing, developed kinds of analysis of the real-time conduct of talk that were more superficial—and more linear and unimodal, more focused on the voice track and dependent on play-script transcription—than what had begun to be done earlier. Cinema film was much more expensive than videotape but it had certain advantages for microanalysis of interaction that analog video could never replace. Only with the advent of digital video are we able to do some things analytically again in ways that were available in the slow-motion analysis of cinema film, in the very first stages of the scholarly analysis of naturally occurring talk that preceded modern discourse analysis.

Implications for Current Research Practice

One implication of my brief history is that for analytic purposes it is usually desirable to consider verbal and nonverbal behavior together in the study of oral discourse. This is not to deny that for some purposes it still makes sense to consider speech by itself in discourse analysis. But the material presented in the various plenary addresses at this conference, as well as much of what was presented here in symposia, shows the myriad extraverbal phenomena that are being attended to by interlocutors as they talk, and this makes a strong case for the proposition that these extraverbal phenomena are deeply implicated in the communication of meaning during the course of human social interaction. When we look by comparison at what has come to be mainstream work in discourse analysis, it is fair to say that the analysis of talk has tended to be "linguocentric" in ways which, in the long run, may prove to be misleading even for those whose primary research interest is in speech phenomena rather than in nonverbal aspects of communication.

Another implication is that we need to explore a wider variety of forms of transcription. Play-script transcription of speech still has its uses and it has been developed ingeniously over the last thirty years. It is not likely to disappear. But a perspective on the conduct of social interaction which sees it as an ecology established in and through the conjoint actions of all parties who are engaged in an interactional activity throughout the course of that activity in real time requires more than play-script transcription of speech to make visible the multidimensionality of that ecology. Even when we try to consider speech by itself, it should be obvious from the various presentations made at this conference that speech does not occur in nature in strips or bursts that are never longer than the width of a sheet of typewriter paper, with space for left and right margins subtracted, nor are the speech sounds that are indicated by equally spaced letters (and blank spaces) in print all of the same duration or volume in their actual performance. Nor can a play-script transcription show continuously what listeners are doing while each speaker is speaking. A line of printed play script is not a way to display speech that models in its graphic form how speech gets done as embodied social action in real time. Rather, that way of displaying speech is an artifact of typesetting, of the printing of book pages, and of the workings of an IBM Selectric typewriter.

One way to break the reifying frame of print and play script is, at the very least, to rotate our page ninety degrees to give enough horizontal room so that (usually) *any* breath group can be shown across its entire course on a single line of text. Another approach is to do more thoroughly "horizontal" transcription in which the verbal and nonverbal behavior of each of the participants in an interactional event is transcribed continuously. (For good examples of this, see the transcriptions in Kendon 1990.) What one gets is a scroll of transcript, constantly read to the right, that looks a bit like an orchestra score. This is rather clumsy still for printers to handle in a page format. Yet with the digitizing of the print production process, the old limits of typesetting need no longer constrain us. We can now publish radically horizontal kinds of transcript much more cheaply than in the past.

A third implication, related to the second, is that the real-time location of verbal and nonverbal microevents within the stream of communicative activity needs to be given more analytic attention and be displayed more graphically in transcription. One way to do this is to use quasi-musical transcription approaches, as Scollon and I have done in the past (Scollon 1982; Erickson 1982, 2003). Another way to display timing is to use machine printouts of various sorts. We now can take advantage of a happy technological coincidence—because micro time-coding is so important in the video editing process, digital video software packages now often include software that can be used to show the timing patterns of syllable production, gesture, and gaze during the course of talking. Inexpensive software also can display the pitch and volume of speech sounds.

At least one more implication bears mention here. That is the tendency in previous studies of talk to focus on a single event rather than to identify patterns of communicative activity which obtain across multiple successive events. "Discourse analysis," as forecast by my teacher Ethel Albert, was a decided advance from the intrasentential focus of American linguistics immediately before and after World War II. Just as the pioneers in early discourse analysis used new equipment to go analytically beyond the level of the sentence, so we now are technically able to go analytically beyond the level of the single event. Digital multimedia data storage and retrieval allows us easily to move back and forth across strips of interaction that occur not only at different places within an event, but also across sets of events over long spans of time. But are we conceptually able to do this? Which particular strips should be selected for comparative analysis across events? What spans of time should we attempt to encompass analytically—successive days, months, years? These issues must now be explored. (For a recent, and particularly elegant, solution to this kind of selection problem, see Duranti's 2003 study of a political candidate's successive deliveries of a campaign "stump" speech.)

It is now practically possible to collect longitudinal data on topics that require monitoring the interactional behavior of persons across a series of successive events—for example, data on the acquisition of fluency in a first or second language by particular speakers, or data on the evolution of interaction with a particular child in a series of pediatric clinic visits, or data on the learning of subject matter in classrooms—all across spans of months or years. How to conceive of such topics theoretically and study them empirically we cannot yet imagine fully, but we know now that we can do such research technically, with the new tools for data storage and retrieval that are available to us in digital information systems.

Material That Requires Multimodal Discourse Analysis: An Example

In the plenary address at the Georgetown Round Table, I covered most of the points presented in the text above. Then, using a laptop computer and projector, I showed the audience a multimedia array of research material collected in a recent study of classroom interaction that is still in process. The multimedia collection included still photographs of children's art and written work and videotape segments from small group and large group lessons with the children, as well as planning sessions among the teachers. The multimedia array shows how three kindergarten–first grade teachers in two adjoining classrooms taught basic ideas in physics, concerning matter, energy, and motion, across the entire course of a school year, culminating in a long-term classroom project, the study and construction of classroom-sized roller coasters by which messages could be sent from one room to the other.

My primary purpose in collecting this audiovisual material was to portray the "how" of this kind of pedagogy; a documentation of skilled teaching practice to be shared with other early grades teachers and teacher educators. This particular video footage also has sociolinguistic interest, and especially for the conduct of multimodal discourse analysis. That is because the commitments of these particular teachers to curriculum and pedagogy involve teaching basic ideas very thoroughly by presenting them in multiple sensory and semiotic media, and by asking children to display their learning by using multiple semiotic systems. (In this, they were following approaches developed at the well-known preschool in the northern Italian city of

Reggio Emilia, approaches that were also used in classic "progressive" pedagogy in the nineteenth and twentieth centuries in Switzerland, Germany, England, and the United States.)

For example, one of the key ideas in the study of matter (on the way to studying energy and motion) was that molecules in differing states of matter "dance" differently—they move more rapidly and across more space as matter changes in state from solid to liquid and then to gas. This metaphoric dancing was demonstrated in talk, writing, graphic displays, and by engaging students in the kinesthetics of actual dancing. To make visible their understanding to themselves and to their teachers and parents, children modeled the motion of molecules in differing states of matter, using clay and found objects. They drew the motion of the molecules. They spoke about molecules. Here is what one kindergartner wrote about what he had modeled in clay:

(Name) 3-1-01

> SoLids are close TogeTher
> my soLid is very close
> TogeTher. my liqui is
> is a LittL Bit and ah LittL Bit
> Fare apart. my gas is very sprd
> apart.

Even this rendering in typescript showing the child's invented spelling and use of uppercase T, L, and B together with lowercase for other letters cannot begin to communicate what a still photograph of the actual writing shows. And my larger point is that without the real-time moving sound and visual imaging of video I cannot show the reader here what the children were doing interactionally as they spoke together, drew, and danced the motions of molecules in differing states of matter. Nor can I show how the teaching and learning that took place in their room evolved over the course of an entire school year.

Rather than try to illustrate any of this with charts and elaborate transcription systems, I want to observe that what is necessary for such display is not print by itself but multimedia hypertext—a combination of written commentary with video clips, still photographs, and analytic charts. Charles Goodwin is becoming adept in the preparation of such multimedia displays. He has a website that contains copies of his recent papers, including elaborate analytic charts and still photographs. Emanuel Schegloff has a website in which he makes available audio material he has transcribed and analyzed in published writing, and he plans soon to include video material (www.sscnet.ucla.edu/soc/faculty/schegloff). Such examples show how the scholar's personal website becomes an alternative/supplementary publishing medium that permits direct communication of multimodal discourse analysis.

Finally, it should be noted that the first doctoral thesis to be presented in the form of a CD-ROM disk rather than a paper document was written by Leslie Jarmon at the University of Texas at Austin in 1996. She had to request special permission to submit the thesis in CD form. It is a study in multimodal discourse analysis and conversation analysis, titled "An ecology of embodied interaction: Turn-taking and interactional syntax in face to face encounters" (Jarmon 1996).

Conclusion

We have come a long way from Muybridge and Edison. It is not so long a distance from the groundbreaking work of Bateson, McQuown, Hall, Barker, Soskin, John, and many others since who have made use of sound cinema film, audiotape, video, still cameras, typewriters, word processors, digital multimedia (plus yellow pads of paper for observational notes and transcript drafts, and more recently "Post-It" notes). Researchers have used these information media tools in increasingly skillful ways in order to study the organization and conduct of human social interaction. In my story of early efforts in such work, by emphasizing the roles of machines I do not mean to have implied a technological determinism. Conceptions and tools evolve together. But the close analysis of human social interaction cannot proceed without use of information storage and retrieval tools and so their particular affordances and their variously jury-rigged uses play an important part in this story.

Meanwhile the multiple streams of oral discourse analysis that have arisen in the last thirty-five years continue on their disparate courses, sometimes in contradistinction to one another, sometimes in parallel play, sometimes in mutual influence. The "multimodality" of everyday discursive practices seems obvious. New attempts to address this multidimensionality more adequately—theoretically, empirically, and technologically—are being invented even as these words are being written. Certainly a future for such work lies before us. Just where the various workers among us will go next remains to be determined, by those of us who continue to do that work. ▩

REFERENCES

Barker, R. G., and L. S. Barker, eds. 1963. *The stream of behavior: Exploration of its structure and content.* New York: Appleton-Century-Crofts.

Bateson, G. 1971. Communication. In Norman McQuown, ed., *The natural history of an interview.* University of Chicago, Joseph Regenstein Library, Microfilm Department, Microfilm Collection of Manuscripts on Cultural Anthropology, Series 15, Nos. 95—98.

Bateson, G., and M. Mead. 1942. *Balinese character: A photographic analysis.* New York: New York Academy of Sciences.

Birdwhistell, R. 1970. *Kinesics and context: Essays on body motion communication.* Philadelphia: University of Pennsylvania Press.

Condon, W., and W. Ogston. 1967. A segmentation of behavior. *Journal of Psychiatric Research* 5:221–35.

Duranti, A. 2003. The voice of the audience in contemporary American political discourse. In D. Tannen and J. E. Alatis, eds., *Georgetown University Round Table on Languages and Linguistics 2001: Linguistics, language, and the real world—Discourse and beyond,* 117–38. Washington, DC: Georgetown University Press.

Erickson, F. 1982. Money tree, lasagna bush, salt and pepper: Social construction of topical cohesion in a conversation among Italian-Americans. In D. Tannen, ed., *Georgetown University Round Table on Languages and Linguistics 1981: Analyzing discourse—Text and talk,* 43–70. Washington, DC: Georgetown University Press.

——. 2003. Some notes on the musicality of speech. In D. Tannen and J. E. Alatis, eds., *Georgetown University Round Table on Languages and Linguistics 2001: Linguistics, language, and the real world—Discourse and beyond,* 11–35. Washington, DC: Georgetown University Press.

Erickson, F., and J. Shultz 1982. *The counselor as gatekeeper: Social interaction in interviews.* New York: Academic Press.

Hall, E. T. 1959. *The silent language.* New York: Fawcett.

——. 1963. A system for the notation of proxemic behavior. *American Anthropologist* 65 (5): 1003–26.

——. 1966. *The hidden dimension.* Garden City, NY: Doubleday.

——. 1974. *Handbook of proxemic research.* Washington, DC: Society for the Anthropology of Visual Communication.

——. 1976. *Beyond culture.* New York: Doubleday.

——. 1992. *An anthropology of everyday life: an autobiography.* New York: Doubleday.

Harris, Z. 1952. Discourse analysis. *Language* 28:1–30.

Jarmon, L. 1996. An ecology of embodied interaction: Turn-taking and interactional syntax in face to face encounters. Ph.D. diss., University of Texas at Austin.

Kendon, A. 1990. *Conducting interaction: Patterns of behavior in focused encounters.* New York: Cambridge University Press.

Kress, G., and T. Van Leeuwen. 2001. *Multimodal discourse analysis: The modes and media of contemporary communication.* London: Edward Arnold.

Muybridge, E. 1955. *The human figure in motion.* New York: Dover Books.

Ruesch, J., and W. Kees. 1956. *Nonverbal communication: Notes on the visual perception of human relations.* Berkeley: University of California Press.

Scollon, R. 1982. The rhythmic integration of ordinary talk. In D. Tannen, ed., *Georgetown University Round Table on Languages and Linguistics 1981: Analyzing discourse—Text and talk,* 335–349. Washington DC: Georgetown University Press.

Soskin, W. F., and V. P. John. 1963. The study of spontaneous talk. In R. G. Barker and L. S. Barker, eds., *The stream of behavior,* 228–81. New York: Appleton-Century-Crofts.

Trager, G. 1958. Paralanguage: A first approximation. *Studies in Linguistics* 13:1–12.

Trager, G., and E. T. Hall. 1954. Culture and communication: A model and an analysis. *Explorations* 3:137–49.

Van Leeuwen, T., and C. Jewitt, eds. 2001. *Handbook of visual analysis.* London: Sage.

Studying Workscapes

MARILYN WHALEN AND JACK WHALEN
with ROBERT MOORE, GEOFF RAYMOND, MARGARET SZYMANSKI, AND ERIK VINKHUYZEN
Palo Alto Research Center

INCREASINGLY, STUDENTS of talk-in-interaction and embodied conduct have come to appreciate that this activity is plainly "the vehicle through which a very great portion of the ordinary business of all the major social institutions (and the minor ones as well) get addressed and accomplished" (Schegloff 1992:1340). Many have then turned their attention to the details and actual methods of this accomplishment, and to the endogenous organization of the settings where it occurs (for discussions of this turn, see Silverman 1997; Whalen and Raymond 2000). Additionally, students of talk-in-interaction have recognized that we are embodied creatures living in a material environment that is populated not only with objects that are natural in origin but also (and progressively) with those that are manufactured. This means that the work of the world accomplished in and through our interactions necessarily—and often essentially—entails engagement with the material features of settings; with technologies, artifacts, the physical configuration of buildings or other social spaces, and the like (Whalen, Whalen, and Henderson 2002; Scollon and Scollon 2003).

This distinct line of research developed an early focus on workplaces as a basic site of institutional ordering. The scope of investigation gradually expanded from attending mainly to vocal interaction, particularly in settings where the exchange of talk was absolutely critical to the accomplishment of the work and the realization of some institutional order (Zimmerman 1984; Drew and Heritage 1992; Whalen and Zimmerman 1987; Boden 1994), or was itself *the* work (news interviewing and plea bargaining, for instance; see Heritage 1985; Clayman 1989; Maynard 1984), to encompass all aspects of human conduct, with extensive use of video recordings as data (see Goodwin and Goodwin 1996). And influenced by Suchman's (1987) groundbreaking study of human-machine interaction, researchers began to pay special attention to how the machines, technologies, and other artifacts that saturate the modern workplace are taken up and enter into the endogenous organization of work tasks (Button 1993; Whalen 1995; Heath and Luff 2000; Luff, Hindmarsh, and Heath 2000). This consideration has in turn produced interesting contributions to the design of work tools and technologies (for a recent example, see Suchman, Trigg, and Blomberg 2002; see also Dourish 2001).

In this paper we outline and illustrate our ongoing research program in "workplace studies," or what we prefer to call the study of workscapes. We also make a case for how such studies depend on and contribute to building a natural observational discipline for the study of human conduct. And we discuss the relationship between this discipline and the design sciences.

We begin with a brief account of what we mean by these two key notions, "natural observational discipline" and "workscapes." We then argue that naturalistic research on workscapes can play an important role in the human centered design of technology. But we go on to maintain that design efforts can and should involve much more than new technology, should encompass the entire workscape. Finally, to illustrate this argument and, especially, our program, we present sketches of recent and current research projects.

A Natural Observational Discipline

The satisfactory study of humans as a social species—indeed, the satisfactory study of any social species—requires (although should of course not necessarily be limited to) *naturalistic* observation and recording of their conduct. By naturalistic, we mean observing conduct as it occurs naturally, rather than under controlled or feigned conditions, and in the species' natural habitats, rather than in laboratories or similarly artificial environments. Moreover, as much as possible, the methods of observation should not directly intervene or interfere with that conduct or those habitats. Of course, this does not mean that observers cannot actively participate in the ordinary activities of subjects' lives, as this may in fact afford detailed understanding of the natural organization of such activities and domains of life, and of the competencies required of participants to produce them.

Recordings, particularly video records, are especially useful for such studies, for they serve as an important control on the limitations and fallibilities of intuition and recollection. If the data is collected in an appropriate manner, it also exposes the researcher to a wide range of natural materials and circumstances, and provides some guarantee that the analytic conclusions will not arise as artifacts of intuitive idiosyncrasy, selective attention or recollection. And perhaps most important, the availability of a taped record enables repeated and close examination of the events in question and hence greatly enhances the range and precision of the observations that can be made (Heritage and Atkinson 1984).

The bare logic of our argument for naturalistic observation can be illustrated by considering the scientific study of a social species other than humans—say, chimpanzees. If you wanted to investigate the behavior of chimpanzees you could of course observe them in captivity—in a zoo or laboratory—and also control and manipulate their actions in various ways in order to isolate or focus on certain aspects of it. And you could learn some important things about chimpanzees that way, like their cognitive abilities and their capacity for using language. But if you wanted to understand how chimpanzees actually organized their lives—their social world, the milieu where their capacities for thought and action are ordinarily employed and have genuine significance—you would have to observe (and, ideally, record) naturally occurring behavior in the places where chimpanzees customarily reside and conduct their business. The situation is no different for studying the human animal. It was indeed fortuitous that ethologists could not ask chimpanzees to tell them about what they did or why they did it, and so could not take shortcuts to direct observation. And it was fairly obvious to them that zoos and laboratories were so removed from the natural habitats of these animals that by restricting studies to those in captivity, you could learn a significant amount only about a very small part of their lives. Unfortunately, students of human behavior, who can usually query their subjects at will and may prefer the apparent scientific security of controlled environments to the supposed disorder of their everyday surroundings, have not been forced to learn these lessons.[1]

Focusing on Workscapes

For some fifteen years now, we have been studying human conduct naturalistically in a particular type of habitat: the locales and settings where people go about their jobs. These sites and jobs include[2]:

- Call centers, both public safety (police, fire, paramedic) communications centers and the various types of "customer support" operations that corporations frequently provide for their customers, who call toll-free numbers to manage their accounts, purchase supplies, place requests for service on their equipment, and the like;
- Other "centers of coordination" (Suchman 1993), such as NASA Mission Control, where the workers—like those staffing public safety communications centers—are responsible for the provision of services across space and time, involving the deployment of people and equipment over distances according either to a canonical timetable or the emergent requirements of response to a time-critical situation;
- Survey research centers, which contract with public and private organizations to conduct studies of public opinion and (reported) behavior through telephone interviews;
- Community psychiatric centers that support a regular set of patients with serious mental illnesses who are attempting to live and work in their community rather than be confined in institutions;
- Print or reprographic businesses that provide a wide variety of document services for their retail and commercial customers;
- Technical service and equipment repair in the field, at customer sites, where the technicians operate out of a van or car, carrying their tools and parts with them;
- Other types of so-called remote work, where a great deal of work gets done away from the worker's home office, such as selling reprographic equipment and office supplies, and brokering real estate transactions.

Our studies are concerned with more than simply sites or jobs, though; our interest is in entire "workscapes," which we define as *distinct configurations* of *people;* their *practices* (the communal methods they use to organize and accomplish their work); the *habitats* or environments where this work gets done; and the *tools, artifacts, and devices* that populate these environments and are in involved in the work's achievement. These phenomena are intimately related, and need to be analyzed in terms of that interrelatedness, and thus holistically, whenever possible. This is certainly not to say that analysis of a specific phenomenon of interest in a workscape, such as the way the workers in a retail setting take up and make use of certain technologies or artifacts while interacting with customers over the counter, cannot be undertaken, only that it should not be done in isolation from the other, related features of that workscape.

. . . but with a Distinct Analytic Stance

Our analysis of these workscapes is built upon more than simply a naturalistic methodology. In our studies, we take a particular analytic stance. We begin with the ethnomethodological principle that any social ordering, however mundane or exotic, simple or complex, is a local and thus thoroughly endogenous production. As Schegloff and Sacks (1973:290) put it, if human activity exhibits a methodical orderliness, it does so "not only to us [the observing analysts], indeed not in the first place for us, but for the co-participants who . . . produced" it. Accordingly, that some activity or encounter is recognizably a "machine service visit," "call to the police," "customer order placement," "psychiatric consultation," or whatever is something that the co-participants can and do realize, procedurally, at each and every moment of the encounter. The task for the analyst is to demonstrate just how they do this. This requires understanding precisely how their activity becomes what it recognizably and accountably is; that is to say, how it acquires its social facticity.

We also assume that this orderliness can be found, in Sacks's (1984) words, "at all points" with respect to human action (see Garfinkel 2002). There are no limits, then, on the scale of phenomena that can be subjected to investigation, and the granularity runs very deep. Nor can you rely on a theoretical scheme, no matter how well articulated or ingenious, to conceptually stipulate this orderliness; there is no alternative but empirical discovery (Schegloff 1996), which then demands rigorous, naturalistic observation.

There is an inductive strategy involved as well. We work at generating preliminary hypotheses or conjectures through our initial observations. We try to then evaluate those notions through more investigations. We then reformulate them, come up with new ones, and go back to the field to do more observing and assessment. We see how that turns out, and then go back to the field yet again to further refine our ideas. And so on. It is always an iterative process.

Naturalistic Research and Technology Design

We are employed by a technology research center, and so our studies are done in collaboration or coordination with those of computer scientists, engineers, computational linguists, mathematicians, physicists, and other physical scientists. These studies are aimed not only at discovering knowledge, but also at turning those discoveries into new technologies; not just investigating and analyzing the world, but designing and building things for that world. The relationship between our discipline and its studies and those of our colleagues' disciplines, like computer science and engineering, which are very closely involved with design is therefore of considerable significance to us.

Our own thinking about design—one shared by many researchers at the Palo Alto Research Center (PARC)—begins from the presumption that truly useful technology supports and enhances natural human capacities and practices. To illustrate this point, let us consider the breakthrough achieved in computer design at PARC (then operated directly by Xerox) in the 1970s, when most of what we now regard as standard, essential features of the personal computer—things that make the computer a device that can be used by ordinary people, not just engineers or "techies," like the graphic user interface and the mouse—were ingeniously brought together in the development of the Xerox Star, which was based on PARC's Alto computer (for a detailed historical account of the Xerox Star, see Johnson et al. 1989).

The Star—and its research forerunner, the Alto—was a machine explicitly designed to capitalize on natural human skills and abilities.[3] The user interface was built around the remarkable visual capacities of humans; that is, the deeply visual ways in which humans perceive, represent, and interact with objects in the world. Moreover, the Alto and Star made use of pictorial representations whose form straightforwardly suggested their meaning (icons), in large part because the images were of familiar office and desktop objects: folders, documents, a trashcan, and the like. The design of this "graphic user interface" thus took ordinary work practice into account; not only the visual capacities of humans but also the ways many of the objects essential for their work could be visually represented, by employing what came to be called the desktop metaphor (the Star relied on icons even more than did the Alto, in an attempt to further simplify the interface). And the mouse was designed to serve as an extension of the body, of the hand, in order to leverage the human predilection for pointing and thus couple the body with the device in a more natural manner than was possible with a keyboard. As the Star's designers once summarized their intentions, "an important design goal was to make the 'computer' as invisible to users as possible" (Johnson et al. 1989:12).

The design of the Star also took into account the common and highly functional human practice of working in concert with others to accomplish shared goals (in many ways a natural way for people to work). It was not conceived primarily as a standalone device, but rather as a tool for cooperation and collaboration in offices and other workplaces. The Xerox corporate strategy at the time centered on building devices that would support the "architecture for information" in the "office of the future." A number of researchers at that time, at PARC and elsewhere, recognized that trafficking in information is an essentially social activity, and that such an "architecture" required computer technology that would allow individuals to collaboratively manage and share their information. If the Star were to effectively support this need, it would require a means of linking many computers and peripherals—such as printers and mass storage devices—and transferring or sharing data between them at high speeds (the Ethernet communications protocol, also invented at PARC contemporaneous and integrated with the development of the Alto, served this purpose quite well).

There were no researchers in the social sciences at PARC at the time of the Alto's development, but the work of the center's engineers and computer scientists unquestionably drew upon a "human centered" philosophy of design. They were committed to the idea of "eat your own dog food," which meant having themselves and their colleagues become users of everything they were designing. And not just "experimental users"—people who might try out this or that for a short time, and give some feedback—but rather "full time users" who had to rely on the system, application, or device in question to do their work. Thus they were forced to confront all its problems and explore all its possibilities.

This incipient human-centered approach can plainly be advanced through the disciplined, formal study of naturally occurring behavior that we argue for above. For what better way is there to learn about human capacities for reasoning and action, and the systematic manner in which people endogenously and concertedly organize their actions, than to closely observe and record their everyday behavior as it takes place in their natural habitats?

Naturalistic observation also makes a prominent contribution to design through studies of people using already existing technologies, investigating the place and significance of this technology in the everyday conduct of human affairs. For these investigations, the key problem to address is not so much *whether* technology is in some fundamental way "social," but rather to show precisely *how* it is social; accordingly, studies of the social life of technology must obviously consider "not only the material objects but the collage of activities involved in making technology into an *instrument* which is incorporated into a weave of working tasks" (Shapiro et al. 1991:3, emphasis in original; see also Brown and Duguid 2000). When carrying out these kinds of highly focused field observations, we nevertheless try to adopt a comprehensive, "workscapes" strategy, and in this way our approach can be distinguished from that normally taken in more limited and narrowly directed "user studies," which tend to rely on laboratory testing or interviews more than naturalistic observation in everyday work environments.

Designing for the Entire Workscape

Design, however, can—and should—involve much more than technology. As we have stated, technology is but one aspect of any workscape. Workscapes also include people and their practices, including here what we can call the epistemological basis of practice: how people commonly learn to do something, to become competent practitioners of some craft, job, or profession, and how they continue to strive to master their work tasks. And as we have also emphasized, workscapes include the habitat or environment for work, the spaces and places where the work is accomplished. From this view, then, the scope of design should be significantly expanded beyond technology alone, taking into account and thus designing for the entire workscape.

To illustrate what it could mean to do complete "workscape design" using naturalistic methods, we will very briefly describe a project undertaken in the mid-1990s, prior to any of us joining PARC, when Marilyn Whalen and Jack Whalen were on leave from the University of Oregon and working at the Institute for Research on Learning (IRL), in Menlo Park, California, along with Erik Vinkhuyzen.[4] The project in question was an experiment by Xerox on integrating what were normally separate customer call center functions for account administration, supply ordering, and equipment service (essentially, they were three distinct businesses) into a single, integrated operation. IRL was contracted by Xerox to assist with this "Integrated Customer Services" (ICS) experiment. The project site was situated just north of Dallas, Texas, in a large company facility that already included all three functions. A key issue to be addressed through this project was whether a single set of workers—call center representatives or "reps"—could do all three kinds of work; that is, whether three previously distinct jobs could be combined or integrated. Solving this problem would require close examination not only of how people could best learn and perform this new, integrated work, but how the work process itself would be organized, what technologies could best support it (including a comparison of paper-based and digital resources), the computer interfaces needed in the ICS system, and how the ICS work area would be designed.

We participated in the experiment as part of the ICS program team, which was in reality a full design team and included seven reps and three call-center managers. We relocated to Dallas for the duration of the project, and worked with the other members of the program team on a daily basis. An unused area of the Xerox facility was dedicated to ICS, and some thirty employees of the separate functions volunteered to participate as "ICS reps."

Our research in the project involved extensive field observations, supplemented by video recordings, and covered three main areas. Research in each of these areas was closely coupled with specific design needs, as indicated below.

1. *Reps on the phone with customers*

Observed and recorded actions of reps when they were on the telephone with customers (see photo 17.1), including their use of various tools and job aids, and analyzed the structure of these conversations . . .

. . . to help reengineer the work process, understand customer requirements, and design a customer-focused learning program for the reps based on these requirements (that is, one based on how customers reasoned about their needs and their problems and their various dealings with the company, as this reasoning was exhibited in their phone calls).

Photo 17.1. Rep on the Phone with Customer.

2. *Computer use during those conversations*

Observed and recorded the details of how reps coordinated their talking, reading, and especially their data entry and retrieval with their computer applications (see photo 17.2). . .

. . . to inform design of the ICS system interface, job aids and information resources, as well as the project learning program (here focused on the information system and ICS applications), and to develop the project's strategy for using an expert diagnostic system during calls for equipment service (since use of this application was required by Xerox on the grounds that it would improve the company's response to customers' equipment problems).

3. *Work environment*

Observed and recorded how reps naturally learned from and taught each other (see photo 17.3), and how their collaboration was supported or undermined by different configurations of both their work stations and the work space taken as a whole . . .

. . . to design a plan for fully integrating work with learning (something quite different from conventional, classroom-based "training"), and to design the experimental ICS facility.

The most significant outcome of ICS was the work on the development of a new learning environment through which ICS reps would be able to quickly and effectively acquire unfamiliar skills and knowledge, and thus deserves additional

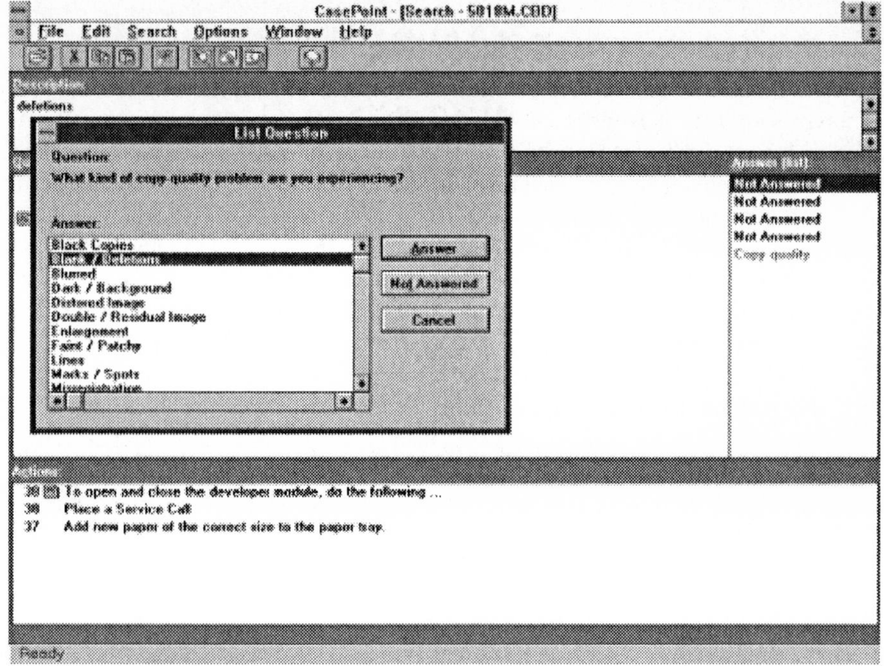

Photo 17.2. Computer Use during Rep Conversation.

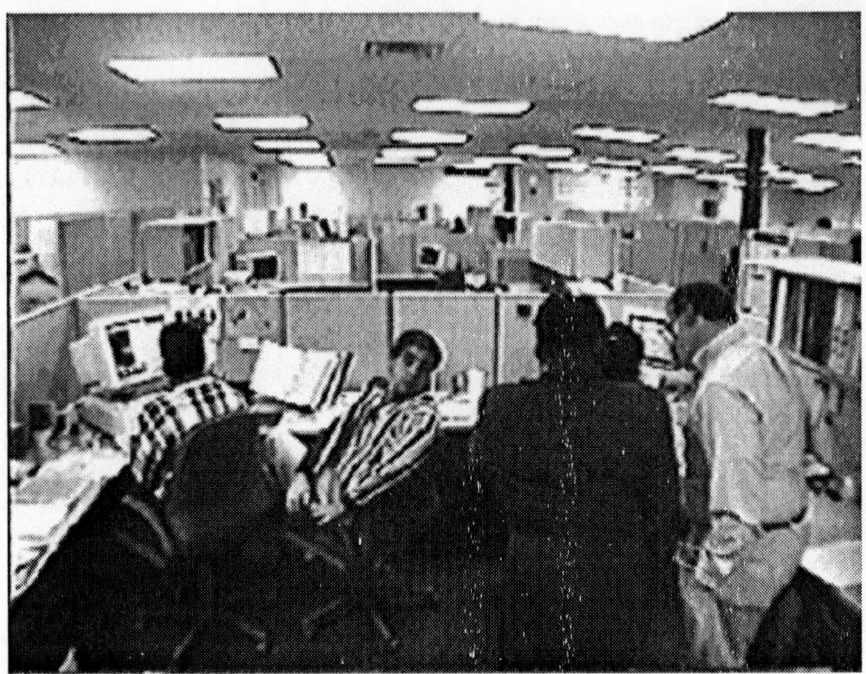

Photo 17.3. Work Environment.

discussion. The catalyst for our focus on learning was the project requirement that ICS reps learn their new tasks and functions while continuing, at least in the beginning of the project, to perform the work tasks they brought with them from their prior, specialized functions. If the project had followed the existing classroom-based, specialist curriculum for the three functional areas it would have taken many months to cover the necessary material, using that delivery method and the numerous specialist curriculums. Plainly, this was not practical. In addition, there was real concern over whether workers who spent such an exorbitant amount of time in the classroom could hope to retain the necessary knowledge and skills to then be effective on the floor.

This learning challenge, equivalent to having to change a tire while the car is moving, required a very different strategy than that followed in conventional Xerox training programs: learning had to be moved out of the classroom and into the workplace as much as possible. Classroom instruction could still be an important delivery method for learning, but it could no longer be the primary method. This alternative strategy was based on a social, interactive model of how meaningful and effective learning takes place, recognizing that "knowing how" depends on engagement in real-world practice. And this is where the data we collected proved so important. As suggested above, our research revealed how employees naturally and routinely collaborate with and learn from each other while engaging in everyday work, and how newly hired employees regularly learn from experienced workers. Our findings also presented a compelling case for how the design of the physical work environment could effectively support learning, and enable quick collaboration between peers and among groups.

Even though Xerox did not take up the ICS experiment as a model for all its call center operations, due primarily to conflicts over disbanding the traditional functional organizations, it was successful in a number of ways. ICS reps were able to equal or better the performance of their peers in Xerox's traditional call centers, despite the fact that those workers had to be concerned only with their specialized work tasks and targets, while workers in ICS had to manage a wide array of tasks and responsibilities. This proved that with the appropriate learning methods and work environment, integrated customer service and support was possible—a single Xerox call center worker could successfully perform all the different functional tasks in a fully integrated environment. Most important, the decisive innovation from the project, which was the close integration of work and learning, was soon adopted by Xerox throughout the corporation and became the linchpin of its learning strategy.

The Eastside Reprographics Project: At the Customer Front

Our experience with call center workscapes, where the interactions between the organization and its customers are technologically mediated (principally by the telephone, of course, but sometimes involving fax machines or email), led us to an investigation of another workscape with a significant "customer front" but where most of the encounters with customers take place face-to-face.

The organization we selected for study, Eastside Reprographics (henceforth, Eastside), owns and operates three local copy shops (the name is a pseudonym; Eastside is a competitor in its own locale to other locally owned document production centers and to franchise operations such as CopyMax). The bulk of Eastside's customers are individuals who walk into their stores with a wide variety of document reproduction needs. Eastside also handles document work from both small and large companies in their area (these jobs typically entail a much higher volume than do jobs submitted by retail "walk in" customers).

Our research interests in the workscape include not only the source of document jobs and the manner of their submission by Eastside's customers—retail or commercial, over the front counter or (much less commonly) electronically, via email—but also:

- how the job orders are produced by Eastside's employees, operating a variety of reprographic machines and other devices;
- how production work is represented, instructed, and tracked by both paper and digital technology;
- the physical arrangement through which all of a store's work and other activities (including the navigation of both workers and customers through the store) are accomplished.

Because of these interests, our observations and recordings are spotlighting several kinds of activity for analysis, including:

- interactions between Eastside's workers and customers at the front counter, at the primary site for where orders are placed and money changes hands;
- filling out the basic, paper-based order recording form at the counter during those interactions (the order is recorded by an Eastside worker);
- making sense of these records at the machines, where job orders are then produced;
- processing digital jobs, where the originals are not paper documents but rather files;
- operating photocopy machines, printers, finishers and other devices to actually run the jobs;
- classroom training for Eastside's workers;
- practices through which Eastside's workers informally teach and help each other, as well as those through which they help or guide customers.

Because of space limitations, we can illustrate only a small part of this research with any detail, selecting for this purpose the placement of job orders at the front counter. Our illustration will focus on a single encounter where some problems that regularly occur with these "walk in" orders are especially evident. Our purpose is not to present findings, as in a research report. Rather, as was the case in our account of ICS, our intent is *programmatic.* Nevertheless, we will here develop a limited analysis of some actual data to demonstrate what the naturalistic, detailed study of action entails, and how this can inform the analysis of a workscape and provide an empirical foundation for design efforts.

A Routine Order Placement

The encounter in question is a markedly routine order placement; that is to say, it would come across, to any casual observer, as an utterly mundane and uneventful sort of encounter. It begins with the customer walking up to the counter, where she then places her order over the course of a brief conversation with the Eastside worker (see photo 17.4), who is in point of fact a manager in this store. After they settle on a time for the job to be completed, the customer takes her leave with a smile and departs.

But now let us look closely at what happens during one part of the exchange at the counter and what turned out to be a particularly significant moment. This action occurs soon after the customer explains she has some documents that need to be reproduced. The Eastside worker has already placed an order recording form on the counter and has started to fill it out. The customer removes a document from her bag. "I want ten copies of these," she says, referring to the document, which is a small poster announcing a yoga class. The Eastside worker asks her if she wants the copies in color (the customer has color originals). The customer responds affirmatively. Then the customer produces an envelope containing another set of documents—drawings of different yoga positions—and after removing them from the envelope, holds them in her right hand. Here is the transcript of the talk and other, related actions (transcribed directly below the talk or silence during which it occurs) that follow.[5]

Photo 17.4. Routine Order Placement.

Customer:	Uh these I'd like
	(0.2) uh:m (0.9)
	((sweeps her left hand))
	half this si:ze?
	((looking at Eastside worker))
	(0.4)
Eastside worker:	Okay.
	((nods while looking at customer's documents))
	(0.4)
	((starts to write on form))
Customer:	An' jus' one copy of each(h).
	((Eastside worker continues to fill out form))
	(1.7)
	((customer watches Eastside worker fill out the form))

Following this exchange and the apparent completion of the work with the order form, the customer asks when the job will be ready for pickup, and the Eastside worker tells her it will be a half hour. The customer is quite pleased with this report. "You guys are fantastic," she proclaims. The encounter closes soon after.

It certainly appears, at first glance, that this is an entirely unproblematic order placement. The customer seems to know just what she wants done, and the Eastside worker seems to understand the customer's request, and can satisfactorily represent it on the order form. However, at closer examination, a few hints about a *possible* source of trouble with the order emerge.

We should notice, for instance, that when the customer says she wants the drawings reproduced at "half this size," her utterance has a rising intonation contour, indicated in the transcript by a question mark. This way of saying "half this size" turns that description into a try marker (Sacks and Schegloff 1979)—a device used to indicate a test of an addressee's recognition of a referent. That is to say, the customer is working at determining whether the addressee of her utterance, the Eastside worker, knows what she means by "half this size." Additionally, the customer looks directly at the Eastside worker as she says "half this size," a further indication of her search for some sign of recognition or confirmation. Moreover, a try marker is ordinarily followed by a hesitation pause, in expectation of a sign from the addressee as to whether the referent is known to them. And in fact the customer does not say anything more for the moment, which spawns a short silence before the Eastside worker says, "okay," and nods her head.

Plainly, the worker's response does exhibit, to the customer, recognition and understanding of the half-size referent. The worker never actually looks up at the customer during or immediately after the "half this size" remark. Instead, she is looking down at the customer's drawings and then at the paper order form, and starts to write on the form. To the customer, the Eastside worker is presumably recording the half-size specification, which would provide further evidence for the customer that the worker understands the order. Nevertheless, we can still assert with some confidence that this data all suggest the "half this size" referent is a *possible* source of trouble insofar as the issue has now been raised *by one of the participants in this encounter* of whether the meaning of "half this size" is recognizable to Eastside, and whether the nature of the requested document production work has thus been clearly understood.

Talking about Reduction

To pursue this matter, we can first ask: What *could* be meant by "half this size"? As it happens, it can mean several different things:

- half the height and length of the image, of the yoga position drawing;
- half of that image area;
- half of the page.

This kind of problem is a common one in reprographics. It is part of the more general problem of how to precisely denote *reduction* and *enlargement* requirements when reproducing documents and images. And not surprisingly, the Eastside order form, like those throughout the reprographics industry, has a specific information field in which to record these requirements, labeled in this instance "Size %." In this field, as indicated by its label, the requirement has to be represented *mathematically* as a percentage, with an accompanying specification of whether this is a reduction or enlargement. On the form, 100 percent is the default, meaning no reduction or enlargement of the original (if nothing is entered in this field, it is assumed no size changes are needed).

Each of the three different understandings of "half this size" listed above have an equivalent representation as a percentage reduction: half the height and length of the original image would be a 50 percent reduction, half the image area would be 71 percent, and half the page (that is, reducing the image so that it fit onto half of an 8.5 x 11-inch page of paper) would be 65 percent. These understandings of "half" and their respective representations as reduction percentages are shown in figure 17.1.

Why is a mathematical representation necessary? Because photocopiers need mathematical instructions stated as percent figures; that is how instructions to the machine are given for reduction and enlargement. This need is thus also built-in, as it were, to the machine's interface, where the user must select or enter a percent figure (with 100 percent, or no reduction or enlargement, again being the default).

What we have, then, is a system for the documentary representation of reduction that originates from the engineering of the machine and is incorporated into the machine's interface, and then transferred directly into the Eastside order form. Accordingly, the task of the Eastside worker is to take the customer's description or account of their reduction (or enlargement) needs and translate it into a percent figure. The order form's use of a label like "Size %" for the relevant field that indicates a percentage figure must be entered serves as an embedded instruction in this regard, reminding them of that special mathematical requirement.

Plainly, these mathematical equivalents of the various "half this size" meanings are not something with which most customers would be familiar; to a large extent, they are naive when it comes to technical matters in reprographic work. Nor is this something that most workers at Eastside appear to know well. In this case, we cannot be sure whether the Eastside worker in our example knew about all the complications that can arise with reduction and enlargement requests, or was fully aware of the

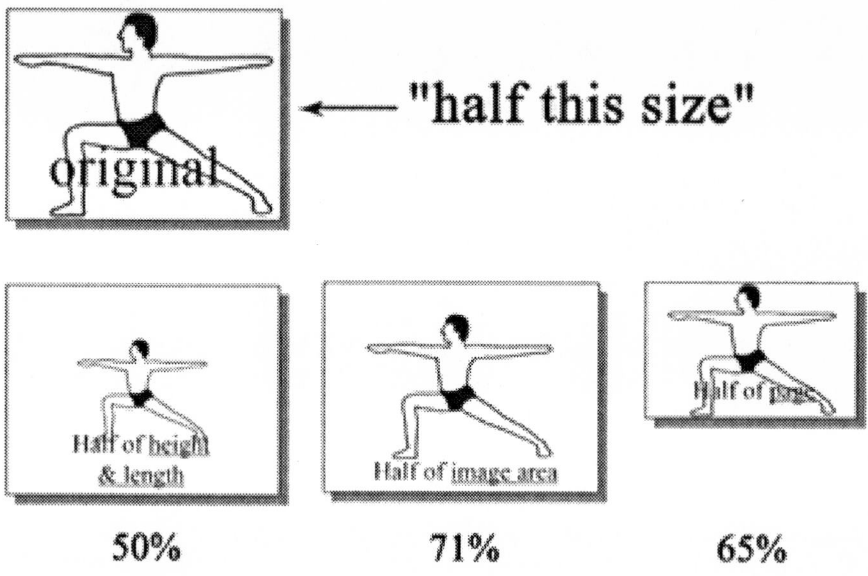

Figure 17.1. "Half this size."

different ways "half this size" might be understood. We do know that the worker did not raise any questions or concerns. She did not query the customer, for example, about what she meant exactly by "half this size." Instead, she simply nodded and said "Okay." And that turned out to have consequences for the work that got done, and the customer's reaction to it.

Problem at Pickup

The customer returns to the store later that day to pick up her job, and an Eastside worker—not the one with whom the order was originally placed—retrieves the finished copies. The customer starts to inspect the work. "Oh," she exclaims. She looks at more copies. And again exhibits some surprise. She looks up at the worker. "I-yeah, half the size," she starts, "but I needed them." She doesn't finish this verbal description, trying instead to demonstrate what she really wanted done with the drawings by making chopping gestures, two on each side of the yoga position image. This apparently is meant to show that she meant "half this size" as something like "half the page," with her gestures indicating a cropping of the original. But whatever she was trying to indicate, the customer is observably struggling to articulate the problem; the meaning of "half this size" remains elusive. Very soon after this, while looking down again at her copies, and with the Eastside worker still silent, the customer observes, "But it seems like it's smaller than half size, though." The following transcript shows how the conversation developed from there.

Customer:	But it seems like it's smaller than half size, though.
Eastside worker:	It's at 50 percent reduction.
	(0.1)
Customer:	It is:? =
Eastside worker:	= Mhm.
	(3.2)
Customer:	It's too sma:ll.
	(2.8)
Eastside worker:	That's[the-
Customer:	[What else c'n I ha:ve.
	(0.9)
Eastside worker:	Well you- (0.2) if you have a (.) specific measurement you wanna give us, (0.2) we c'n (0.1) work with tha:t.
	(0.3)
Eastside worker:	Bu:t.
	(2.3)
	((worker leafs through the documents, looking for the order form))
Eastside worker:	The order form said 50 percent so that's what we did

It is now reasonably clear what occurred. The Eastside worker who took the order interpreted "half this size" as "50 percent" (reduction) and recorded that figure on the envelope form. The worker who produced the job entered that same figure into the photocopier, which then produced copies that were half the height and length of the original images—copies that were, in the customer's words, "smaller than half size," at least as *she* understood the meaning of that term. Eastside ended up making a new set of copies, after the worker and the customer reached a shared and openly formulated understanding of the size reduction requirement for these drawings, and the customer was quite satisfied at the end with the results.

Orders, Forms, Workscapes

These order placement and pickup sequences point to at least three "practitioners' problems" that Eastside faces in its everyday operations and, especially, its order and production process. Identifying these problems and developing a systematic understanding of their origin and features was possible only through naturalistic observation and recording, followed by the kind of detailed analysis presented above that such naturalistic data affords.

First, there appears to be a significant knowledge problem when it comes to reduction and enlargement (and perhaps other document services). In this example, all three parties—the worker who took the order, the customer, and, at least to some degree, the worker who retrieved the completed order—display a lack of knowledge of the issues involved with such matters. This leads directly to trouble with the production of the job. Although it was technically correct insofar as the result matched what was recorded on the order form, the customer was not satisfied with those results, and complained that what Eastside took to be "half size" (as translated into the 50 percent figure recorded on the form) was not what she intended by that referent, with the consequence that the job had to be redone. Eastside had to bear the cost of this; the customer could not be charged for copying the drawings a second time.

Second, our analysis points to the related problem of achieving shared understanding during front counter transactions. In our example, the difficulty we identify is found in all forms of human interaction: a listener thinks she understand what a speaker meant by what they said, or what was meant by a particular referent that was used, but in fact her understanding is not that of the speaker. Moreover, in this instance the difference between the two understandings is not identified during the initial encounter, but rather at a later time. This, too, is not uncommon in social life.[6]

Still, while the problem of different understandings that go undetected (for whatever period of time) may be an ordinary enough concern, when the purpose of an interaction is to record specific requirements for work or a service to be performed, then avoiding such confusion acquires a special importance, with potential economic consequences. And not having enough knowledge to quickly recognize the possible problems that can develop with vernacular descriptions of certain procedures like reduction and their translation into technical (here, mathematical) reprographic equivalents plainly compounds the difficulties in this instance for all the parties.

Third, there is the problem of properly representing, on the Eastside order form, the actions requested by customers, so that these actions and the jobs of which they are a part can then be done to the customer's satisfaction. In this kind of representational work, Eastside workers (like all standard form users) are necessarily faced, on each and every occasion of the form's use, with the problem of how to administer that form in the context of what are, irremediably, singular events and sets of circumstances: *this* customer's job, with *these* requirements, as they are described and explained in *these* ways. That is to say, they recurrently face the problem of appropriating the form, and more generally, their available configurations of working practices and representational conventions, to meet the requirements of those singular events. At the same time, however, this appropriating action necessarily obliges them to rework the event in order to meet the requirements of the form (Suchman and Whalen 1994; Whalen 1995). We want to emphasize that this is a "normal" problem; it is not anything special, but an everyday, inescapable exigency of work with standardized forms.

We can put this in terms of the data we have been examining. The customer says, among other things, "half this size." It is only through use of the order form that this vernacular description, and anything else this customer requests, can be worked up into an organizationally relevant and actionable "job." The worker has to literally make the form do this; that is what "appropriating" the form means. And this unavoidable appropriating activity obliges the worker to then render the customer's vernacular description into a mathematical representation, because this is the only way the form can denote size: the description must be "reworked" into a percent figure.

Intimately related to this is another normal and inescapable problem with documentary representations, although perhaps especially with standard business forms, where those documents have to be used to organize and instruct activities, typically involving actors separated by time and space, and in quite fundamental ways. At Eastside, workers who are responsible only for handling business at the front counter typically fill out the envelope order forms. The production workers who operate the machines then have to interpret the form—always in relation to the originals inside the envelope—at a later time in order to run the job. Occasionally, a worker assigned to production will take an order at the counter, but this same manager or worker will almost never end up running that particular job. It is thus highly unlikely that a worker trying to make sense of a form when running a job will have any knowledge of what transpired during the counter interaction when that form was assembled, of what the customer said that was then translated into markings on the form. And they do not often have the opportunity to speak with the worker took the order, who does have that knowledge and did that translation. Consequently, they commonly have only those markings to go by, to use as instructions for what they are to do at the machine.

In most cases, production workers who are about to run a job, and who are thus scrutinizing the original documents to be copied or the files to be printed, are easily able to make sense of what the form instructs them to do with those originals and so can produce the job without any great difficulty. But to say "easily" does not mean there is no significant work involved, no more than we could say no significant work is required for filling out a form. Understanding the details of this work with forms, and the practices and conventions that organize it, is crucial to understanding the organization of the entire Eastside workscape. Indeed, the successful operation of their business depends so heavily on the successful use of the form that new workers are given a special training class, lasting two days, on how to properly fill out and follow it.

In the "half size" encounter, there is no problem with filling out the form in terms of what we might call its *procedural* correctness; that is to say, the worker at the counter recorded a proper, recognizable figure in the "Size %" field, representing one possible mathematical representation of "half this size." And as far as we know, the production worker had no difficulty understanding that instruction, and properly entered the "50%" figure into the machine to make copies of the drawings. It also appears that there were no procedural or technical problems for these workers with any other representations on the form. But we can point to the manner in which the form was actually taken up and appropriated during the encounter as a source of concern, and suggest how its highly standardized requirements entered into the organization and character of that conversation.

In the action that occurs prior to the "half size" exchange we have been examining, the Eastside worker pulls out a blank form and places it on the counter almost as soon as the customer walks up. By the time the customer brings out her drawings, the worker has already recorded the job specifications for the first set of documents she presented, the posters, and continues to attend to the form as the customer explains what she wants done with the drawings. The worker does more than closely attend to and regularly write on the form, though. She has asked, and continues to ask, questions about the order, and these questions are observably oriented, in both their ordering and subject matter, to certain fields on the form, ones made relevant by the features of this customer's document needs, and to the requirements concerning what can be entered in those fields. An organizational agenda is hearably operating (see Whalen 1995): the worker is seeking to control the exchange, so as to economically obtain the information she deems most important, with the form serving to guide and instruct her actions. Of course, this is why standardized business forms were invented: to help coordinate and control organizational practice, creating a highly stylized—and to some extent, scripted—form of "conversation" between the form and the person filling it out (Yates 1989; Levy 2001). In this instance this structure enters into the conversation between the worker and the customer. In a sense, then, the Eastside worker has become a talking order form. And there will be instances where such close adherence to the form, and somewhat "scripted" questioning, may lull the worker into a false sense of security, so that things like the different meanings of "half this size" are overlooked.

At this very early stage of the Eastside project, we are not yet in a position to develop major design recommendations. But in identifying these three interrelated problem areas, we have been able to start working with a team of Eastside employees on solutions. The solutions will unquestionably involve a learning strategy to address the lack of knowledge about reprographic processes and their regular conundrums. Again, as we suggested earlier in our discussion of the ICS project, this strategy would not be based on a training course, but rather organized around methods for developing practical expertise and know-how through peer-to-peer teaching and collaboration, thus integrating learning with everyday work activities (see Whalen and Vinkhuyzen 2000:132–38).

The development of new work practices will also be required, as well as better support for existing ones, in order to manage interactions with customers at the front counter and understand their true needs. Issues with appropriating standardized forms with care, and attentively translating vernacular expressions and descriptions to meet the form's requirements will certainly be addressed as well. And we are closely studying the practices around form use more generally in the hope that this scrutiny will inform the design of digital, Web-based forms for the reprographics industry that customers fill out on their own. In short, we have plenty of research and design work to do.

Designing for the Workscape: Final Thoughts

We stated earlier that the scope of design should include more than technology. However, this is not to say that we reject design that focuses primarily on technology itself. In fact, a certain amount of our work on the ICS project was specifically dedicated to informing the design of tools and job aids. And one lesson that has come out of our technology design work is that simpler and older technologies often turn out to be very valuable for workers, and often in ways that would be difficult to equal by designing new ones. In ICS, for example, Xerox had allocated a quarter of a million dollars to take all of the information reps used that was currently on paper and put it online, which was thought to make the information more accessible and searchable. But after we had spent a considerable amount of time examining how people in the traditional call center environments used their paper documents, we discovered that some of the most important paper documents were already available online, and that that no one used the digital version. They all preferred the paper version. Why was this so? There were some critical and unique affordances of paper that were tremendously helpful for the kind of work done in call centers. What came out of that research was a set of plans for paper job aids, which not only were more useful for workers but also saved Xerox money.

This experience also provided a foundation for more research, in other projects, on the use of paper as a technology in different types of work sites; in particular, how paper documents are actually taken up and enter into the organization of various activities. And this is similar to the process by which our ICS research on telephone interactions with customers served as the starting point for our investigations on service worker-customer front counter interactions in the Eastside Reprographics project, and greatly helped us identify and analyze problems with control and mutual understanding. From each specific project, then, and each set of findings about a specific site or activity, we have been able to develop more general analyses about human conduct and the organization of workscapes.

This story from ICS or Eastside is thus not really about technology design or customer interactions. It is surely more about workscapes, and how technologies have to somehow live in them, in these real-world environments of humans and their practices. That is, all technologies have to live in a world in which the kind of things that get done, the kind of information that might be needed for the task at hand, in the environment in which people have to do that task might necessarily require or be done more easily with certain means of action, and not others. A critical part of good design is achieving an appropriate fit—what Lucy Suchman (personal communication) terms "artful integration"—between technological capacities, techniques, and means on one hand and the natural organization of human habitats and practices on the other. It is not about what can be built as much as it is about what should be built in this instance.

NOTES

1. Our argument about a natural observational *discipline* shares much in common with the position Sacks (1984) takes concerning the possibilities for sociology being a natural observational *science.* But we eschew the word "science" because of the unfortunate tendency toward *scientism*—the belief that the investigative methods of the physical sciences are applicable in all fields of inquiry, and in fact define what "science" is—among students of human conduct. We want to also make clear in this regard that in advocating for the continued development of this kind of naturalistic discipline, we are not proposing that by taking it up, researchers studying humans can then (or only then) become truly "scientific." The road to a more detailed and accurate understanding of human behavior—and after all, this is what "science" is really about, empirically grounded knowledge of phenomena—cannot be achieved by *design,* on a philosophical understanding of "the truth" or "the scientific method" (Sharrock and Read 2002:99–130). Finally, the term *natural* also can have unfortunate interpretations associated with scientism, if it is used in studies of social life to mean that social processes or states of affairs are necessarily determined by or in accordance with "nature," are the result of "natural laws." This view could not be more different from our own. We follow the more ordinary usage of "natural": something that is the opposite of artificial or contrived.
2. Some of these studies were done in collaboration with our colleagues Don H. Zimmerman (University of California, Santa Barbara), Douglas Maynard (University of Wisconsin), William Clancey (NASA Ames Research Center), and Elizabeth Churchill (FX Palo Alto Laboratory).
3. The Apple Macintosh, which was inspired in part by a visit to PARC by Steve Jobs in 1979, went on to achieve the commercial success that always eluded Xerox. To be sure, though, Apple's first attempt in this regard, the Lisa, was a commercial failure. A brief but useful discussion of why, in contrast to the Star and Lisa, the Macintosh succeeded can be found in Baecker et al. (1995).
4. Two other researchers working with IRL, Kathryn Henderson and Susan Allen, also participated in the project.
5. We are using the basic transcription orthography developed initially by Gail Jefferson and followed in conversation analysis research, but in a greatly simplified version for this chapter.
6. The fact that this occurs without notice by the parties during that initial order taking exchange and thus without consequences *for the interactional course* of their encounter should serve as a useful reminder that phenomena like "intersubjectivity" and "mutual intelligibility"—a common orientation to the world and its workings, a shared recognition of words or actions and their meaning—are *procedural accomplishments,* locally organized and interactionally managed, and furthermore, that they are always and only achieved "for all practical purposes," to use Garfinkel's (1984) apt description. A genuine cognitive consensus, an intersection of minds and their contents, is plainly unnecessary for parties to reach temporarily situated "agreement" regarding their intentions and meanings, or to carry out, for practical purposes, what they experience as a trouble free encounter.

REFERENCES

Baecker, R. M., J. Grudin, W. A. S. Buxton, and S. Greenberg. 1995. The emergence of graphical user interfaces. In R. M. Baecker et al., eds., *Human-computer interaction: Toward the year 2000,* 49–52. San Francisco: Morgan Kaufmann.

Boden, D. 1994. *The business of talk: Organizations in action.* Oxford: Polity Press.

Brown, J. S., and P. Duguid. 2000. *The social life of information.* Cambridge, MA: Harvard Business School Press.

Button, G., ed. 1993. *Technologies in working order: Studies of work, interaction and technology.* London: Routledge.

Clayman, S. E. 1989. The production of punctuality: Social interaction, temporal organization, and social structure. *American Journal of Sociology* 95:659–91.

Dourish, P. 2001. *Where the action is.* Cambridge, MA: MIT Press.

Drew, P., and J. Heritage, eds. 1992. *Talk at work: Interaction in institutional settings.* Cambridge, MA: Cambridge University Press.

Garfinkel, H. 1984. *Studies in ethnomethodology.* Cambridge: Polity Press.

——. 2002. *Ethnomethodology's program: Working out Durkheim's aphorism.* Ed. A. W. Rawls. Lanham, MD: Rowman and Littlefield.

Goodwin, C., and M. H. Goodwin. 1996. Seeing as a situated activity: Formulating planes. In Y. Engeström and D. Middleton, eds., *Cognition and communication at work,* 61–95. Cambridge: Cambridge University Press.

Heath, C., and P. Luff. 2000. *Technology in action.* Cambridge: Cambridge University Press.

Heritage, J. 1985. Analyzing news interviews: Aspects of the production of talk for an overhearing audience. In T. A. Van Dijk, ed., *Handbook of discourse analysis,* vol. 3, 95–117. London: Academic Press.

Heritage, J., and J. M. Atkinson. 1984. Introduction. In J. M. Atkinson and J. Heritage, eds., *Structures of social action: Studies in conversation analysis,* 1–15. Cambridge: Cambridge University Press.

Johnson J., T. L. Roberts, W. Verplank, D. C. Smith, C. H. Irby, M. Beard, and K. Mackey. 1989 [1995]. The Xerox Star: A retrospective. *IEEE Computer* 22, no. 9: 11–29. Reprinted in R. M. Baecker, J. Grudin, W. A. S. Buxton, and S. Greenberg, eds., *Readings in Human-Computer Interaction: Toward the Year 2000,* 53–70. San Francisco: Morgan Kaufmann.

Levy, D. M. 2001. *Scrolling forward: Making sense of documents in the digital age.* New York: Arcade.

Luff, P., J. Hindmarsh, and C. Heath, eds. 2000. *Workplace studies: Recovering work practice and informing system design.* Cambridge: Cambridge University Press.

Maynard, D. 1984. *Inside plea bargaining: The language of negotiation.* New York: Plenum.

Sacks, H. 1984. Notes on methodology. In J. M. Atkinson and J. Heritage, eds., *Structures of social action: Studies in conversation analysis,* 167–90. Cambridge: Cambridge University Press.

Sacks, H., and E. A. Schegloff. 1979. Two preferences in the organization of reference to persons in conversation and their interaction. In G. Psathas, ed., *Everyday language: Studies in ethnomethodology,* 7–14. New York: Irvington.

Schegloff, E. A. 1992. Repair after next turn: The last structurally provided defense of intersubjectivity in conversation. *American Journal of Sociology* 98:1295–1345.

——. 1996. Confirming allusions: Towards an empirical account of action. *American Journal of Sociology* 104:161–216.

Schegloff, E. A., and H. Sacks. 1973. Opening up closings. *Semiotica* 7:289–327.

Scollon, R., and S. W. Scollon. 2003. *Discourses in place: Language in the material world.* London: Routledge.

Shapiro, D., J. Hughes, R. Harper, S. Ackroyd, and K. Soothill. 1991. Policing information systems: The social context of success and failure in introducing information systems in the police service. Technical Report EPC-91-117. Rank Xerox Limited, Cambridge EuroPARC.

Sharrock, W., and R. Read. 2002. *Kuhn: Philosopher of scientific revolution.* Cambridge: Polity.

Silverman, D. 1997. Studying organizational interaction: Ethnomethodology's contribution to the "new institutionalism." *Administrative Theory and Praxis* 19:178–95.

Suchman, L. 1987. *Plans and situated actions: The problem of human-machine communication.* Cambridge: Cambridge University Press.

———. 1993. Technologies of accountability: Of lizards and aeroplanes. In G. Button, ed., *Technologies in working order: Studies of work, interaction and technology,* 113–26. London: Routledge.

Suchman, L., R. Trigg, and J. Blomberg. 2002. Working artefacts: Ethnomethods of the prototype. *British Journal of Sociology* 53:163–79.

Suchman, L., and J. Whalen. 1994. Standardizing local events and localizing standard forms: A comparative analysis. Paper presented at the annual meeting of the Society for Social Study of Science, New Orleans.

Whalen, J. 1995. A technology of order production: Computer-aided dispatch in public safety communications. In P. ten Have and G. Psathas, eds., *Situated order: Studies in the social organization of embodied activities,* 187–230. Washington: University Press of America.

Whalen, J., and G. Raymond. 2000. Conversation analysis. In E. F. Borgatta and M. L. Borgatta, eds., *The encyclopedia of sociology* (2d ed.), 431–41. New York: Macmillan.

Whalen, J., and E. Vinkhuyzen. 2000. Expert systems in (inter)action: diagnosing document machine problems over the telephone. In P. Luff, J. Hindmarsh, and C. Heath, eds., *Workplace studies: Recovering work practice and informing system design,* 92–140. Cambridge: Cambridge University Press.

Whalen, J., M. Whalen, and K. Henderson. 2002. Improvisational choreography in teleservice work. *British Journal of Sociology* 53:239–58.

Whalen, M., and D. H. Zimmerman. 1987. Sequential and institutional contexts in calls for help. *Social Psychology Quarterly* 50:172–85.

Yates, J. 1989. *Control through communication.* Baltimore: Johns Hopkins University Press.

Zimmerman, D. H. 1984. Talk and its occasion: The case of calling the police. In D. Schiffrin, ed., *Georgetown University Round Table on Language and Linguistics 1983: Meaning, form, and use in context—Linguistic applications,* 210–18. Washington, DC: Georgetown University Press.

Printed in the United Kingdom
by Lightning Source UK Ltd.
103153UKS00003B/127-129

9 781589 011014